W9-ATE-597

OXFORD WORLD'S CLASSICS

THE FLOWERS OF EVIL

CHARLES BAUDELAIRE was born in Paris in 1821. His father died when Baudelaire was 5 and his mother's remarriage in 1828 had a traumatic effect on him. In 1841 his stepfather sent him on a voyage that was meant to take him to Calcutta, but the homesick and rebellious Baudelaire insisted on leaving the ship after visiting Réunion and Mauritius and returned to France. In the following year he inherited 100,000 francs, which he proceeded to spend with such speed that his family appointed a lawyer to manage his fortune. Constantly in debt, Baudelaire led a life increasingly marked by poverty, disorder, and illness, though he remained something of a dandy, known to his friends for his elegance of taste, dress, and expression. He was an active, discerning critic of contemporary painting and an enthusiastic translator and promoter of the work of Edgar Allan Poe. His major work, *The Flowers of Evil*, published in 1857, was prosecuted for outrage to public decency. Ordered by the court to suppress six of the poems, Baudelaire revised and enlarged the collection and republished it in 1861. Meanwhile, he wrote a number of ironic and allegorical prose poems, collected after his death as *Paris Spleen* or *Short Poems in Prose*. In 1864 he went to lecture in Belgium in the vain hope of earning money and establishing his fame. In 1866 he suffered a series of strokes, leading to paralysis and aphasia, and was brought back to Paris, where he died in 1867. In addition to *The Flowers of Evil* and the prose poems, his works include studies of intoxicants and numerous essays on painting, caricature, and contemporary literature.

JAMES MCGOWAN is Professor of English, Illinois Wesleyan University, Bloomington, Illinois. His published works include a collection of poems, *Each Other—Where We Are* (1978, 1980), and *66 Translations from Charles Baudelaire's 'Les Fleurs Du Mal'* (1985). He also co-edited *Benchmark: An Anthology of Illinois Poetry* (1988).

JONATHAN CULLER is the author of numerous studies of French literature and literary theory, including *Flaubert: The Uses of Uncertainty* (1974), *Structuralist Poetics* (1975), *On Deconstruction* (1982), *Framing the Sign* (1988), and *Literary Theory: A Very Short Introduction* (1997). Professor of English and Comparative Literature at Cornell University, Ithaca, NY, he is completing a study of Baudelaire, entitled *The Devil's Part: Baudelaire's Poetry*.

OXFORD WORLD'S CLASSICS

*For almost 100 years Oxford World's Classics have brought
readers closer to the world's great literature. Now with over 700
titles—from the 4,000-year-old myths of Mesopotamia to the
twentieth century's greatest novels—the series makes available
lesser-known as well as celebrated writing.*

*The pocket-sized hardbacks of the early years contained
introductions by Virginia Woolf, T. S. Eliot, Graham Greene,
and other literary figures which enriched the experience of reading.
Today the series is recognized for its fine scholarship and
reliability in texts that span world literature, drama and poetry,
religion, philosophy and politics. Each edition includes perceptive
commentary and essential background information to meet the
changing needs of readers.*

OXFORD WORLD'S CLASSICS

CHARLES BAUDELAIRE

The Flowers of Evil

Translated with Notes by
JAMES McGOWAN

With an Introduction by
JONATHAN CULLER

Oxford   New York
OXFORD UNIVERSITY PRESS

Oxford University Press, Great Clarendon Street, Oxford OX2 6DP

Oxford New York

Athens Auckland Bangkok Bogotá Buenos Aires Calcutta
Cape Town Chennai Dar es Salaam Delhi Florence Hong Kong Istanbul
Karachi Kuala Lumpur Madrid Melbourne Mexico City Mumbai
Nairobi Paris São Paulo Singapore Taipei Tokyo Toronto Warsaw

and associated companies in Berlin Ibadan

Oxford is a registered trade mark of Oxford University Press

First published as a World's Classics paperback 1993
Reissued as an Oxford World's Classics paperback 1998

British Library Cataloguing in Publication Data

Data available

Library of Congress Cataloging in Publication Data

Baudelaire, Charles, 1821–1867.
[Fleurs du mal. English]
The flowers of evil / Charles Baudelaire; translated by James McGowan;
with an introduction by Jonathan Culler.
p. cm.—(Oxford World's classics)
I. McGowan, James. II. Title. III. Series.
PQ2191.F6E5 1993 841'.8—dc20 92–28008
ISBN 0–19–283545–9

1 3 5 7 9 10 8 6 4 2

Printed in Great Britain by
Caledonian International Book Manufacturing Ltd.
Glasgow

CONTENTS

INTRODUCTION

I

Les Fleurs du Mal, the most celebrated collection of verse in the history of modern poetry, first appeared on the horizon in 1845 in an advertisement on a book cover: 'To be published shortly: *The Lesbians* by Baudelaire-Dufaÿs'. Charles Baudelaire, who was trying out different versions of his name (Dufaÿs was his mother's name), was a 24-year-old man of letters who had published only one poem. The announcement of *The Lesbians* was repeated on several book covers in 1846 and 1847, including that of Baudelaire's own substantial pamphlet reviewing the annual art exhibit, *The Salon of 1846*. By 1848 the title had changed to *Limbo*, whose publication was announced as imminent, and in 1850 and 1851 some poems from the future *Flowers of Evil* were published as extracts from *Limbo*. Finally in 1855 the *Revue des deux mondes* printed eighteen poems under the title, *Les Fleurs du Mal*, and the complete collection appeared in 1857.

The evolution of titles is certainly intriguing. Why 'The Lesbians'?[1] *The Flowers of Evil* contains only three poems that obviously fit this title: 'Lesbos' and the two 'Condemned Women'. It is very unlikely that Baudelaire had written others which were then abandoned, though of course he might have planned a substantial sequence. Marcel Proust, a great admirer of Baudelaire's poetry, wondered 'how he could have been so especially interested in lesbians to go as far as wanting to use their name as the title of his whole splendid collection'.

---

[1] Claude Pichois, Baudelaire's biographer and editor of the best edition of his work, maintains that for Baudelaire's contemporaries, the French title 'Les Lesbiennes' would have meant only 'female inhabitants of Lesbos', but there is much evidence to confute this. For example, an article in the *Revue des deux mondes* of 1847 by Baudelaire's schoolfriend Émile Deschanel speaks of Sappho as 'a Lesbian in the full sense of the word'. Moreover, the young Baudelaire, out to shock, would scarcely have chosen an innocent, archaic-sounding title.

Baudelaire's three lesbian poems offer some answers. His lovers are presented as adventurers into the unknown, explorers of forbidden love, 'seekers of the infinite', driven by over-whelming passion: 'This fierce and moaning monster nothing can assuage', declares Hippolyta ('Condemned Women: Delphine and Hippolyta'). They suffer the condemnation of men and God and, more than that, the lacerations of passion itself. Their island, Lesbos, is a land of exotic, often masochistic sensuality:

> Lesbos, where love is like the wild cascades
> That throw themselves into the deepest gulfs,
> And twist and run with gurglings and with sobs
> Stormy and secret, swarming underground.
>
> ('Lesbos')

Baudelaire, who wrote in his *Intimate Journals* that 'the unique and supreme pleasure of making love lies in the certitude of doing evil', identifies with this transgressive eroticism and with the experience of torment.

> O maidens, demons, monsters—martyrs all,
> Spirits disdainful of reality,
> Satyrs and seekers of the infinite
> With rain of tears or cries of ecstasy,
>
> You whom my soul has followed to your hell,
> Poor sisters, let me pity and approve—
> For all your leaden griefs, for slakeless thirsts,
> And for your hearts, great urns that ache with love!
>
> ('Condemned Women')

'Disdainful of reality' in that they refuse to accept what is permitted but seek the unknown, Baudelaire's lesbians are imagined as ineluctably damned—and in this, soul-mates of his speaker. The patron of this love, Sappho, is 'Fairer than Venus' because her dark beauty is tinged with the melancholy of an insatiable passion. Delphine and Hippolyta, in the harshest poem of this group, suffer the torment and damnation of those who 'run at [the] limits of desire':

The harsh sterility of all your acts of lust
Will bring a dreadful thirst and stiffen out your skin,
And your concupiscence become a furious wind
To snap your feeble flesh like an old, weathered flag.

The critic Pierre Emmanuel writes that 'beneath the cover
of female homosexuality, all the themes dear to Baudelaire,
difficult to treat in the form in which he lived them, are sys-
tematically exacerbated to the furthest extreme of their dizzy-
ing logic'.[2] As willing victims of a passion held in horror by
Baudelaire's world, his lesbians make plausible this powerful
representation of passion as a sought-for hell. Baudelaire
imagines lesbians as the most compelling embodiments of lust
and desire because for him desire is always defeated, and acts
of desire are in this sense sterile. Male lovers delude themselves
that they desire something they may actually get from women
(at least, they often seem to think that they can get what they
are after if the woman yields); lesbians, however, may seem to a
male imagination driven by insatiable longing, by passions
which can find no satisfaction but only provoke further desire.
They are thus embodiments of what in fact is the general
character of passion in *The Flowers of Evil*: provoked by some-
thing intangible and intensified by the very impossibility of
fulfilment.

Calling his volume of poetry *The Lesbians* was also
Baudelaire's challenge to the discourses of his day about
women. A friend, Louis Veuillot, wrote that the century that
followed the Age of Voltaire could be called the Age of the
Virgin Mary. In 1854 the Catholic Church proclaimed the
doctrine of the Immaculate Conception, which maintained not
just that Mary was a virgin when she conceived Jesus but that
she herself had been born free of the taint of original sin. This
was only the climax of a movement of mariolatry which sought
to make the Virgin Mother, the supreme example of the purity
of women, the feminine ideal. Juxtaposed with this was a debate
about prostitution, whose terms were set in the pioneering

[2] Pierre Emmanuel, *Baudelaire, la femme, et Dieu* (Paris: Seuil, 1982), 82.

sociological investigation by the erstwhile inspector of the Paris sewers, Alexandre Parent-Duchatelet. His *On Prostitution in the City of Paris* declared that prostitutes are as inevitable in a large city as sewers, slaughterhouses, and refuse dumps, and that the government ought to adopt the same policy as in these other cases: to control them and to keep them out of sight. What these two discourses share is the attempt to de-eroticize women, and in proposing to call his collection of poems 'The Lesbians', Baudelaire not only endows women with sexual desire but counters the discourses of male passion which represent women as objects of male desire who find fulfilment in the love of a man.

There was a small vogue of plays and novels about Sappho in early nineteenth-century France, but most authors followed Ovid in treating Sappho as a tragic figure, an abandoned woman who leaped into the sea when she was spurned by the young boatman Phaon, for whom she was consumed by passion. Baudelaire is the first nineteenth-century author to portray Sappho as a lesbian; speaking of her as 'lover and poet', he imagines her as the priestess of a cult based on the impossibility for women to find satisfaction with men; she died, he imagines,

> When she, against the rite the cult devised,
> Let her sweet body be the rutting-ground
> For a brute . . .
>
> ('Lesbos')

Baudelaire's identification with his imagined lesbians emphasizes above all that men and women do not enter symmetrical sexual relations or find satisfaction together. In this respect, the lesbians would have been the central and representative figures for a book of poems about the impossible structure of desire, its diverse dramas, and the poet's relation to infinite longings.[3]

[3] F. W. Leakey, who has collected and presented the evidence that many of *Les Fleurs du Mal* were composed before 1850, has imagined an arrangement of poems that would have given the collection a certain narrative order. See his *Baudelaire: Collected Essays* (Cambridge: Cambridge University Press, 1990).

In shifting from *The Lesbians* to *The Flowers of Evil*, Baudelaire moved from a classical setting to a modern one, and, in essence, replaced lesbians with prostitutes as his representative female figures—figures who, like lesbians, do not find satisfaction in relations with men. What persists through these changes is the lack of symmetrical sexual relations between men and women.

II

In the form it was published in 1857, *Les Fleurs du Mal* consisted of five sections. Seventy-seven of the hundred and one poems were placed in the opening section, 'Spleen and the Ideal'.[4] The three lesbian poems come early in the second section, entitled 'Flowers of Evil'. Their placement at the beginning of the section that bears the title of the collection as a whole makes them seem paradigmatic instances of the exfoliation of evil that the book explores. Then there follow three short sections, 'Revolt', 'Wine', and 'Death', which include only eleven poems all told.

Much has been written about the 'secret architecture' of *The Flowers of Evil*. The phrase comes from Baudelaire's friend Barbey D'Aurévilly, who in 1857 defended the book against charges of immorality by arguing that it had a secret architecture which made it a moral book. Since he didn't reveal the secret, attempting to work it out has been an obvious task for critics ever since. Certainly the way the poems are ordered has important effects, though one may be sceptical about a 'secret architecture'. In December 1856, Baudelaire wrote to his publisher Poulet-Malassis that they should meet 'to arrange together the order of materials—together, do you hear, for the

---

[4] The term *spleen* was in vogue in Baudelaire's day: a number of minor French Romantic poets had used the term for a state of depression or youthful world-weariness, marked by a sense of the oppressiveness of life. The four poems entitled 'Spleen' in *The Flowers of Evil* give the notion a particular intensity. *The ideal* is more difficult to define: most generally it is whatever provokes effort and aspiration, including the world of ideal forms and beauty itself. It is thus both opposed to spleen and, in its inaccessibility, a cause of spleen.

question is important; we must make a volume composed only of good pieces, a small amount of material but which looks like a lot and is very eye-catching' (*très voyante*). On 29 January he says he needs just a day to 'put a bit of order in the collection' and that he will take this day shortly. This sounds less like the imposing of a secret architecture than an attempt to work out, with a friend's help, what arrangement might be most effective.[5]

In fact, the volume proved all too 'eye-catching', attracting the attention of the police. The edition was seized and Baudelaire and his publisher prosecuted for 'offence to public decency'. Gustave Flaubert's *Madame Bovary* had earlier that year been prosecuted but found innocent. Baudelaire's lawyer argued, at his client's suggestion, that the book must be judged as a whole, that Baudelaire presents evil in order to inspire hatred and disgust, and that the licentiousness of the indicted pieces was no greater than that of many works by celebrated authors, past and present. The judges were not convinced, deciding that whatever Baudelaire's intentions, some of the scenes he presents 'necessarily lead to the excitement of the senses by a crude realism offensive to decency'. Baudelaire's earlier intuition that a lesbian subject would shock proved well founded: while anti-religious poems, such as 'St Peter's Denial' and the 'Litanies of Satan', were indicted for offence to *religious* morality, Baudelaire was found innocent on this charge but guilty on the other, and the six poems banned by the verdict included two of the three lesbian poems—despite the fact that just before publication Baudelaire had rewritten the end of 'Condemned Women: Delphine and Hippolyta' to emphasize the condemnation of their illicit passion.

More shocking, though, to nineteenth-century readers than scenes of love between women, which had occured in both pornographic and 'serious' literature,[6] was the linking of sex

---

[5] For discussion of the changes made in the second edition and their effect on the volume as a whole, see Note on the Text, below.

[6] Honoré de Balzac's 'The Girl with Green Eyes' and Théophile Gautier's *Mademoiselle de Maupin*, like the much reprinted anonymous French pornographic novel *Gamiani, or Two Nights of Excess*, involve

with sadism and death in *The Flowers of Evil*. By 1859 there was one poem ineluctably tied to the name Baudelaire: 'A Carcass'. The opening lines of this poem, addressing the beloved as his 'soul' in the past tense of the greatest formality—'Rappelez-vous l'objet que nous vîmes, mon âme, | Ce beau matin d'été si doux' ('Remember, my love, the object we saw | That beautiful morning in June')—install us in the universe of Petrarchan love poetry and exalted sentiments, but the object the lovers saw proves to be not a flower but a rotting corpse, and the lengthy, disgusting description makes it a sexual object:

> Her legs were spread out like a lecherous whore,
>   Sweating out poisonous fumes,
> Who opened in slick invitational style
>   Her stinking and festering womb.

The end of the poem enforces the juxtaposition:

> —And you, in your turn, will be rotten as this:
>   Horrible, filthy, undone,
> O sun of my nature and star of my eyes,
>   My passion, my angel in one!

No wonder a journalist complained that Baudelaire had invented 'carcass literature' ('la littérature-charogne'). Though evocations of rotting corpses are relatively infrequent in *The Flowers of Evil*—just a few set a tone—one suspects that complaints about corpses are a convenient outlet for discomforts with aspects of this poetry more difficult to define, such as its general negativity, its relentless irony, and its refusal of the sentimental or heartwarming gesture. But complaints about corpses may also be a way of objecting to a sadism of which it was difficult to speak—though one reviewer of the 1857 edition maintained that 'Never has one seen so many breasts bitten or even chewed in so few pages'.

---

lovemaking between women; but all put forward the suggestion that, ultimately, women would find greater satisfaction with men—a note completely absent from Baudelaire's poems.

Clearly the poems about love, which comprise a considerable portion of the first section of *The Flowers of Evil*, struck contemporaries as unusual. They are likely to seem so to us as well—for their diversity. *The Flowers of Evil* contains the most extraordinary body of love poetry, or poetry about love, we possess—extraordinary, first, for the variety of amorous relations explored and, second, for the surprising combination of attitudes, the involutions of the passion they explore. By turn tender, reverent, vicious, sententious, suppliant, declamatory, mocking, and insinuating, these poems often shift abruptly from one tone to another, enacting the instabilities of fantasy so central to passion. It is as though Baudelaire, inheritor of the tradition of Renaissance and Baroque love poetry and an adept of the discourse of modern urban debauchery, had wagered that the range and complexity of human passion could be as great as the rhetorical and imaginative resources of his language. That the visions of his poems have been found compelling suggests that he was right.

Critics have generally not seen the love poetry in this way, as a demonstration that the complications of amorous experience can be as great as our possibilities of rhetorical invention. In fact, they have coped with the extraordinary diversity of the love poetry, the daring of its rhetorical exuberance, by dividing the poems into 'cycles' addressed to different women. Thus poems 22–39 are the cycle of the 'Black Venus', a mulatto named Jeanne Duval, sometime prostitute, with whom Baudelaire lived on and off for most of his adult life; poems 40–48 form the cycle of the 'White Venus', Apollonie Sabatier, a celebrated beauty whose salon was a meeting place for artists and writers, and to whom Baudelaire anonymously sent a number of these poems; and poems 49–57, called the cycle of 'the Green-eyed Venus' have been linked to an actress named Marie Daubrun, whom Baudelaire pursued briefly in 1854–5 and again in 1859. As anyone reading these poems for the first time can see, the references to identifiable qualities of specific women are relatively rare. (Given the poems in a random order and asked to sort them into three groups, no one could come up with the groups we have; it is even hard to tell, without looking it up, where one cycle is supposed to end and another begin.)[7] In using the figures of these three women to think about the poems of love, critics have obscured the tremendous variety of amorous relations dramatized by Baudelaire. It simply is not true that the Black Venus represents a sensual, sinful love, the White Venus an idealized, Platonic love, and the Green-Eyed Venus some combination of the two. Each group contains a variety of attitudes and relations (which is why critics have to speak of 'cycles'—a word Baudelaire never used).

Thus the poems to or about Madame Sabatier are supposed to be the cycle of an idealized love: she is his 'dear Goddess, lucid, pure and wise' ('The Spiritual Dawn'). But 'To One Who Is Too Cheerful', which was banned by the court, speaks of a desire to creep up while she sleeps and

> To bruise your ever-tender breast
> And carve in your astonished side
> An injury both deep and wide,
> To chastize your too-joyous flesh.
>
> And, sweetness that would dizzy me!
> In these two lips so red and new
> My sister, I have made for you,
> To slip my venom, lovingly!

The speaker would punish her self-sufficiency and physical vibrancy by sadistically inventing his own 'dizzying' sexual relation to a mutilated body, creating what he imagines as a more exciting simulacrum of a vagina, into which he can infuse the poison of his own nature, making her like him.

The poems linked with Marie Daubrun are especially striking in their combination of attitudes. She is 'My sister, my child' whom the famous 'Invitation to the Voyage' invites to a land

---

[7] Baudelaire himself never speaks of three cycles, and if he had wished readers to treat the poems as about specific women, nothing would have been easier than for him to use subheadings, such as 'Poems to Jeanne', to make readers construct a single figure in each case. The fact that he declined to do this gives the poems a much greater power of generalization, as they come to refer not to qualities of a single individual but to general aspects of possible relationships.

of order and beauty 'that resembles you', and also the 'soft enchantress' and 'majestic child' of 'The Splendid Ship', But 'Poison' tells us that the poison which flows from her eyes is more powerful than wine or opium.

> But all that is not worth the prodigy
>   Of your saliva, girl,
> That bites my soul, and dizzies it, and swirls
>   It down remorselessly,
> Rolling it, fainting, to the underworld!

And 'To a Madonna' joins a tradition of poetic celebration, where the poet imagines various aspects of his passion as ornaments for the beloved, with a blasphemous version of allegorical representations of the Virgin, in which the seven deadly sins are seven daggers piercing her heart. In order to complete the role of worshipped Madonna in which he is casting her

> Full of a dark, remorseful joy, I'll take
> The seven deadly sins, and of them make
> Seven bright Daggers; with a juggler's lore
> Target your love within its deepest core,
> And plant them all within your panting Heart,
> Within your sobbing Heart, your streaming Heart!

The phantasms of this remorseful joy take us beyond relations to any woman in particular to a claim about the imbrication of sadism, passion, and veneration.

The longest cycle, Jeanne Duval's, contains a remarkable variety of tones and utterance. The speaker vituperates:

> You'd entertain the universe in bed,
> Foul woman . . .
>
>   ('You'd entertain the universe . . .')

He fondly mocks:

> Your childlike head lolls with the weight
>   Of all your idleness,
> And sways with all the slackness of
>   A baby elephant's.
>
>   ('The Dancing Serpent')

He surrenders:

> I cry in every fibre of my flesh:
> 'O my Beelzebub, I worship you!'
>
> ('The Possessed')

He supplicates:

> I beg your pity, you, my only love.
>
> ('*De profundis clamavi*')

He tenderly remembers:

> Evenings . . .
> We often told ourselves imperishable things.
>
> .   .   .   .
>
> In my fraternal hands, your feet would go to sleep.
>
> ('The Balcony')

He summons a fusion of love and oblivion:

> I want to sleep! to sleep and not to live!
> And in a sleep as sweet as death, to dream
> Of spreading out my kisses without shame
> On your smooth body, bright with copper sheen.
>
> ('Lethe')

Or he performs speech acts yet unnamed, as when a declaration of love ('I love you as I love the night's high vault, | O silent one') turns into utterance that resists interpretation as communication to the beloved:

> I climb to the assault, attack the source,
> A choir of wormlets pressing towards a corpse,
> And cherish your unbending cruelty,
> This iciness so beautiful to me.
>
> ('I love you as I love . . .')

The self-reflective irony in such strange modes of address (comparing yourself in lovemaking to a choir of wormlets!) places the utterance of poems such as this in a world of poetic action, where the workings of fantasy in the confection of a passionate self can be tested.

Baudelaire's poems of love are exciting for the particular combinations of attitudes they achieve, for the rhetorical daring that weaves declamatory moments with soothing rhythms or sardonic anti-climaxes, for the surprising images—like the 'choir of wormlets' above—which seem very far from empirical situations and for that very reason suggest deeper insights into the mechanisms of desire and the intense farces and tragedies of its realization. Baudelaire's is a poetry of the body, but while most love poetry identifies the woman with her body, the object of the male gaze, Baudelaire's is more explicit than most in its engagement with the body as site of phantasms, stimulus to imagination and reverie, and prompter of memory. The woman herself, we might say, is left aside as the gestures and textures of bodies, conceived as if in memory, produce dramas or exchanges, direct fantasies, prompt utterance and reflection. This poetry suggests that imagination never works harder than when love is 'physical'; conversely, it displays the sadism and physicality of the most spiritual love.

What is missing from Baudelaire's love poetry is the note of satisfied mutuality that we occasionally find elsewhere. The idea of concord, he suggests, is a delusion: when making love 'the man sighs, "O my angel!" The woman cries, "Mama!" And these two imbeciles are persuaded that they are thinking as one' (*Intimate Journals*). Even in moments of contentment, as when the speaker imagines sleeping in the shade of a young giantess, there is no satisfied mutuality or reciprocity. Is this part of Baudelaire's modernity, or is it, rather, a subversion of our dearest 'modern' belief, that we can find love?

III

Until now this discussion has not mentioned what is usually emphasized in discussions of Baudelaire, his modernity. What is it that leads poets and critics to speak of Baudelaire as the founder of modern poetry? We could certainly say that Baudelaire, in his social existence—fleeing creditors, hanging out with prostitutes, living in cheap hotel rooms, struggling to sell articles to journals—helped contribute to a shift in the idea of the poet: the modern poet is not a seer or public spokesman, like Victor Hugo, Wordsworth, or Pope, but a social misfit, a *poète maudit*, cursed and ostracized because of his commitment to poetry. But there were many other poets living on the fringes of a hostile society, so this does little to explain Baudelaire's significance. Paul Verlaine, one of the first to declare Baudelaire's overwhelming importance, claimed that 'the profound originality of Charles Baudelaire is to represent powerfully and essentially modern man'—'modern man, made what he is by the refinements of excessive civilization, modern man with his sharpened and vibrant senses, his painfully subtle mind, his brain saturated with tobacco, and his blood poisoned by alcohol'. And T. S. Eliot writes, 'Baudelaire is indeed the greatest exemplar in *modern* poetry in any language, for his verse and language is the nearest thing to a complete renovation that we have experienced. But his renovation of an attitude towards life is no less radical and no less important.' Baudelaire is seen not only as the creator of a new sort of poetry but as instigator of something like modern experience, an experience of life that we regard as modern. Clearly there is more to this than alcohol, tobacco, and nervousness, and one wants to know what it is about *The Flowers of Evil*, given its conservatism in matters of poetic form, that makes it seem to explore the possibility of a distinctly modern experience.

A first answer is this poetry's ability to bring into verse the banal, the prosaic, or the disgusting—thought to loom especially large in modern life—and give it a poetic function. Praising the power of the beloved's saliva as well as her eyes ('Poison'), comparing the sky to the lid of a pot ('Spleen (IV)'), or suggesting that we become attached to feeling remorse, 'as beggars take to nourishing their lice' ('To the Reader'), Baudelaire produces dissonant combinations, which can be seen as reflecting the dissociated character of modern experience, where consciousness is confronted by objects, sensations, and experiences that do not go together. Dissonant images may also be seen, though, as models for combining or synthesizing disparate :nsations, offering moderns a way of appreciating and thus dealing with inchoate experience, encouraging a poetic attitude to the alienation said to characterize modern life. The very title, *The Flowers of Evil*, underlines an aesthetic of bizarre combinations. In addition, dissonant images foreground the operations of language themselves and the problem of sense-making that is so central to the play of modern literature.

Second, Baudelaire is a poet of the city, the first, as Albert Thibaudet wrote, to create a new situation for poetry by taking as the norm life in large cities and the new human relationships and temporality that urban life creates, as men and women pass among people they do not know in settings marked by an ever-changing history.[8] In his *Salon of 1846* Baudelaire writes that Parisian life is 'fertile in poetic and marvellous subjects', and he singles out 'the spectacle of the elegant world and of the thousands of floating existences which circulate in the subterranean labyrinths of a great city—criminals and prostitutes'—all of whom appear in *The Flowers of Evil*. But this is not descriptive poetry of the city, glorying in sights and sounds. The section called 'Parisian Scenes' would surprise anyone expecting urban descriptions, for it begins with 'Landscape', in which the poet, looking out over the roof-tops, claims he will close his shutters and conjure up a world out of his imagination. And when we do get description, it may be something like this:

> Meanwhile, corrupting demons of the air
> Slowly wake up like men of great affairs.
> And, flying, bump our shutters and our eaves.
> Against the glimmerings teased by the breeze
> Old Prostitution blazes in the streets;
> She opens out her nest-of-ants retreat;
> Everywhere she clears the secret routes,
> A stealthy force preparing for a coup;
> She moves within this city made of mud,
> A worm who steals from man his daily food.

----

[8] Albert Thibaudet, 'Baudelaire', *Intérieurs* (Paris: Plon, 1924), 7–35. This forgotten essay of Thibaudet's is among the best, most original discussions of Baudelaire. Many of its insights are developed in Walter Benjamin's *Charles Baudelaire: A Lyric Poet in the Era of High Capitalism* (London: New Left Books, 1973).

One hears the hissing kitchens close at hand,
The playhouse screech, the blaring of a band.
The tables at the inns where gamesmen sport
Are full of swindlers, sluts, and all their sort.
Robbers who show no pity to their prey
Get ready for their nightly work-a-day
Of cracking safes and deftly forcing doors,
To live a few days more and dress their whores.

('Dusk')

Poetry of the city, no doubt, but poetry whose most prosaic details (kitchens, safes) seem to have much the same status as the patently unrealistic (the corrupting demons of the air), as though the true subject were the strange realm produced by their intersection. This poetry creates a level of event at which personifications, such as Prostitution, can act along with the demons and the robbers, swindlers, beggars, and other urban types. The low-life figures who parade through the Parisian scenes—sinister old men, broken-down old women, gamblers, criminals, and prostitutes—are figures as much imagined as observed, like the seven appalling and identical creatures of 'The Seven Old Men' who, appearing one after another before the speaker, threaten his sanity and cast him loose like a mastless ship on a monstrous sea.

Some of Baudelaire's greatest poems—'The Swan', 'The Little Old Women', 'The Seven Old Men'—belong to 'Parisian Scenes', but as their narrators wander through the 'sinuous coils of the old capitals', the encounters with these grotesque figures become above all struggles over meaning, attempts to understand their mystery. These struggles can produce pleasure—the satisfaction of empathy in 'The Little Old Women'—or melancholy at the oppressiveness of the interpretive process:

Paris may change, but in my melancholy mood
Nothing has budged! New palaces, blocks, scaffoldings,
Old neighbourhoods, are allegorical for me
And my dear memories are heavier than stone.

('The Swan')

or fright at the tenuousness of meaning:

> Bedazzled, like a double-visioned drunk,
> I staggered home and shut the door, aghast,
> Shaking and sick, the spirit feverous,
> Struck by this mystery, this absurdity!
>
> ('The Seven Old Men')

City life in this poetry is not modern inventions, commerce, and progress but dangerous passage through a forest of anonymous figures imbued with mystery, who produce a vivid sense of a world not masterable except by arbitrary and unstable acts of imagination.

But Victor Hugo had written poems of the city—about beggars, prostitutes, and working men, among others—and Baudelaire declared Hugo 'the most gifted, the most visibly elected to express through poetry what I will call the *mystery of life*'. What was different about Baudelaire's poetry?

The repudiation of sentimental themes is a major aspect of Baudelaire's modernity. Baudelaire complained about Hugo's prostitutes with hearts of gold and criminals with consciences, and proposed to write a story of an unrepentant criminal enjoying the fruits of his crimes. Hugo wrote a poem called 'Never Insult a Woman who is Falling', but Baudelaire always insults, while lamenting and celebrating at the same time. His 'Little Old Women' are 'singular beings with appalling charms':

> These dislocated wrecks were women once . . .
> . . . . .
> They toddle, every bit like marionettes,
> Or drag themselves like wounded animals.

They 'trudge on, stoic, without complaint, Through the chaotic city's teeming waste', and the poet who follows them, as other men would follow a beautiful young woman, observes 'with tenderness, and restless eye intent', imaginatively sharing their 'lost days', their secret pleasures and fears. They are 'Ruins! my family! my fellow-minds!'.

These energetic verses, whose tone shifts radically from irony to empathy, from cruelty and detachment to declamation, are more modern in their discontinuities than anything Hugo wrote. As in the poems about lesbians and about heterosexual love, the harshness and shifts of mood give this verse what seems a modern complexity.

These changes of tone are part of the irony and self-consciousness that mark Baudelaire's verse, where the speakers often turn and reflect upon what they have been saying or doing and its implications. '*Heautontimoroumenos*' (the self-torturer) is the most extreme example, where the speaker begins by announcing an intention to strike the beloved coldly, without anger, for sadistic pleasure, but the very formulation of this intention brings an ironic self-reflection, in which he becomes a victim of his own self-consciousness,

> Thanks to voracious Irony
> Who gnaws on me and shakes me hard.
>
> She's in my voice, in all I do!
> Her poison flows in all my veins!

The irony described here is inseparable from a process of poetic self-dramatization: the rhetorical resources of the poetic imagination become a source of self-torture as well as of perverse satisfaction.

Less extreme and grandiloquent, and perhaps the more sinister, is the movement of 'Gaming', which begins with the description of decrepit gamblers and prostitutes in a shabby gaming house. This turns out to be a dream or vision of the speaker, in which he sees himself mutely envying 'these men's tenacious lust, | The morbid gaiety of these old whores'. Reflecting on the implications of this vision, though, he is frightened that he should envy 'this poor lot | Who rush so fervently to the abyss'. It is indeed a peculiar condition, of the sort these poems excel in portraying.

When the focus of interest in the poem is not objects and events themselves but the speaker's relation to them and his responses to this relation, then we have dramas of consciousness which readers and critics have found particularly modern. The second 'Spleen' poem is a compelling example: it describes a loss of self in images that make unreal the experiences they purport to capture. The poem begins:

> More memories than if I'd lived a thousand years!
>
> A giant chest of drawers, stuffed to the full,
> With balance sheets, love letters, lawsuits, verse
> Romances, locks of hair rolled in receipts,
> Hides fewer secrets than my sullen skull.
> It is a pyramid, a giant vault,
> Holding more corpses than a common grave.
> —I am a graveyard hated by the moon
> Where like remorse the long worms crawl, and turn
> Attention to the dearest of my dead.

What could be thought of as a wealth of memories is experienced as excessive or oppressive, unmasterable as the experience of a subject. The imaginative operations of an ironic, self-reflective consciousness transform this heterogeneous series of writings and documents into so much dead matter: first more corpses than the common grave, and then, in an image which one contemporary reviewer quoted as summing up *The Flowers of Evil*, 'a graveyard hated by the moon'.

As the accumulated memories become dead matter, ennui takes on immortal proportions. Ennui is the force of boredom and depression that 'To the Reader' calls the ugliest, meanest, most obscene monster in the human zoo. The self, further depersonalized and addressed just as 'living matter' (*matière vivante*), is identified with a granite monument forgotten in the desert.

> —Henceforth, o living flesh, you are no more!
> You are of granite, wrapped in a vague dread,
> Slumbering in some Sahara's hazy sands,
> An ancient sphinx lost to a careless world,
> Forgotten on the map, whose haughty mood
> Sings only in the glow of setting sun.

The poem began with the question of what becomes of the self among this excess of discourses and experiences which cannot be mastered or integrated—a condition more frustrating, even ridiculous, than tragic—but it ends with an identification of the self with the lurid figure of a sphinx forgotten in a desert, singing to the setting sun. The very hyperbole of the images—a graveyard hated by the moon, a piece of granite wrapped in a vague dread—suggests that we are dealing not with empirical incidents or predicaments but with the drama of a generalized modern consciousness. The poem's emphatic denial that any of the experiences or memories are themselves of interest leaves the impression that any value must lie in the operations of consciousness themselves, such as memory, revulsion, or self-criticism. Such operations of consciousness, this poetry shows, can even give an interest and value to the most horrendous conditions—such as being more full of dead bodies than a common grave. The perverse pleasure that the modern subject dramatized in the poem takes in representing itself as a forgotten sphinx grumpily singing in the desert suggests that there are ways of surviving the disintegration and depersonalization of the self described here, that whatever the modern threats to the self, a certain poetic consciousness can salvage at least itself from the collapse of signification and value, and that, thus, the subject remains the source of meaning and untranscendable horizon. If Baudelaire is seen as the prophet of modernity, it is no doubt because his lyrics can be read as asking how one can experience or come to terms with the modern world and as offering poetic consciousness as a solution—albeit a desperate one, requiring a passage through negativity.

IV

But this model does not exhaust *The Flowers of Evil*. Baudelaire's irony often works in a different way, without involving the dramatization of the ironic attitude of a speaker. Frequently, for example, irony results from readers' perceptions of discrepancies between poems: it is not so much that a speaker is being ironic as that the formulations of one poem undercut or ironically frame those of another. For example, the opening poem of 'Spleen and the Ideal', 'Benediction', recounts the birth of the poet, his persecution by his mother and wife, and his presumption that these sufferings are the price of glory and that God will, of course, make him a halo of pure light, far outshining earth's richest jewels. In a prose poem, Baudelaire writes ironically of the poet losing his halo as he dashes across a muddy street and deciding not to advertise for its return—a more modern attitude, no doubt. Alerted by this text and by the self-consciousness of others, one can notice odd things about 'Benediction': while the poet of 'To the Reader' claimed, in a convincing conclusion, to be the twin of or brother to the hypocrite reader, the poet described in the very next poem, 'Benediction', has no relation to earthly readers. A parody of the visionary poet, he pays no attention to what happens around him and nothing earthly is good enough for him. The blinding light of his majestic intellect, we are told, blots out the sight of angry mortals, such as his wife and mother. This poet, one realizes, could not have written this poem, much of whose energy comes from its representation of the fury and plottings of mother and wife; therefore, one can scarcely accept as gospel the poem's account of the poet. It seems to present a traditional myth of the poet, which will be gradually undercut by the actual workings of the poems of *The Flowers of Evil*.

The fourth poem in the collection, 'Correspondences', is often read as Baudelaire's affirmation of a traditional notion: that the poet's task is to convey correspondences between things terrestrial and celestial, revealing the spiritual significance of earthly matters. In fact, the poem gives us a much stranger, more uncertain vision. A literal translation of the opening quatrains would read: 'Nature is a temple where living pillars often let emerge confused words; man passes through forests of symbols which observe him with familiar looks. Like long echoes which heard from afar are confused together in a shadowy and profound unity, as vast as night and as luminescence, smells, colours, and sounds answer one another.' Compared with poems of Victor Hugo and Alphonse de Lamartine, which asserted that nature was a temple, in that each thing testified to the glory of God, Baudelaire's version is an ironic, potentially demystifying reflection on this tradition and on the notion of poet as decipherer of spiritual significance.[9]

Another important feature of Baudelaire's verse which is not reducible to the experience of a subject or consciousness is its use of personification or abstract agents to establish dramas of meaning. I can experience anguish but if Anguish plants its black flag in my bowed skull, as happens in the fourth 'Spleen' poem, this is not the experience of a subject but a risky attempt to describe problems of the human condition more powerfully by abandoning the level of individual experience for a different kind of narrative. This sort of writing has often been called allegorical, but that term simplifies rather than clarifies the strange procedures of Baudelairian verse, which we observed earlier: in 'Dusk' a series of most diverse protagonists—the demons who get up heavily like businessmen, Prostitution which lights up in the streets, and the robbers and whores who go about their business—converge in a special linguistic space. In these non-realistic narratives we find operating a host of Baudelairian figures: Evil, Ennui, Spleen, Pain, Demons, and, perhaps most important, the Devil himself.

V

The Devil—here is one thing that makes Baudelaire seem scarcely modern. Surely the Devil is an archaic myth, an outmoded piece of mythological machinery, no longer taken very seriously even by practising Christians. What can an enlightened religion do with a scrawny red man with horns, hooves, tail, and pitchfork? But the opening poem of *The Flowers of Evil*, 'To the Reader', firmly declares, 'Truly the Devil pulls on all our strings!' and 'Close, swarming, like a million writhing worms, | A demon nation [*un peuple de Démons*] riots in our brains'. Baudelaire considered himself a Catholic, but his

---

[9] For discussion see Jonathan Culler, 'Baudelaire's "Correspondances": Intertextuality and Interpretation', in Christopher Prendergast, ed., *Nineteenth-Century French Poetry* (Cambridge: Cambridge University Press, 1990).

Catholicism is most unorthodox (others consider him a heretic, a Christian without Christ). The poems frequently play upon religious imagery, but the clearest sign of religion in his poetry and prose is the Devil. Modern critics who concur on little else seem to agree that this side of Baudelaire—the Baudelaire of Satan, Demons, and Evil with a capital E—is of little interest or importance, not part of Baudelaire's and our modernity but the stale remnant of a gothic Romanticism which boldly invoked infernal powers. This consensus suggests, at the very least, that there might be something disquieting at issue in this aspect of Baudelaire's poetry and that we should at least ask about the significance of the Devil in what are, after all, 'The Flowers of Evil'.

'To the Reader' tells us that we are puppets of Satan: he holds the strings that move us.

> On evil's pillow lies the alchemist,
> Satan Thrice-Great, who lulls our captive soul,
> And all the richest metal of our will
> Is vaporized by his hermetic arts.

Sometimes he makes us act, sometimes prevents us from having the will to act as we would. The first seven stanzas of 'The Irremediable' present a series of images of human oppression and entrapment which, the poem suggests, illustrate Satan's effectiveness:

> Pure emblems, a perfect tableau
> Of an irremediable evil,
> Which makes us think that the Devil
> Does well what he chooses to do!

But the phrase 'makes us think' leaves open the possibility that we may be mistaken. Perhaps the Devil isn't really responsible for these disasters and entrapments after all. Since the poem immediately proceeds to speak of the 'Sombre and limpid tête-à-tête | Of a heart become its own mirror', it is possible that the earlier images show not the Devil's ubiquity but the heart's power of projection. What is most diabolical about the Devil, we might say, is that we can never be sure when he is at work. 'He swirls around me like a subtle breeze', says the speaker of 'Destruction', the opening poem of the section 'Flowers of Evil'. I swallow him; he inspires eternal and guilty desires; he leads me into the plains of Ennui. Sometimes he takes 'a woman's form—most perfect, most corrupt'. Elsewhere Baudelaire speaks of love as a 'Satanic religion' and of an 'ineluctable Satanic logic' whereby fleshly pleasure leads to the delights of crime. The speaker of 'The Possessed' reports that every fibre of his body cries to his beloved, 'O my Beelzebub, I worship you!' There is always a question, it seems, whether a woman is a Satanic manifestation. 'From Heaven or Hell, who cares!' exclaim Baudelairian narrators in moments of desperation, but that this should come as the climax of agonized reflection shows that usually they care very much whether they are dealing with the Devil, though they can never know for sure. When the sinister old man in 'The Seven Old Men' seems to multiply himself seven times, the speaker suspects a diabolical plot, but it could also be just 'wicked chance' that humiliates him by making him suspect a plot.

We might say that the figure of the Devil poses the general question of whether there is a meaning to the scenarios in which we are caught up or misfortunes that befall us, or whether they are simply accidents. Can we escape our sense that there are malignant forces that operate independently of human intentions or that the world often works against us? 'Everyone *feels* the Devil but no one believes in him', wrote Baudelaire. As the prose poem 'The Generous Gambler' puts it, 'the Devil's subtlest ruse is to convince us that he doesn't exist'.

If the Devil is the name of a force that works on us against our will—if, as Baudelaire says in 'To the Reader', 'all the richest metal of our will | Is vaporized by his hermetic arts'— isn't he just a personification of aspects of what Freud called the Unconscious or the Id, forces that make us do what our conscious selves might reject? To make Baudelaire modern can't we just cross out *Devil* and write in *Unconscious* or, better, *Death Drive*, or *Repetition Compulsion*? There is something to be said for this view, though one would have to work out the analogy and the substitution more precisely. Baudelaire, though, had thought about this possibility and in his prose poem 'The Bad Glazier' speaks of 'that mood [*humeur*] termed hysterical by doctors and Satanical by those who think rather more clearly than doctors, which pushes us unresisting towards a host of dangerous or unsuitable actions'. The Satanical hypothesis is clearer thinking, one surmises, because it adduces not an individual disorder but impersonal structures and forces. When Gustave Flaubert objected to Baudelaire that he 'insisted too much on the *Evil Spirit*' (*l'Esprit du Mal*), Baudelaire replied, 'I have always been obsessed by the impossibility of accounting for some of man's sudden actions or thoughts without the hypothesis of the intervention of an evil force outside him— Here's a scandalous avowal for which the whole nineteenth century won't make me blush'.

Christian theology introduces the Devil to account for the presence of evil in the world. If God is not to be held responsible for evil, there must be another creature whose free choice in deviating from good introduced evil. The Devil, thus, is not a symbol of evil but an agent or personification whose ability to act is essential. *The Flowers of Evil* make him an actor as well, along with other unexpected agents: Prostitution, which lights up in the streets; Anguish, which plants its black flag in my skull; Ennui, who puffs on his hookah and dreams of gallows; and many other figures who people these poems. To dismiss Satan as just a 'personification' of evil requires remarkable confidence about what can and what cannot act. Behind this may lie the wishful presumption that only human individuals can act, that they control the world and that there are no other agents; but the world would be a very different place if this were true. Much of its difficulty as well as its mystery comes from the effects produced by actions of other sorts of agents—history, language, 'the market'—which our grammars may personify. These poems, in which Anguish, Autumn, Beauty, Ennui, Hope, Hate and others do their work, pose questions about the constituents and boundaries of persons, about the forces that can act in the world, and about whether this level of allegorical action does not best capture the realities of body, spirit, and history.

This is, finally, a question about the sort of rhetoric best suited to explore our condition. In his 'Epigraph for a Condemned Book', Baudelaire takes up again the distinction between the hysterical and the Satanic that we encountered in 'The Bad Glazier' and urges any reader who has not studied rhetoric with Satan to throw away this 'Saturnian book':

> unless you've learned
> Your rhetoric in Satan's school
> You will not understand a word,
> You'll think I am hysterical.

To study rhetoric with Satan is to complete your education ('Rhetoric' was the name of the last year of *lycée*, or grammar school). Satan the tempter or seducer is a master of persuasive discourse, but rhetoric in this sense would work on novices as well as experts, so the epigraph must rather have in view rhetoric as a way of analysing and articulating the world. When Baudelaire speaks of the best contemporary literature as 'essentially Satanic', he hints at such a notion. To see *The Flowers of Evil* as a Satanic rhetoric is to read it as an exposition or articulation of uncanny forces (forces of evil) that structure our lives and imaginings.

Many readers of Baudelaire's time did think him hysterical, but Baudelaire was convinced that, as he put it in 'To the Reader', whatever our hypocritical claims, we are thoroughly familiar with the forces and figures that people such a world, such as Ennui, 'this dainty monster'. Whether we know it or not, we *have* studied with Satan and may hope to understand Baudelaire's book.

NOTE ON THE TEXT

The first edition of *Les Fleurs du Mal* was published in 1857 by Poulet-Malassis et De Broise, a firm run by a young publisher, Auguste Poulet-Malassis. It contained one hundred poems, plus the prefatory poem 'To the Reader': the vast majority of these poems, seventy-seven, comprised the first section, 'Spleen and the Ideal'; twelve were included in the section entitled 'Flowers of Evil', three in 'Revolt', five in 'Wine', and three in the final section, 'Death'. A table listing the poems of this edition and their placement follows on pp. xxxix–xlv. In the trial of 1857, six poems were condemned for offence to public morals; the copies of the first edition were seized and the six poems were forbidden to be published in France. (In fact, the decision condemning them was reversed only in 1949, nearly a century later, although editions of *Les Fleurs du Mal* containing the banned poems had been sold for some time without attracting the attention of the police.)

Since most of the first edition had been confiscated, Baudelaire and Poulet-Malassis needed to produce a second edition. With considerable irritation, Baudelaire went back to work: 'To have to start again on these damned *Fleurs du Mal*!' he complained (19 Feb. 1858). He undertook to compose twenty new poems, but in fact 1858–60 turned out to be one of his greatest periods of creativity and the new edition, which finally appeared early in 1861, contained thirty-five new poems. (In addition, Baudelaire made some changes, mostly minor, to the poems already published.) This 1861 edition, also published by Poulet-Malassis, is the one generally followed by modern editions of Baudelaire and is the one used here. It has the disadvantage, however, of omitting from the body of the work the six banned poems; we have chosen to reinsert them according to their place in the 1857 edition. This procedure has the advantage of enriching the sections to which these six poems belong and of preventing readers from considering them above all as poems that were banned. The table below indicates which are the poems added in 1861, where they were inserted, and where poems from the 1857 edition were arranged differently in 1861.

Arrangement of Poems in the First Two Editions of 'Les Fleurs du Mal'

A dash (—) in the 1861 column indicates that the poem listed on the same line in the 1857 column appears here in 1861. Poems whose names appear in the 1861 list are new, unless their former place in the 1857 edition is indicated in brackets.

	1857		*1861*
	To the Reader		To the Reader
	Spleen and the Ideal		*Spleen and the Ideal*
1.	Benediction	1.	—
2.	The Sun [87 in 1861]	2.	The Albatross
3.	Elevation	3.	—
4.	Correspondences	4.	—
5.	'I love the thought . . .'	5.	—
6.	The Beacons	6.	—
7.	The Sick Muse	7.	—
8.	The Venal Muse	8.	—
9.	The Wretched Monk	9.	—
10.	The Enemy	10.	—
11.	Ill Fortune	11.	—
12.	A Former Life	12.	—
13.	Gypsies Travelling	13.	—
14.	Man and the Sea	14.	—
15.	Don Juan in Hell	15.	—
16.	Punishment for Pride	16.	—
17.	Beauty	17.	—
18.	The Ideal	18.	—

The 1861 edition of *The Flowers of Evil*, which we are reprinting here, brought four major changes.

(1) A new section was added: 'Parisian Scenes' (*Tableaux parisiens*). This section not only contains what are now some of Baudelaire's most celebrated poems, such as 'The Swan', 'The Seven Old Men', and 'The Little Old Women'; its intense yet ironical engagement with urban life and its phantasmagoria

today seems quintessentially Baudelairian, the soul of *The Flowers of Evil*.

(2) Thirteen poems were removed from the end of 'Spleen and the Ideal', where they had formed something of a miscellany, and were placed as appropriate: in 'Parisian Scenes', among the poems about or addressed to women in the middle of 'Spleen and the Ideal', or among the poems about the poet's meditations which follow the poems to and about women. This rearrangement, together with the insertion at the end of 'Spleen and the Ideal' of a number of poems about self-torment and the oppressions of life, gave this section a different, more intense ending—indeed, a climax that had been lacking in 1857.

(3) The rearrangement and the addition of new love poems gave this part of 'Spleen and the Ideal' a new diversity, in the sorts of amorous relations conceived.

(4) The section 'Wine' was moved from its place just before 'Death' in 1857 to follow the new 'Parisian Scenes' in 1861, so that emphasis came to fall less on wine as an escape and prelude to death and more on the diverse characters of the city—ragpickers, murderers, lovers, artists—whose lives wine touches.

Critics agree that the 1861 edition is a stronger collection, not only because of the new poems, but because of the rearrangement Baudelaire produced.

Later in the 1860s, Baudelaire wished to publish a further edition of *The Flowers of Evil* as part of a collected edition of his works but had not succeeded in negotiating arrangements with a publisher before he fell ill. In 1865 Baudelaire and Poulet-Malassis decided to reprint the banned poems along with some others in Belgium, where books banned in France were often published. *Les Épaves de Charles Baudelaire* ('Charles Baudelaire's Waifs' or 'Cast-offs') appeared in 1866. The cover claimed that it was published in Amsterdam 'At the Sign of the Cock' but it was actually printed by Poulet-Malassis in Brussels. An unsigned Editor's Note stated: 'This collection consists of poems, for the most part banned or unpublished, which Mr. Charles Baudelaire did not wish to place in the definitive edition of *The Flowers of Evil*.' The note also claimed that the collection was published without the author's knowledge, by a friend to whom he had given the poems and who wished to share his pleasure in them.

The Waifs contained twenty-three poems, including the six banned poems (grouped together as poems II–VII under the heading 'Banned Poems Taken from *The Flowers of Evil*') and 'Praises for My Francisca', which in fact appeared in every edition of *The Flowers of Evil*. We print the other sixteen poems in the order in which they appeared.

After Baudelaire's death in 1867, his friends Charles Asselineau and Théodore de Banville undertook to produce a new edition of the poems for the complete works, to be published by Michel Lévy. This volume, the third edition of *The Flowers of Evil*, appeared in 1868. In producing this edition, Asselineau and Banville used a copy of the 1861 edition in which Baudelaire himself had inserted eleven further poems. It is not known for certain which poems these were, much less where Baudelaire would have liked to have had them inserted, if indeed he had made any such decision (in 1867, when Michel Lévy visited Baudelaire during his illness and expressed a wish to begin publishing the complete works straight away, Baudelaire, though he could not speak, made it clear by gestures, pointing to dates in a diary, that he wanted Levy to wait three months—presumably in the hope that he would have recovered and could have a hand in the arrangement).[1] In addition to these eleven poems, Asselineau and Banville decided to add further poems as well, some of which scarcely seem to belong to *The Flowers of Evil*, to a total of twenty-five: they reprinted twelve poems from *The Waifs*, despite the explicit statement there that these were poems Baudelaire did not see fit to include in *The Flowers of Evil*, a poem to Banville himself ('To Théodore de Banville'), a translation from Longfellow's *Song of Hiawatha* (which we have omitted), and an 'Epigraph for a Condemned Book'. We print the eleven new poems along with

---

[1] Charles Asselineau, Biography of Baudelaire, in Jacques Crépet and Claude Pichois, eds. *Baudelaire et Asselineau* (Paris: Nizet, 1953), 148–9.

'To Théodore de Banville' and 'Epigraph for a Condemned Book' as 'Additional Poems from the Third Edition of *The Flowers of Evil*'.

In the 1868 edition of *The Flowers of Evil*, twenty of the twenty-five additional poems were placed by Asselineau and Banville together in a group towards the end of 'Spleen and the Ideal', between no. 82, 'Congenial Horror', and no. 83, '*Heautontimoroumenos*'. The other five were inserted as follows (I have marked with an asterisk those eleven poems which, by best critical estimates, Baudelaire might have wished to include):

'To Théodore de Banville', after no. 15, 'Don Juan in Hell'

'Poem on the Portrait of Honoré Daumier', after no. 59, 'Sisina'

'Lola de Valence' and 'The Insulted Moon'* in 'Parisian Scenes' after no. 87, 'The Sun'

'Epigraph for a Condemned Book' at the beginning of the 'Flowers of Evil' section, before no. 109, 'Destruction'.

The order of the other twenty poems in the 1868 edition is as follows (after 'Congenial Horror', no. 82): 'The Peacepipe, after Longfellow'; 'Prayer of a Pagan';* 'The Pot Lid';* 'The Unforeseen'; 'Midnight Examination';* 'Sad Madrigal';* 'The Cautioner';* 'To a Girl of Malabar'; 'The Voice'; 'Hymn'; 'The Rebel';* 'Bertha's Eyes'; 'The Fountain'; 'The Ransom'; 'Very Far from France';* 'The Setting of the Romantic Sun'; 'On *Tasso in Prison*, by Eugène Delacroix'; 'The Gulf';* 'Lament of an Icarus';* 'Meditation'.*

SELECT BIBLIOGRAPHY

PROSE WRITINGS OF BAUDELAIRE

Most of Baudelaire's prose has been translated into English. The following list of editions is not exhaustive:

The Prose Poems and La Fanfarlo, trans. Rosemary Lloyd (Oxford: Oxford University Press, 1991), a companion volume to this in the World's Classics series.

Intimate Journals, trans. Christopher Isherwood (London: Methuen, 1949); *My Heart Laid Bare and Other Prose Writings*, trans. Norman Cameron (London: Weidenfeld and Nicolson, 1950).

The Painter of Modern Life and Other Essays, trans. Jonathan Mayne (London: Phaidon Press, 1955).

Art in Paris, 1845–1862: Salons and Other Exhibitions Reviewed by Charles Baudelaire, trans. Jonathan Mayne (London: Phaidon Press, 1965).

Selected Writings on Art and Artists, trans. P. E. Carret (Harmondsworth. Penguin, 1972).

Artificial Paradises; on Hashish and Wine as Means of Expanding Individuality, trans. Ellen Fox (New York: Herder & Herder, 1971); 'Artificial Paradises' in *Hashish, Wine, Opium*, ed. and trans. M. Strong (London: Calder & Boyars, 1972).

Baudelaire as Literary Critic: Selected Essays, trans. Lois Boe Hyslop (University Park: Pennsylvania State University Press, 1964).

'The Essence of Laughter' and Other Essays, ed. Peter Quennell (New York: Meridian Books, 1956).

BIOGRAPHY

There are several biographies; much the best is Claude Pichois and Jean Ziegler, *Baudelaire*, trans. Graham Robb (London: Hamish Hamilton, 1989).

CRITICAL WRITINGS

There is an abundant critical literature in English on Baudelaire and *The Flowers of Evil*. The following are recommended.

Arac, Jonathan, 'Charles Baudelaire and Emily Dickinson', *Critical*

Genealogies (New York: Columbia University Press, 1987). A surprising and revealing comparison.

Benjamin, Walter, *Charles Baudelaire: A Lyric Poet in the Era of High Capitalism* (London: New Left Books, 1973). Extremely influential.

Bersani, Leo, *Baudelaire and Freud* (Berkeley: University of California Press, 1977). A brilliant, resourceful reading focused especially on the love poetry.

Bloom, Harold, ed., *Charles Baudelaire* (New York: Chelsea House, 1987). A selection of valuable essays on the poet.

Burton, Richard, *Baudelaire in 1859* (Cambridge: Cambridge University Press, 1988). Studies Baudelaire's most creative period.

Butor, Michel, *Histoire Extraordinaire: Essay on a Dream of Baudelaire's*, trans. Richard Howard (London: Jonathan Cape, 1969). A splendid reading of *The Flowers of Evil*, which takes a dream as a point of departure and means of integration.

De Man, Paul, 'Anthropomorphism and Trope in the Lyric', *The Rhetoric of Romanticism* (New York: Columbia University Press, 1983). A challenging discussion of 'Correspondences' and of the problem of the lyric.

Eliot, T. S., 'Baudelaire', *Selected Essays* (London: Faber, 1972). A short essay on the importance of Baudelaire and his poetry.

Houston, John Porter, *The Demonic Imagination: Style and Theme in French Romantic Poetry* (Baton Rouge: Louisiana State University Press, 1969). Excellent chapter on Baudelaire as a late Romantic.

Leakey, F. W., *Baudelaire and Nature* (Manchester: Manchester University Press, 1969). A study of key themes.

—— *Baudelaire: Collected Essays* (Cambridge: Cambridge University Press, 1990). Efficient scholarly essays on a range of topics.

Mossop, D. J., *Baudelaire's Tragic Hero* (Oxford: Oxford University Press, 1961). Seeks to elucidate *Les Fleurs du Mal* as a story with a plot.

Peyre, Henri, ed., *Baudelaire*, 20th Century Views (New York: Prentice Hall, 1957). Includes classic essays by Marcel Proust, T. S. Eliot, Erich Auerbach, and others.

Sartre, Jean-Paul, *Baudelaire*, trans. Martin Turnell (London: Hamish Hamilton, 1964). A controversial, rewarding 'existential psychoanalysis', which presents Baudelaire as choosing his fate.

Turnell, Martin, *Baudelaire: A Study of His Poetry* (London: Hamish Hamilton, 1953). A useful overview.

A CHRONOLOGY OF CHARLES BAUDELAIRE

1821   9 April: birth, in Paris, of Charles-Pierre Baudelaire, son of Joseph-François Baudelaire (age 63, painter and administrative officer in the Senate) and Caroline Archenbaut-Dufaÿs (age 28).

1827   Death of Baudelaire's father.

1828   Baudelaire's mother marries Major Jacques Aupick.

1832   Aupick is stationed in Lyons, where Baudelaire attends school.

1836   Aupick is transferred to Paris, where Baudelaire attends Lycée Louis-le-Grand.

1839   Baudelaire is expelled from school for refusing to surrender a note passed to him but is allowed to take his Baccalauréat exam (which he passes).

1839–40   Bohemian existence in Paris with a circle of young poets.

1841   Sent by his parents on a voyage to India designed to remove him from his bohemian milieu, Baudelaire disembarks in Mauritius and Réunion and, refusing to go further, returns to Paris.

1842   On turning 21, Baudelaire inherits 100,000 francs from his father, which would have given him a modest but adequate income, similar to Gustave Flaubert's. Becomes involved with Jeanne Duval, a mulatto actress with whom he lives off and on for most of his life.

1842–4   Collaborates on various literary projects with his friends, writes poetry, including some of the poems of *The Flowers of Evil*, and contracts substantial debts.

1844   Because Baudelaire has been spending his capital and acquiring debts quickly, his family undertakes a judicial procedure to have his money removed from his control and placed in trust for him, under a 'conseil judiciaire' or trustee (Narcisse Ancelle, the family lawyer). This

arrangement, to Baudelaire's great irritation, will last for
the rest of his life.

1845   April–May: first publications: the sonnet 'To a Creole
Lady', later collected in *The Flowers of Evil*, and the *Salon
of 1845*, a substantial article on the annual exhibition of
contemporary painting and sculpture.
June: announces to Ancelle his intention to kill himself
but recovers quickly from a slight wound.
October: advertisement of the imminent publication
of *The Lesbians*, a collection of poems (which never
appeared).

1846   Collaboration on a newspaper *Le Corsaire-Satan*; pub-
lication of further essays and of *The Salon of 1846*, a
wide-ranging discussion of painting and art generally.

1848   February: Baudelaire throws himself into the February
Revolution against the July Monarchy. Works on a short-
lived left political journal, *The Public Good* (*Le Salut
public*) (Feb–March), and for a moderate paper, *The
National Tribune* (April–May).
July: participates in the uprisings against the conservative
turn of new legislature created after the success of the
February Revolution. Baudelaire's first translation of Poe
is published ('The Mesmeric Revolution').
October: appointed editor of a conservative provincial
journal, *The Indre Herald*, but leaves after a few days.
A collection of his poems entitled *Limbo* is announced.

1851   Eleven poems from the projected collection *Limbo* are
published (they will be collected in *The Flowers of Evil*).
Publication of part of *Artificial Paradises*.

1852   The first of three long articles on Edgar Allan Poe is
published.

1852–4 Over a fifteen-month period sends six poems anonym-
ously to Mme Sabatier, a beauty in whose salon artists
and writers met.

1855   Eighteen poems of *The Flowers of Evil* are published
under this title in the prestigious *Revue des deux mondes*.

1857   April: death of General Aupick.
June: publication of *The Flowers of Evil*.
July: seizure of the edition.
August: trial and conviction of Baudelaire and his

publisher, Auguste Poulet-Malassis, for outrage to public decency. They are sentenced to pay fines and six poems are banned.

August: publication of six prose poems.

1859   Period of great productivity during a short stay with his mother at Honfleur.

1860   Publication of *Artificial Paradises*, on hashish and opium.

1861   February: second edition of *The Flowers of Evil*, containing thirty-two new poems. Publication of nine critical articles on contemporary writers.

November: publication of nine prose poems.

December: to the amazement of friends and enemies, Baudelaire presents himself as a candidate for a vacant seat in the French Academy, finally withdrawing as it becomes obvious he is gaining no votes.

1862   Publication of twenty prose poems. Signs of poor health appear.

1863   Publication of seven more prose poems and the important essay, 'The Painter of Modern Life'.

1864   Publication of more prose poems under the title 'Paris Spleen'. Goes to Brussels to give lectures, where, despite his reiterated dislike for Belgium, he remains for two years.

1866   Physical condition worsens.

February: *Les Épaves* (*The Waifs*), a collection of twenty-three miscellaneous poems, including the six condemned *Flowers of Evil*, is published in Brussels.

March: Baudelaire collapses in Namur, Belgium. Beginnings of aphasia and paralysis. 'New Flowers of Evil' (16 poems) published in the journal *Contemporary Parnassus* in Paris.

August: Baudelaire is brought back to Paris.

1867   Baudelaire receives many visitors. He never recovers the power of speech and dies on 31 August.

1868   The third edition of *The Flowers of Evil* is published by Michel Lévy, as volume 1 in the *Complete Works* of Baudelaire.

1949   The Paris Appeals Court overturns the conviction of Baudelaire and Poulet-Malassis for outrage to public decency.

TRANSLATOR'S PREFACE

The translator's pleasures and responsibilities are both heady and humbling. Presuming to translate a great poet, Charles Baudelaire, I was poignantly aware that he had not chosen me to be his collaborator, and that he would have no active say in what his work was to become in my hands. My first allegiance, then, is to Baudelaire, to be a colleague in some way worthy of him. But I have another allegiance as well, to the English-speaking reader of poetry, which requires me to produce in every case, to the best of my creative ability, a poem that will provide the kind of satisfaction to be gained from reading poetry originally created in English. It is unfortunately true that no translator succeeds in this ambition more than part of the time; still, one tries all of the time. As John Frederick Nims has put it, 'the greatest infidelity is to pass off a bad poem in English as representing a good poem in another language'. I act as a poet when I am devising my translations, and it is as a poet that I hope to serve both Baudelaire and the modern reader.

Can there be too many translations of a poet of central importance like Charles Baudelaire? Perhaps so, but will there ever be enough good ones: accurate and poetic? Each translator necessarily brings himself into the equation, so that in each new version Baudelaire will be found transmuted, not only presented in an alien language, but alloyed with an alien sensibility, no two translations ever being alike. The reader with little or no French who would come to Baudelaire should try several routes—read several translations. As translator I have studied all other translations I have come across, while remaining faithful, I trust, to the voice (or voices) in which I myself can best replicate Baudelaire's poetic effects. As 'modern', as frequently outrageous as Baudelaire is in subject and imagery, he is most often traditional in form. What I've tried most to capture, then, is this tension between modern or romantic subject, and classical form (I oversimplify, but the point must be made), which is for me the wonder of Baudelaire's poetic voice. The translator must attempt in some way, in every poem, to capture this tension: to miss it is to lose Baudelaire, indeed to betray him.

Concerning Baudelaire's formality, all of his poems rhyme, and many are written in the classic, 12-syllable alexandrine line. Here arise two major problems, and matters for decision, for translators into English. Most translators have made their choices and have stuck to them programmatically. Edna St Vincent Millay, for instance, insisted on rhyming every poem, and maintaining the 12-syllable line. Richard Howard, on the other hand, has given over the alexandrine in favour of that standby in English, the iambic pentameter line, and he does not attempt regular rhyme, employing other technical devices to try to represent Baudelaire's formality of sound. As for me, I have worked on a case-by-case basis, varying my practice as need be. I often translate first into a long line version, then I try reducing the line to the pentameter. If this reduction does not involve losing or distorting crucial imagery, and if (as is usually true) it produces a livelier movement in English, I use the shorter, more familiar line. I the case of some poems, though, the alexandrine does seem to work gracefully in English, and I have stayed with it (e.g. in translating 'Landscape', a poem of leisurely pace and sumptuous imagery). As for rhyme, I have tried hard to get it, but have not always succeeded. I try not to corrupt imagery or meaning, or even distort meaningful syntax, to force rhyme. In 'The Death of the Poor', for instance, the last stanza depends for its impact on strict syntactical parallelism; I could not rhyme the poem and still replicate this parallelism, so I dropped the rhyme. I had better luck with 'Heautontimoroumenos', where in the penultimate stanza a similar parallelism occurs; this I was able to reproduce while maintaining the rhyming pattern of the original. I have found, then, what Stephen Mitchell found in translating Rilke: 'Translating poems into equivalent formal patterns is to some extent a matter of luck, or grace, and this is especially true of rhymed poems'. Mitchell cites Rilke, who called rhyme 'a goddess of secret and ancient coincidences', and said that 'she comes as happiness comes, hands filled with an achievement that is already in flower'. One works to prepare the way for this goddess, but if rhyme does not appear one must concentrate on other dimensions of form to devise the equivalencies that will show readers at least something of what they would find in the techniques of the original.

A related problem for the translator has to do with rhythms. French is not an accented language, and its poetic lines do not move in the iambic, trochaic, anapaestic, or dactylic rhythmic patterns of English. It is well enough to use the 'standard' English iambic pentameter in place of the 'standard' French alexandrine, and I have often done so. Still, these lines differ not only in length, but in movement, and there are times in my translations when I deviate from the iambic into triple metre (as in 'Beauty'), or into a line in which I count accents rather than syllables (e.g. 'A Carcass'). I sometimes use an accentual line when Baudelaire's line is shorter than the alexandrine, as in 'Alchemy of Suffering', simply because in some poems accentual verse seems to my ear to convey the movement of the French better than would a strict iambic metre. I am not being simply arbitrary in these decisions, but am following, in good faith, my own taste and judgement, poem by poem. Ultimately, it is true, the rhythms of all these translations are those of English rather than French, but it can not be otherwise; French and English rhythms will not turn into one another any more than will the sounds of these languages, or their vocabularies.

When I began thinking about translating Baudelaire and putting my thoughts into practice, I was encouraged by two friends who were then my colleagues at Illinois Wesleyan University, Sue Huseman and Salvador J. Fajardo. Later I received valuable help and encouragement from my colleague James Matthews. I thank the National Endowment for the Humanities for sponsoring my participation in the 1983 summer seminar of Albert Sonnenfeld (then of Princeton), who encouraged my Baudelaire work. Enthusiastic support at this time was also provided by Frank Jones of the University of Washington, and Richard Berchan of the University of Utah. The sponsorship of Robert Sutherland, of *The Pikestaff Forum*, led to my winning an Illinois Arts Council award in 1984 for my translation of 'The Cracked Bell'. My special thanks go to David Pichaske, whose Spoon River Poetry Press published in 1985 my *66 Translations from Charles Baudelaire's 'Les Fleurs Du Mal'*. The reception of this book encouraged me to finish the job of translating all the *Fleurs*, which I accomplished thanks in large part to a sabbatical leave from Illinois Wesleyan in 1990. *Laudes* for my wife, Anne W. McGowan, who provided a literal rendition of the Latin of 'Praises for My Francisca' and spent many hours proofreading these translations in their various forms. Finally, thanks to Jonathan Culler and to Oxford University Press for their critiques both of my translations and of the notes for this volume; for infelicities that may remain after their painstaking scrutiny, the sole responsibility is mine.

J. McG.

The following translations by James McGowan have been published previously (some in slightly different form or with different titles) in *66 Translations from Charles Baudelaire's 'Les Fleurs Du Mal'* (Peoria, Illinois: Spoon River Poetry Press, 1985):

To the Reader, The Albatross, Elevation, Correspondences, The Sick Muse, The Venal Muse, The Enemy, A Former Life, Man and the Sea, Don Juan in Hell, Beauty, The Giantess, Hymn to Beauty, Head of Hair, 'You'd entertain the universe...', A Carcass, *De profundis clamavi*, Lethe, Remorse after Death, *Duellum*, The Balcony, A Phantom, 'I give to you these verses...', The Flask, The Cat, Invitation to the Voyage, Conversation, Autumn Song, For a Creole Lady, Sorrows of the Moon, Cats, A Fantastical Engraving, The Cracked Bell, Spleen (I), Spleen (II), Spleen (III), Spleen (IV), Landscape, The Swan, The Seven Old Men, The Little Old Women, Dusk, The Love of Illusion, 'I have not forgotten...', Mists and Rains, Dawn, The Solitary's Wine, Destruction, Lesbos, Condemned Women: Delphine and Hippolyta, Condemned Women, The Two Good Sisters, The Fountain of Blood, Allegory, A Beatrice, The Metamorphoses of the Vampire, A Voyage to Cythera, St Peter's Denial, The Death of Lovers, The Death of the Poor, The Death of Artists, Voyaging, The Fountain, The Voice, Lament of an Icarus, Meditation.

Journals that have published James McGowan's translations from the *Flowers* are:

Hiram Poetry Review: 'A Former Life', 'Harmony of the Evening', 'Spleen I and II', 'The Blind'.

Nebo: 'Congenial Horror', 'Very Far from France'.

Northeast: 'Sorrows of the Moon'.

Pikestaff Forum: 'To the Reader', 'The Enemy', 'The Cracked Bell', 'The Metamorphoses of the Vampire', 'A Voyage to Cythera', 'St Peter's Denial', 'The Death of Lovers'.

Poetry Miscellany: 'The Taste for Nothingness', 'A Face Makes Promises'.

Spoon River Quarterly: 'Music', 'The Jewels'.

Southern Humanities Review: 'For a Creole Lady'.

Translation: 'Dusk'.

THE FLOWERS OF
EVIL

TO THE IMPECCABLE POET

To The Perfect Magician of French Letters

To My Dearest and Most Admired

MASTER AND FRIEND

Théophile Gautier*

With Feelings

Of The Most Profound Humility

I Dedicate

These Sickly Flowers

C.B.

Au lecteur

La sottise, l'erreur, le péché, la lésine,
Occupent nos esprits et travaillent nos corps,
Et nous alimentons nos aimables remords,
Comme les mendiants nourrissent leur vermine.

Nos péchés sont têtus, nos repentirs sont lâches;
Nous nous faisons payer grassement nos aveux,
Et nous rentrons gaiement dans le chemin bourbeux,
Croyant par de vils pleurs laver toutes nos taches.

Sur l'oreiller du mal c'est Satan Trismégiste
Qui berce longuement notre esprit enchanté,
Et le riche métal de notre volonté
Est tout vaporisé par ce savant chimiste.

C'est le Diable qui tient les fils qui nous remuent!
Aux objets répugnants nous trouvons des appas;
Chaque jour vers l'Enfer nous descendons d'un pas,
Sans horreur, à travers des ténèbres qui puent

Ainsi qu'un débauché pauvre qui baise et mange
Le sein martyrisé d'une antique catin,
Nous volons au passage un plaisir clandestin
Que nous pressons bien fort comme une vieille orange.

Serré, fourmillant, comme un million d'helminthes,
Dans nos cerveaux ribote un peuple de Démons,
Et, quand nous respirons, la Mort dans nos poumons
Descend, fleuve invisible, avec de sourdes plaintes.

Si le viol, le poison, le poignard, l'incendie,
N'ont pas encor brodé de leurs plaisants dessins
Le canevas banal de nos piteux destins,
C'est que notre âme, hélas! n'est pas assez hardie.

To the Reader

Folly and error, stinginess and sin
Possess our spirits and fatigue our flesh.
And like a pet we feed our tame remorse
As beggars take to nourishing their lice.

Our sins are stubborn, our contrition lax;
We offer lavishly our vows of faith
And turn back gladly to the path of filth,
Thinking mean tears will wash away our stains.

On evil's pillow lies the alchemist
Satan Thrice-Great,* who lulls our captive soul,
And all the richest metal of our will
Is vaporized by his hermetic arts.

Truly the Devil pulls on all our strings!
In most repugnant objects we find charms;
Each day we're one step further into Hell,
Content to move across the stinking pit.

As a poor libertine will suck and kiss
The sad, tormented tit of some old whore,
We steal a furtive pleasure as we pass,
A shrivelled orange that we squeeze and press.

Close, swarming, like a million writhing worms,
A demon nation riots in our brains,
And, when we breathe, death flows into our lungs,
A secret stream of dull, lamenting cries.

If slaughter, or if arson, poison, rape
Have not as yet adorned our fine designs,
The banal canvas of our woeful fates,
It's only that our spirit lacks the nerve.

Mais parmi les chacals, les panthères, les lices,
Les singes, les scorpions, les vautours, les serpents,
Les monstres glapissants, hurlants, grognants, rampants,
Dans la ménagerie infâme de nos vices,

Il en est un plus laid, plus méchant, plus immonde!
Quoiqu'il ne pousse ni grands gestes ni grands cris,
Il ferait volontiers de la terre un débris
Et dans un bâillement avalerait le monde;

C'est l'Ennui! — l'œil chargé d'un pleur involontaire,
Il rêve d'échafauds en fumant son houka.
Tu le connais, lecteur, ce monstre délicat,
— Hypocrite lecteur, — mon semblable, — mon frère!

But there with all the jackals, panthers, hounds,
The monkeys, scorpions, the vultures, snakes,
Those howling, yelping, grunting, crawling brutes,
The infamous menagerie of vice,

One creature only is most foul and false!
Though making no grand gestures, nor great cries,
He willingly would devastate the earth
And in one yawning swallow all the world;

He is Ennui!*—with tear-filled eye he dreams
Of scaffolds, as he puffs his water-pipe.
Reader, you know this dainty monster too;
—Hypocrite reader,—fellowman,—my twin!

Spleen et idéal

Spleen and the Ideal

1. Bénédiction

Lorsque, par un décret des puissances suprêmes,
Le Poëte apparaît en ce monde ennuyé,
Sa mère épouvantée et pleine de blasphèmes
Crispe ses poings vers Dieu, qui la prend en pitié:

— 'Ah! que n'ai-je mis bas tout un nœud de vipères,
Plutôt que de nourrir cette dérision!
Maudite soit la nuit aux plaisirs éphémères
Où mon ventre a conçu mon expiation!

Puisque tu m'as choisie entre toutes les femmes
Pour être le dégoût de mon triste mari,
Et que je ne puis pas rejeter dans les flammes,
Comme un billet d'amour, ce monstre rabougri,

Je ferai rejaillir ta haine qui m'accable
Sur l'instrument maudit de tes méchancetés,
Et je tordrai si bien cet arbre misérable,
Qu'il ne pourra pousser ses boutons empestés!'

Elle ravale ainsi l'écume de sa haine,
Et, ne comprenant pas les desseins éternels,
Elle-même prépare au fond de la Géhenne
Les bûchers consacrés aux crimes maternels.

Pourtant, sous la tutelle invisible d'un Ange,
L'Enfant déshérité s'enivre de soleil,
Et dans tout ce qu'il boit et dans tout qu'il mange
Retrouve l'ambroisie et le nectar vermeil.

Il joue avec le vent, cause avec le nuage,
Et s'enivre en chantant du chemin de la croix;
Et l'Esprit qui le suit dans son pèlerinage
Pleure de le voir gai comme un oiseau des bois.

1. Benediction

When, by an edict of the powers supreme,
The Poet in this bored world comes to be,
His daunted mother, eager to blaspheme,
Rages to God, who looks down piteously:

—'Rather than have this mockery to nurse
Why not a nest of snakes for me to bear!
And may that night of fleeting lust be cursed,
When I conceived my penance,* unaware!

Since from all women you chose me to shame,
To be disgusting to my grieving spouse,
And since I can't just drop into the flames
Like an old love-note, this misshapen mouse,

I'll turn your hate that overburdens me
Toward the damned agent of your spiteful doom,
And I will twist this miserable tree
So its infected buds will never bloom!'

She swallows thus her hatred's foaming spit
And, never grasping the divine design,
She makes herself within Gehenna's* pit
The pyre suited to a mother's crimes.

Still, with an angel guarding secretly,
The misfit child grows drunk on sunny air;
In all he drinks or eats in ecstasy
He finds sweet nectar and ambrosia there.

Free as a bird, he plays with clouds and wind,
Sings of the Passion with enraptured joy;
Tending his pilgrimage, his Guardian
Must weep to see the gladness of the boy.

Tous ceux qu'il veut aimer l'observent avec crainte,
Ou bien, s'enhardissant de sa tranquillité,
Cherchent à qui saura lui tirer une plainte,
Et font sur lui l'essai de leur férocité.

Dans le pain et le vin destinés à sa bouche
Ils mêlent de la cendre avec d'impurs crachats;
Avec hypocrisie ils jettent ce qu'il touche,
Et s'accusent d'avoir mis leurs pieds dans ses pas.

Sa femme va criant sur les places publiques:
'Puisqu'il me trouve assez belle pour m'adorer,
Je ferai le métier des idoles antiques,
Et comme elles je veux me faire redorer;

Et je me soûlerai de nard, d'encens, de myrrhe,
De génuflexions, de viandes et de vins,
Pour savoir si je puis dans un cœur qui m'admire
Usurper en riant les hommages divins!

Et, quand je m'ennuierai de ces farces impies,
Je poserai sur lui ma frêle et forte main;
Et mes ongles, pareils aux ongles des harpies,
Sauront jusqu'à son cœur se frayer un chemin.

Comme un tout jeune oiseau qui tremble et qui palpite,
J'arracherai ce cœur tout rouge de son sein,
Et, pour rassasier ma bête favorite,
Je le lui jetterai par terre avec dédain!'

Vers le Ciel, où son œil voit un trône splendide,
Le Poëte serein lève ses bras pieux,
Et les vastes éclairs de son esprit lucide
Lui dérobent l'aspect des peuples furieux:

— 'Soyez béni, mon Dieu, qui donnez la souffrance
Comme un divin remède à nos impuretés
Et comme la meilleure et la plus pure essence
Qui prépare les forts aux saintes voluptés!

Those he would love watch him with jaundiced eye,
Or, growing bold with his tranquillity,
Look for a certain way to make him cry,
Testing on him their own ferocity.

In bread and wine intended for his mouth
They muddle filthy spit with dirt and ash;
Hypocrites, all that he touches they throw out,
And blame their feet for walking in his path.

His woman cries to all the countryside:
'Since he has found me worthy to adore
I'll let the heathen idols be my guide
And gild myself, as they have done before;

I'll sate myself with incense, myrrh, and nard,
With genuflections, meats and wines galore,
To prove I can in that admiring heart
Laughingly claim the homage due the Lord!

I'll set on him my frail, determined hand
When I am bored with this blasphemous farce;
My fingernails, like harpies' talons,* can
Claw out a bloody pathway to his heart.

I'll dig the bright red heart out of his breast,
A pitiful and trembling baby bird;
To satisfy the dog I like the best
I'll toss it to him, with a scornful word!'

Toward Heaven, where he sees a throne of gold,
The Poet lifts his arms in piety,
And brilliant flashes from his lucid soul
Block from his sight the people's cruelty:

—'Be praised, my God, who gives us suffering
As remedy for our impurities,
And as the best and purest nurturing
To fit the strong for holy ecstasies!

Je sais que vous gardez une place au Poëte
Dans les rangs bienheureux des saintes Légions,
Et que vous l'invitez à l'éternelle fête
Des Trônes, des Vertus, des Dominations.

Je sais que la douleur est la noblesse unique
Où ne mordront jamais la terre et les enfers,
Et qu'il faut pour tresser ma couronne mystique
Imposer tous les temps et tous les univers.

Mais les bijoux perdus de l'antique Palmyre,
Les métaux inconnus, les perles de la mer,
Par votre main montés, ne pourraient pas suffire
A ce beau diadème éblouissant et clair;

Car il ne sera fait que de pure lumière,
Puisée au foyer saint des rayons primitifs,
Et dont les yeux mortels, dans leur splendeur entière,
Ne sont que des miroirs obscurcis et plaintifs!'

2. L'Albatros

Souvent, pour s'amuser, les hommes d'équipage
Prennent des albatros, vastes oiseaux des mers,
Qui suivent, indolents compagnons de voyage,
Le navire glissant sur les gouffres amers.

A peine les ont-ils déposés sur les planches,
Que ces rois de l'azur, maladroits et honteux,
Laissent piteusement leurs grandes ailes blanches
Comme des avirons traîner à côté d'eux.

Ce voyageur ailé, comme il est gauche et veule!
Lui, naguère si beau, qu'il est comique et laid!
L'un agace son bec avec un brûle-gueule,
L'autre mime, en boitant, l'infirme qui volait!

I know in Heaven there's a place for me
Kept for the poet in celestial zones,
And that I'll feast throughout eternity
With Virtues, Powers, Dominations, Thrones.*

Man's sorrow is a nobleness, I trust,
Untouchable by either earth or hell;
I know to weave my mystic crown I must
Tax all the times, the universe as well.

But treasure lost from old Palmyra's wealth,*
The unknown metals, pearls out of the sea,
Can't equal, though you mounted them yourself,
This diadem of dazzling clarity,

Since it is perfect luminosity,
Drawn from the holy hearth of primal rays,
Of which men's eyes, for all their majesty,
Are only mournful mirrors, dark and crazed!'

2. The Albatross

Often, when bored, the sailors of the crew
Trap albatross, the great birds of the seas,
Mild travellers escorting in the blue
Ships gliding on the ocean's mysteries.

And when the sailors have them on the planks,
Hurt and distraught, these kings of all outdoors
Piteously let trail along their flanks
Their great white wings, dragging like useless oars.

This voyager, how comical and weak!
Once handsome, how unseemly and inept!
One sailor pokes a pipe into his beak,
Another mocks the flier's hobbled step.

Le Poëte est semblable au prince des nuées
Qui hante la tempête et se rit de l'archer;
Exilé sur le sol au milieu des huées,
Ses ailes de géant l'empêchent de marcher.

3. Élévation

Au-dessus des étangs, au-dessus des vallées,
Des montagnes, des bois, des nuages, des mers,
Par delà le soleil, par delà les éthers,
Par delà les confins des sphères étoilées,

Mon esprit, tu te meus avec agilité,
Et, comme un bon nageur qui se pâme dans l'onde,
Tu sillonnes gaiement l'immensité profonde
Avec une indicible et mâle volupté.

Envole-toi bien loin de ces miasmes morbides:
Va te purifier dans l'air supérieur,
Et bois, comme une pure et divine liqueur,
Le feu clair qui remplit les espaces limpides

Derrière les ennuis et les vastes chagrins
Qui chargent de leur poids l'existence brumeuse,
Heureux celui qui peut d'une aile vigoureuse
S'élancer vers les champs lumineux et sereins;

Celui dont les pensers, comme des alouettes,
Vers les cieux le matin prennent un libre essor,
—Qui plane sur la vie, et comprend sans effort
Le langage des fleurs et des choses muettes!

The Poet is a kinsman in the clouds
Who scoffs at archers, loves a stormy day;
But on the ground, among the hooting crowds,
He cannot walk, his wings are in the way.*

3. Elevation

Above the valleys, over rills and meres,
Above the mountains, woods, the oceans, clouds,
Beyond the sun, past all ethereal bounds,
Beyond the borders of the starry spheres,

My agile spirit, how you take your flight!
Like a strong swimmer swooning on the sea
You gaily plough the vast immensity
With manly, inexpressible delight.

Fly far above this morbid, vaporous place;
Go cleanse yourself in higher, finer air,
And drink up, like a pure, divine liqueur,
Bright fire, out of clear and limpid space.

Beyond ennui, past troubles and ordeals
That load our dim existence with their weight,
Happy the strong-winged man, who makes the great
Leap upward to the bright and peaceful fields!

The man whose thoughts, like larks, take to their wings
Each morning, freely speeding through the air,
—Who soars above this life, interpreter
Of flowers' speech, the voice of silent things!

4. Correspondances

La Nature est un temple où de vivants piliers
Laissent parfois sortir de confuses paroles;
L'homme y passe à travers des forêts de symboles
Qui l'observent avec des regards familiers.

Comme de longs échos qui de loin se confondent
Dans une ténébreuse et profonde unité,
Vaste comme la nuit et comme la clarté,
Les parfums, les couleurs et les sons se répondent.

Il est des parfums frais comme des chairs d'enfants,
Doux comme les hautbois, verts comme les prairies,
— Et d'autres, corrompus, riches et triomphants,

Ayant l'expansion des choses infinies,
Comme l'ambre, le musc, le benjoin et l'encens,
Qui chantent les transports de l'esprit et des sens.

5. 'J'aime le souvenir . . .'

J'aime le souvenir de ces époques nues,
Dont Phœbus se plaisait à dorer les statues.
Alors l'homme et la femme en leur agilité
Jouissaient sans mensonge et sans anxiété,
Et, le ciel amoureux leur caressant l'échine,
Exerçaient la santé de leur noble machine.
Cybèle alors, fertile en produits généreux,
Ne trouvait point ses fils un poids trop onéreux,
Mais, louve au cœur gonflé de tendresses communes,
Abreuvait l'univers à ses tetines brunes.
L'homme, élégant, robuste et fort, avait le droit
D'être fier des beautés qui le nommaient leur roi;
Fruits purs de tout outrage et vierges de gerçures,
Dont la chair lisse et ferme appelait les morsures!

4. Correspondences

Nature is a temple, where the living
Columns sometimes breathe confusing speech;
Man walks within these groves of symbols, each
Of which regards him as a kindred thing.

As the long echoes, shadowy, profound,
Heard from afar, blend in a unity,
Vast as the night, as sunlight's clarity,
So perfumes, colours, sounds may correspond.

Odours there are, fresh as a baby's skin,
Mellow as oboes, green as meadow grass,*
— Others corrupted, rich, triumphant, full,

Having dimensions infinitely vast,
Frankincense, musk, ambergris, benjamin,
Singing the senses' rapture, and the soul's.

5. 'I love the thought...'

I love the thought of ancient, naked days
When Phoebus* gilded statues with his rays.
Then women, men in their agility
Played without guile, without anxiety,
And, while the sky stroked lovingly their skin,
They tuned to health their excellent machine.
Cybele,* in offering her bounty there,
Found mortals not a heavy weight to bear,
But, she-wolf full of common tenderness,
From her brown nipples fed the universe.*
Man had the right, robust and flourishing,
Of pride in beauties who proclaimed him king;
Pure fruit unsullied, lovely to the sight,
Whose smooth, firm flesh went asking for the bite!

Le Poëte aujourd'hui, quand il veut concevoir
Ces natives grandeurs, aux lieux où se font voir
La nudité de l'homme et celle de la femme,
Sent un froid ténébreux envelopper son âme
Devant ce noir tableau plein d'épouvantement.
Ô monstruosités pleurant leur vêtement!
Ô ridicules troncs! torses dignes des masques!
Ô pauvres corps tordus, maigres, ventrus ou flasques,
Que le dieu de l'Utile, implacable et serein,
Enfants, emmaillota dans ses langes d'airain!
Et vous, femmes, hélas! pâles comme des cierges,
Que ronge et que nourrit la débauche, et vous, vierges,
Du vice maternel traînant l'hérédité
Et toutes les hideurs de la fécondité!

Nous avons, il est vrai, nations corrumpues,
Aux peuples anciens des beautés inconnues:
Des visages rongés par les chancres du cœur,
Et comme qui dirait des beautés de langueur;
Mais ces inventions de nos muses tardives
N'empêcheront jamais les races maladives
De rendre à la jeunesse un hommage profond,
— A la sainte jeunesse, à l'air simple, au doux front,
A l'œil limpide et clair ainsi qu'une eau courante,
Et qui va répandant sur tout, insouciante
Comme l'azur du ciel, les oiseaux et les fleurs,
Ses parfums, ses chansons et ses douces chaleurs!

6. Les Phares

Rubens, fleuve d'oubli, jardin de la paresse,
Oreiller de chair fraîche où l'on ne peut aimer,
Mais où la vie afflue et s'agite sans cesse,
Comme l'air dans le ciel et la mer dans la mer;

Today, the Poet, when he would conceive
These native grandeurs, where can now be seen
Women and men in all their nakedness,
Feels in his soul a chill of hopelessness
Before this terrible and bleak tableau.
Monstrosities that cry out to be clothed!
Bodies grotesque and only fit for masques!
Poor twisted trunks, scrawny or gone to flab,
Whose god, implacable Utility,*
In brazen wraps, swaddles his progeny!
And pale as tapers, all you women too
Corruption gnaws and nourishes, and you
O virgins, heir to all maternal vice
And all the squalor of the fecund life!

It's true, we have in our corrupted states
Beauties unknown to ancient people's tastes:
Visages gnawed by sores of syphilis,
And one might say, beauties of listlessness;
But these inventions of our tardy muse
Never avert the sickly modern crew
From rendering to youth their deepest bow,
—To holy youth, to smooth, untroubled brow,
To limpid eye, to air of innocence,
Who pours out on us all, indifferent
As flowers, birds, the blue of sky or sea,
His perfumes, songs, his sweet vitality!

6. The Beacons

Rubens,* garden of sloth, stream of oblivion,
Pillow of blooming flesh where no one can make love,
But where life's spirit flows and tosses ceaselessly,
As wind does in the sky, or seas within the sea;

Léonard de Vinci, miroir profond et sombre,
Où des anges charmants, avec un doux souris
Tout chargé de mystère, apparaissent à l'ombre
Des glaciers et des pins qui ferment leur pays;

Rembrandt, triste hôpital tout rempli de murmures,
Et d'un grand crucifix décoré seulement,
Où la prière en pleurs s'exhale des ordures,
Et d'un rayon d'hiver traversé brusquement;

Michel-Ange, lieu vague où l'on voit des Hercules
Se mêler à des Christs, et se lever tout droits
Des fantômes puissants qui dans les crépuscules
Déchirent leur suaire en étirant leurs doigts;

Colères de boxeur, impudences de faune,
Toi qui sus ramasser la beauté des goujats,
Grand cœur gonflé d'orgueil, homme débile et jaune,
Puget, mélancolique empereur des forçats;

Watteau, ce carnaval où bien des cœurs illustres,
Comme des papillons, errent en flamboyant,
Décors frais et légers éclairés par des lustres
Qui versent la folie à ce bal tournoyant;

Goya, cauchemar plein de choses inconnues,
De fœtus qu'on fait cuire au milieu des sabbats,
De vieilles au miroir et d'enfants toutes nues,
Pour tenter les démons ajustant bien leurs bas;

Delacroix, lac de sang hanté des mauvais anges,
Ombragé par un bois de sapins toujours vert,
Où, sous un ciel chagrin, des fanfares étranges
Passent, comme un soupir étouffé de Weber;

Ces malédictions, ces blasphèmes, ces plaintes,
Ces extases, ces cris, ces pleurs, ces *Te Deum*,
Sont un écho redit par mille labyrinthes;
C'est pour les cœurs mortels un divin opium!

Leonardo,* a mirror, sombre and profound,
Where charming angels with ingratiating smiles
Burdened with mystery, are seen within the shades
Of glaciers and of pines that border the terrain;

Rembrandt,* sad hospital full of strange whispering,
The one adornment there, a giant crucifix,
Where prayer is full of tears, and rises from the filth—
Abrupt across the room, a ray of winter sun;

And Michelangelo, vague place where Hercules
Mingles with forms of Christ,* and rising very straight
Above are mighty ghosts, which in the dusky light
Will stretch their fingers out, and tear their winding-sheets;

Rage of the boxing-ring, impudence of a faun,
You who could call to beauty vassals in the camp,
Great heart puffed up with pride, feeble and jaundiced man,
Puget,* sad and forlorn, the convicts' emperor;

Watteau,* this carnival, where many famous hearts
Wander about like bright, flamboyant butterflies,
Decor is cool and light under the chandeliers
That pour down madness on this ever-circling dance;

Goya,* a nightmare full of things unspeakable,
Of foetuses one cooks for midnight revellers,
Old women at the mirror, children fully nude,
Dressing to tempt the devils, very carefully;

Delacroix,* lake of blood, the evil angels' haunts,
Shaded within a wood of fir-trees always green;
Under a gloomy sky, strange fanfares pass away
And disappear, like one of Weber's* smothered sighs;

These curses, blasphemies, these maledictions, groans
These ecstasies, these pleas, cries of Te Deum,* tears
Echo respoken by a thousand labyrinths,—
An opium divine for hungry mortals' hearts!

C'est un cri répété par mille sentinelles,
Un ordre renvoyé par mille porte-voix;
C'est un phare allumé sur mille citadelles,
Un appel de chasseurs perdus dans les grands bois!

Car c'est vraiment, Seigneur, le meilleur témoignage
Que nous puissions donner de notre dignité
Que cet ardent sanglot qui roule d'âge en âge
Et vient mourir au bord de votre éternité!

7. La Muse malade

Ma pauvre muse, hélas! qu'as-tu donc ce matin?
Tes yeux creux sont peuplés de visions nocturnes,
Et je vois tour à tour réfléchis sur ton teint
La folie et l'horreur, froides et taciturnes.

Le succube verdâtre et le rose lutin
T'ont-ils versé la peur et l'amour de leurs urnes?
Le cauchemar, d'un poing despotique et mutin,
T'a-t-il noyée au fond d'un fabuleux Minturnes?

Je voudrais qu'exhalant l'odeur de la santé
Ton sein de pensers forts fût toujours fréquenté,
Et que ton sang chrétien coulât à flots rythmiques

Comme les sons nombreux des syllabes antiques,
Où règnent tour à tour le père des chansons,
Phœbus, et le grand Pan, le seigneur des moissons.

It is a call passed by a thousand sentinels,
An order shouted through a thousand speaking horns;
It is a beacon on a thousand citadels,
A cry of hunters lost within a mighty wood!

For it is truly, Lord, best witness in the world
That we might give to you of human dignity,
This ardent sob that rolls onward from age to age
And comes to die in meeting your eternity!

7. The Sick Muse

My wretched muse, what does the morning bring?
Dream visions haunt your eyes, and I discern,
Reflected in the shadings of your skin,
Madness and horror, cold and taciturn.

Have they—green succubus* and rosy imp—
Poured on you fear and love out of their urns?
Has nightmare with his proud unruly grip
Sunk you within some fabulous Minturnes?*

I'd wish your breast to breathe the scent of health,
Your mind to think great thoughts the whole day long,
Your Christian blood to flow in waves that scan

With varied sounds of ancient syllables,
Where reign in turn the father of all song,
Apollo, and the harvest-lord, great Pan.*

8. La Muse vénale

Ô muse de mon cœur, amante des palais,
Auras-tu, quand Janvier lâchera ses Borées,
Durant les noirs ennuis des neigeuses soirées,
Un tison pour chauffer test deux pieds violets?

Ranimeras-tu donc tes épaules marbrées
Aux nocturnes rayons qui percent les volets?
Sentant ta bourse à sec autant que ton palais,
Récolteras-tu l'or des voûtes azurées?

Il te faut, pour gagner ton pain de chaque soir,
Comme un enfant de chœur, jouer de l'encensoir,
Chanter des *Te Deum* auxquels tu ne crois guère,

Ou, saltimbanque à jeun, étaler tes appas
Et ton rire trempé de pleurs qu'on ne voit pas,
Pour faire épanouir la rate du vulgaire.

9. Le Mauvais Moine

Les cloîtres anciens sur leurs grandes murailles
Étalaient en tableaux la sainte Vérité,
Dont l'effet, réchauffant les pieuses entrailles,
Tempérait la froideur de leur austérité.

En ces temps où du Christ florisssaient les semailles,
Plus d'un illustre moine, aujourd'hui peu cité,
Prenant pour atelier le champ des funérailles,
Glorifiait la Mort avec simplicité.

8. The Venal Muse

O muse of mine, in love with palaces,
Will you, when January flings his winds,
In the black tedium of snowy nights,
Find half-burned logs to warm your purple feet?

Your mottled shoulders, will they flush to warmth
As moonbeams slip inside our window glass?
Knowing your purse and palate both are dry,
Will you glean gold out of the azure vaults?

You must, to earn your meagre evening bread,
Like a bored altar boy swing censers, chant
Te Deums* to the never present gods,

Or, starving clown, put up your charms for sale,
Your laughter steeped in tears for no one's eyes,
To bring amusement to the vulgar crowd.

9. The Wretched Monk

Old monasteries under steadfast walls
Displayed tableaux of holy Verity,
Warming the inner men in those cold halls
Against the chill of their austerity.

Those times, when seeds of Christ would thrive and grow,
More than one monk, now in obscurity,
Taking the graveyard as his studio,
Ennobled Death, in all simplicity.

— Mon âme est un tombeau que, mauvais cénobite,
Depuis l'éternité je parcours et j'habite;
Rien n'embellit les murs de ce cloître odieux.

Ô moine fainéant! quand saurai-je donc faire
Du spectacle vivant de ma triste misère
Le travail de mes mains et l'amour de mes yeux?

10. L'Ennemi

Ma jeunesse ne fut qu'un ténébreux orage,
Traversé çà et là par de brillants soleils;
Le tonnerre et la pluie ont fait un tel ravage,
Qu'il reste en mon jardin bien peu de fruits vermeils

Voilà que j'ai touché l'automne des idées,
Et qu'il faut employer la pelle et les râteaux
Pour rassembler à neuf les terres inondées,
Où l'eau creuse des trous grands comme des tombeaux.

Et qui sait si les fleurs nouvelles que je rêve
Trouveront dans ce sol lavé comme une grève
Le mystique aliment qui ferait leur vigueur?

— Ô douleur! ô douleur! Le Temps mange la vie,
Et l'obscur Ennemi qui nous ronge le cœur
Du sang que nous perdons croît et se fortifie!

11. Le Guignon

Pour soulever un poids si lourd,
Sisyphe, il faudrait ton courage!
Bien qu'on ait du cœur à l'ouvrage,
L'Art est long et le Temps est court.

— My soul's a tomb that, wretched cenobite,*
I travel in throughout eternity;
Nothing adorns the walls of this sad shrine.

O slothful monk! Oh, when may I assign
This living spectacle of misery
To labour of my hands, my eyes' delight?

10. The Enemy

When I was young I lived a constant storm,
Though now and then the brilliant suns shot through,
So in my garden few red fruits were born,
The rain and thunder had so much to do.

Now are the autumn days of thought at hand,
And I must use the rake and spade to groom,
Rebuild and cultivate the washed-out land
The water had eroded deep as tombs.

And who knows if the flowers in my mind
In this poor sand, swept like a beach, will find
The food of soul to gain a healthy start?

I cry! I cry! Life feeds the seasons' maw
And that dark Enemy who gnaws our hearts
Battens on blood that drips into his jaws!

11. Ill Fortune*

One must have courage as strong
As Sisyphus',* lifting this weight!
Though the heart for the work may be great,
Time is fleeting, and Art is so long!*

Loin des sépultures célèbres,
Vers un cimetière isolé,
Mon cœur, comme un tambour voilé,
Va battant des marches funèbres.

— Maint joyau dort enseveli
Dans les ténèbres et l'oubli,
Bien loin des pioches et des sondes;

Mainte fleur épanche à regret
Son parfum doux comme un secret
Dans les solitudes profondes.

12. La Vie antérieure

J'ai longtemps habité sous de vastes portiques
Que les soleils marins teignaient de mille feux,
Et que leurs grands piliers, droits et majestueux,
Rendaient pareils, le soir, aux grottes basaltiques.

Les houles, en roulant les images des cieux,
Mêlaient d'une façon solennelle et mystique
Les tout-puissants accords de leur riche musique
Aux couleurs du couchant reflété par mes yeux.

C'est là que j'ai vécu dans les voluptés calmes,
Au milieu de l'azur, des vagues, des splendeurs
Et des esclaves nus, tout imprégnés d'odeurs,

Qui me rafraîchissaient le front avec des palmes,
Et dont l'unique soin était d'approfondir
Le secret douloureux qui me faisait languir.

Far from the tombs of the brave
Toward a churchyard obscure and apart,
Like a muffled drum, my heart
Beats a funeral march to the grave.

— But sleeping lies many a gem
In dark, unfathomed caves,
Far from the probes of men;

And many a flower waves
And wastes its sweet perfumes
In desert solitudes.

12. A Former Life

I once lived under vast and columned vaults
Tinged with a thousand fires by ocean suns,
So that their grand, straight pillars would become,
In evening light, like grottoes of basalt.

In surges rolled the images of skies;
With solemn, mystic force the sea combined
Its harmonies, all-powerful, sublime,
With sunset colours, glowing in my eyes.

So there I lived, in a voluptuous calm
Surrounded by the sea, by splendid blue,
And by my slaves, sweet-scented, handsome, nude,

Who cooled my brow with waving of the palms,
And had one care—to probe and make more deep
What made me languish so, my secret grief.

13. Bohémiens en voyage

La tribu prophétique aux prunelles ardentes
Hier s'est mise en route, emportant ses petits
Sur son dos, ou livrant à leurs fiers appétits
Le trésor toujours prês des mamelles pendantes.

Les hommes vont à pied sous leurs armes luisantes
Le long des chariots où les leurs sont blottis,
Promenant sur le ciel des yeux appesantis
Par le morne regret des chimères absentes.

Du fond de son réduit sablonneux, le grillon,
Les regardant passer, redouble sa chanson;
Cybèle, qui les aime, augmente ses verdures,

Fait couler le rocher et fleurir le désert
Devant ces voyageurs, pour lesquels est ouvert
L'empire familier des ténèbres futures.

14. L'Homme et la mer

Homme libre, toujours tu chériras la mer!
La mer est ton miroir; tu contemples ton âme
Dans le déroulement infini de sa lame,
Et ton esprit n'est pas un gouffre moins amer.

Tu te plais à plonger au sein de ton image;
Tu l'embrasses des yeux et des bras, et ton cœur
Se distrait quelquefois de sa propre rumeur
Au bruit de cette plainte indomptable et sauvage.

13. Gypsies Travelling

That tribe of prophets with the burning eyes
Is on the road, their babies on their backs,
Who satisfy their appetite attacks
With treasured breasts that always hang nearby.

On foot, with weapons shining, go the men
Beside the carts in which their people lie,
With sorrow-laden eyes searching the sky,
Yearning for vanished chimeras* again.

The cricket, as he sees them pass along,
Deep in his lair redoubles his shrill song;
Cybele,* their friend, augments her greenery,

Turns rocks to springs, brings flowers from the sand
Before these sojourners, empowered to see
Their future darkness, that familiar land.

14. Man and the Sea

Free man, you'll love the ocean endlessly!
It is your mirror, you observe your soul
In how its billows endlessly unroll—
Your spirit's bitter depths are there to see.

You plunge in joy to your reflection's core,
With eyes and heart seizing it all along;
Your heart sometimes neglects its proper song
Distracted by the ocean's savage roar.

Vous êtes tous les deux ténébreux et discrets:
Homme, nul n'a sondé le fond de tes abîmes,
Ô mer, nul ne connaît tes richesses intimes,
Tant vous êtes jaloux de garder vos secrets!

Et cependant voilà des siècles innombrables
Que vous vous combattez sans pitié ni remord,
Tellement vous aimez le carnage et la mort,
Ô lutteurs éternels, ô frères implacables!

15. Don Juan aux enfers

Quand Don Juan descendit vers l'onde souterraine
Et lorsqu'il eut donné son obole à Charon,
Un sombre mendiant, l'œil fier comme Antisthène,
D'un bras vengeur et fort saisit chaque aviron.

Montrant leurs seins pendants et leurs robes ouvertes,
Des femmes se tordaient sous le noir firmament,
Et, comme un grand troupeau de victimes offertes,
Derrière lui traînaient un long mugissement.

Sganarelle en riant lui réclamait ses gages,
Tandis que Don Luis avec un doigt tremblant
Montrait à tous les morts errant sur les rivages
Le fils audacieux qui railla son front blanc.

Frissonnant sous son deuil, la chaste et maigre Elvire,
Près de l'époux perfide et qui fut son amant,
Semblait lui réclamer un suprême sourire
Où brillât la douceur de son premier serment.

Tout droit dans son armure, un grand homme de pierre
Se tenait à la barre et coupait le flot noir;
Mais le calme héros, courbé sur sa rapière,
Regardait le sillage et ne daignait rien voir.

The two of you are subtle, shadowy:
Man, none has sounded your profound recess;
O sea, none knows the richness of your depths
Since you protect your secrets jealously!

And yet, because you both love death and strife,
You've fought each other through the endless years
With no remorse, without a pitying tear—
Relentless brothers, enemies for life!

15. Don Juan in Hell

When Don Juan had descended to the waves
Of Hell, and given coin for Charon's chores,*
A beggar with Antisthenes' proud gaze*
Took an avenger's grip around the oars.

Showing their hanging breasts through open gowns,
Sad women* writhed beneath that blackened sky;
Like victims chosen for the killing ground
They trailed behind him, lowing mournfully.

Sganarelle badgered him to get his pay,
While Don Luis, with trembling gesture there,
Showed all the dead who lined the waterway
That shameless son, who'd mocked his old grey hair.

Quivering with grief, Elvira, chaste and thin,
Near to her lover and unfaithful spouse,
Seemed to be begging one last smile of him,
In which would shine the grace of his first vows.

A great stone man,* stiff in his uniform,
Was the stern helmsman on that gloomy run,
But our calm hero, bent upon his sword,
Stared at the wake, and gave his glance to none.

16. Châtiment de l'orgueil

En ces temps merveilleux où la Théologie
Fleurit avec le plus de sève et d'énergie,
On raconte qu'un jour un docteur des plus grands,
— Après avoir forcé les cœurs indifférents;
Les avoir remués dans leurs profondeurs noires;
Après avoir franchi vers les célestes gloires
Des chemins singuliers à lui-même inconnus,
Où les purs Esprits seuls peut-être étaient venus, —
Comme un homme monté trop haut, pris de panique,
S'écria, transporté d'un orgueil satanique:
'Jésus, petit Jésus! je t'ai poussé bien haut!
Mais, si j'avais voulu t'attaquer au défaut
De l'armure, ta honte égalerait ta gloire,
Et tu ne serais plus qu'un fœtus dérisoire!'

Immédiatement sa raison s'en alla.
L'éclat de ce soleil d'un crêpe se voila;
Tout le chaos roula dans cette intelligence,
Temple autrefois vivant, plein d'ordre et d'opulence,
Sous les plafonds duquel tant de pompe avait lui.
Le silence et la nuit s'installèrent en lui,
Comme dans un caveau dont la clef est perdue.
Dès lors il fut semblable aux bêtes de la rue,
Et, quand il s'en allait sans rien voir, à travers
Les champs, sans distinguer les étés des hivers,
Sale, inutile et laid comme une chose usée,
Il faisait des enfants la joie et la risée.

16. Punishment for Pride

When in brave days of old, Theology
Flourished with utmost sap and energy,
A celebrated doctor,* it is said,
—When he had force-fed some indifferent heads;
Had stirred them in their blackest lethargy—
Vaulted himself towards holy ecstasy
By mystic processes he scarcely knew,
A state pure souls alone were welcomed to.
This man who'd tried to grasp beyond his reach,
Flushed with Satanic pride, made bold in speech:
'O little Jesus! I have raised you high!
But if I chose to take the other side,
Thou helpless one, I'd bring thy glory low,
The Christ child an outlandish embryo!'

At once his Reason's sentence had begun.
Shrouded in crepe was this once-blazing sun;
All chaos rolled in this intelligence
Before, a temple, ordered, opulent,
Where he'd held forth in pomp beneath its dome.
Now in him silence, darkness made their home,
As in a cellar vault without a key.
And when he crossed the fields unseeingly,
As unaware of winter as of spring,
Useless and ugly as a wornout thing,
He was no better than a common beast,
And was the jeering children's special treat.

17. La Beauté

Je suis belle, ô mortels! comme un rêve de pierre,
Et mon sein, où chacun s'est meurtri tour à tour,
Est fait pour inspirer au poëte un amour
Éternel et muet ainsi que la matière.

Je trône dans l'azur comme un sphinx incompris;
J'unis un cœur de neige à la blancheur des cygnes;
Je hais le mouvement qui déplace les lignes,
Et jamais je ne pleure et jamais je ne ris.

Les poëtes, devant mes grandes attitudes,
Que j'ai l'air d'emprunter aux plus fiers monuments,
Consumeront leurs jours en d'austères études;

Car j'ai, pour fasciner ces dociles amants,
De purs miroirs qui font toutes choses plus belles:
Mes yeux, mes larges yeux aux clartés éternelles!

18. L'Idéal

Ce ne seront jamais ces beautés de vignettes,
Produits avariés, nés d'un siècle vaurien,
Ces pieds à brodequins, ces doigts à castagnettes,
Qui sauront satisfaire un cœur comme le mien.

Je laisse à Gavarni, poëte des chloroses,
Son troupeau gazouillant de beautés d'hôpital,
Car je ne puis trouver parmi ces pâles roses
Une fleur qui ressemble à mon rouge idéal.

Ce qu'il faut à ce cœur profond comme un abîme,
C'est vous, Lady Macbeth, âme puisssante au crime,
Rêve d'Eschyle éclos au climat des autans;

17. Beauty

I am lovely, o mortals, a stone-fashioned dream,*
And my breast, where you bruise yourselves all in your turn,
Is made so that love will be born in the poet—
Eternal, and silent as matter is timeless.

I reign in the air like a puzzling sphinx;*
My heart is of snow and is pure as the swans.
I hate only impulse, the breaking of line,
And I never will cry, nor will ever show smile.

The poets, in view of my lofty design—
The style, as it seems, of the finest of statues—
Will spend all their days in their painstaking studies

Since I have a charm for these suppliant suitors:
Pure mirrors, which transform to beauty all things—
My eyes, my wide eyes, clear as air, clear as time.

18. The Ideal

It will not be these beauties of vignettes,*
Poor products of a worthless century,
Feet in half-boots, fingers in castanets,
Who satisfy the yearning heart in me.

That poet of chlorosis,* Gavarni,*
Can keep his twittering troupe of sickly queens,
Since these pale roses do not let me see
My red ideal, the flower of my dreams.

' need a heart abyssal in its depth,
A soul confirmed in crime, Lady Macbeth,
Aeschylus' dream,* storm-born out of the south,

Ou bien toi, grande Nuit, fille de Michel-Ange,
Qui tors paisiblement dans une pose étrange
Tes appas façonnés aux bouches des Titans!

19.　La Géante

Du temps que la Nature en sa verve puissante
Concevait chaque jour des enfants monstrueux,
J'eusse aimé vivre auprès d'une jeune géante,
Comme aux pieds d'une reine un chat voluptueux.

J'eusse aimé voir son corps fleurir avec son âme
Et grandir librement dans ses terribles jeux;
Deviner si son cœur couve une sombre flamme
Aux humides brouillards qui nagent dans ses yeux;

Parcourir à loisir ses magnifiques formes;
Ramper sur le versant de ses genoux énormes,
Et parfois en été, quand les soleils malsains,

Lasse, la font s'étendre à travers la campagne,
Dormir nonchalamment à l'ombre de ses seins,
Comme un hameau paisible au pied d'une montagne.

20.　Le Masque

Statue allégorique dans
le goût de la Renaissance

A Ernest Christophe, statuaire

Contemplons ce trésor de grâces florentines;
Dans l'ondulation de ce corps musculeux
L'Élégance et la Force abondent, sœurs divines.
Cette femme, morceau vraiment miraculeux,

Or you, great Night of Michelangelo's,*
Who calmly twist in an exotic pose
Those charms he fashioned for a Titan's mouth.

19. The Giantess

In times* when madcap Nature in her verve
Conceived each day a hatch of monstrous spawn,
I might have lived near some young giantess,
Like a voluptuous cat before a queen —

To watch her body flower with her soul,
And grow up freely in her dreadful play;
To guess about a passion's sombre flame
Born in the mists that swim within her eyes.

At leisure to explore her mighty forms;
To climb the slopes of her enormous knees,
And sometimes, when the summer's tainted suns

Had lain her out across the countryside,
To drowse in nonchalance below her breast,
Like a calm village in the mountain's shade.

20. The Mask

Allegorical Statue in the Style of
the Renaissance

*for Ernest Christophe, sculptor**

Let us observe this prize, of Tuscan charm;
In how the muscles of the body flow
Those holy sisters, Grace and Strength, abound.
This woman, this extraordinary piece,

Divinement robuste, adorablement mince,
Est faite pour trôner sur des lits somptueux,
Et charmer les loisirs d'un pontife ou d'un prince.

— Aussi, vois ce souris fin et voluptueux
Où la Fatuité promène son extase;
Ce long regard sournois, langoureux et moqueur;
Ce visage mignard, tout encadré de gaze,
Dont chaque trait nous dit avec un air vainqueur:
'La Volupté m'appelle et l'Amour me couronne!'
A cet être doué de tant de majesté
Vois quel charme excitant la gentillesse donne!
Approchons, et tournons autour de sa beauté.

Ô blasphème de l'art! ô surprise fatale!
La femme au corps divin, promettant le bonheur,
Par le haut se termine en monstre bicéphale!

— Mais non! ce n'est qu'un masque, un décor suborneur,
Ce visage éclairé d'une exquise grimace,
Et, regarde, voici, crispée atrocement,
La véritable tête, et la sincère face
Renversée à l'abri de la face qui ment.
Pauvre grande beauté! le magnifique fleuve
De tes pleurs aboutit dans mon cœur soucieux;
Ton mensonge m'enivre, et mon âme s'abreuve
Aux flots que la Douleur fait jaillir de tes yeux!

— Mais pourquoi pleure-t-elle? Elle, beauté parfaite
Qui mettrait à ses pieds le genre humain vaincu,
Quel mal mystérieux ronge son flanc d'athlète?

— Elle pleure, insensé, parce qu'elle a vécu!
Et parce qu'elle vit! Mais ce qu'elle déplore
Surtout, ce qui la fait frémir jusqu'aux genoux,
C'est que demain, hélas! il faudra vivre encore!
Demain, après-demain et toujours! — comme nous!

Divinely robust, admirably slim,
Was made to be enthroned on sumptuous beds
As entertainment for a pope or prince.

—Also, observe the fine voluptuous smile
Where Self-conceit parades its ecstasy;
This long, sly, languorous and mocking gaze;
This dainty visage, with its filmy veil,
Each trait of which cries out triumphantly,
'Pleasure invites me, and I wear Love's crown!'
In this creation of such majesty
Excitement flows from her gentility!
Let us approach and look from every side!

O blasphemy of art! fatal surprise!
This woman fashioned to embody bliss
Is at the top a monster with two heads!

—But no! it's just a mask, a trick design,
This visage lit by an exquisite air,*
And look, see here how cruelly it is clenched,
The undissembling face of the true head,
Turned to the shelter of the face that lies.
O beauty, how I pity you! the great
Stream of your tears ends in my anxious heart;
Your lie transports me, and my soul drinks up
The seas brought forth by Sorrow from your eyes!

—But what has made her cry? A beauty who
Could have all mankind conquered at her feet,
What secret pain gnaws at her hardy flank?

—The reason, fool, she cries is that she's lived!
And that she lives! But what she most deplores,
What makes her tremble even to her knees,
Is that tomorrow she'll be living still!
Tomorrow, every day!—And so will we!

21. Hymne à la Beauté

Viens-tu du ciel profond ou sors-tu de l'abîme,
Ô Beauté? ton regard, infernal et divin,
Verse confusément le bienfait et le crime,
Et l'on peut pour cela te comparer au vin.

Tu contiens dans ton œil le couchant et l'aurore;
Tu répands des parfums comme un soir orageux;
Tes baisers sont un philtre et ta bouche une amphore
Qui font le héros lâche et l'enfant courageux.

Sors-tu du gouffre noir ou descends-tu des astres?
Le Destin charmé suit tes jupons comme un chien;
Tu sèmes au hasard la joie et les désastres,
Et tu gouvernes tout et ne réponds de rien.

Tu marches sur des morts, Beauté, dont tu te moques;
De tes bijoux l'Horreur n'est pas le moins charmant,
Et le Meurtre, parmi tes plus chères breloques,
Sur ton ventre orgueilleux danse amoureusement.

L'éphémère ébloui vole vers toi, chandelle,
Crépite, flambe et dit: Bénissons ce flambeau!
L'amoureux pantelant incliné sur sa belle
A l'air d'un moribond caressant son tombeau.

Que tu viennes du ciel ou de l'enfer, qu'importe,
Ô Beauté! monstre énorme, effrayant, ingénu!
Si ton œil, ton souris, ton pied, m'ouvrent la porte
D'un Infini que j'aime et n'ai jamais connu?

De Satan ou de Dieu, qu'importe? Ange ou Sirène,
Qu'importe, si tu rends, — fée aux yeux de velours,
Rythme, parfum, lueur, ô mon unique reine! —
L'univers moins hideux et les instants moins lourds?

21. Hymn to Beauty

O Beauty! do you visit from the sky
Or the abyss? infernal and divine,
Your gaze bestows both kindnesses and crimes,
So it is said you act on us like wine.

Your eye contains the evening and the dawn;
You pour out odours like an evening storm;
Your kiss is potion from an ancient jar,
That can make heroes cold and children warm.

Are you of heaven or the nether world?
Charmed Destiny, your pet, attends your walk;
You scatter joys and sorrows at your whim,
And govern all, and answer no man's call.

Beauty, you walk on corpses, mocking them;
Horror is charming as your other gems,
And Murder is a trinket dancing there
Lovingly on your naked belly's skin.

You are a candle where the mayfly dies
In flames, blessing this fire's deadly bloom.
The panting lover bending to his love
Looks like a dying man who strokes his tomb.

What difference, then, from heaven or from hell,
O Beauty, monstrous in simplicity?
If eye, smile, step can open me the way
To find unknown, sublime infinity?

Angel or siren, spirit, I don't care,
As long as velvet eyes and perfumed head
And glimmering motions, o my queen, can make
The world less dreadful, and the time less dead.

21a. Les Bijoux

La très-chère était nue, et, connaissant mon cœur,
Elle n'avait gardé que ses bijoux sonores,
Dont le riche attirail lui donnait l'air vainqueur
Qu'ont dans leurs jours heureux les esclaves des Mores.

Quand il jette en dansant son bruit vif et moqueur,
Ce monde rayonnant de métal et de pierre
Me ravit en extase, et j'aime à la fureur
Les choses où le son se mêle à la lumière

Elle était donc couchée et se laissait aimer,
Et du haut du divan elle souriait d'aise
A mon amour profond et doux comme la mer,
Qui vers elle montait comme vers sa falaise.

Les yeux fixés sur moi, comme un tigre dompté,
D'un air vague et rêveur elle essayait des poses,
Et la candeur unie à la lubricité
Donnait un charme neuf à ses métamorphoses;

Et son bras et sa jambe, et sa cuisse et ses reins,
Polis comme de l'huile, onduleux comme un cygne,
Passaient devant mes yeux clairvoyants et sereins;
Et son ventre et ses seins, ces grappes de ma vigne,

S'avançaient, plus câlins que les Anges du mal,
Pour troubler le repos où mon âme était mise,
Et pour la déranger du rocher de cristal
Où, calme et solitaire, elle s'était assise.

21a. The Jewels

Knowing my heart, my dearest one was nude,
Her resonating jewellery all she wore,
Which rich array gave her the attitude
Of darling in the harem of a Moor.

When dancing, ringing out its mockeries,
This radiating world of gold and stones
Ravishes me to lovers' ecstasies
Over the interplay of lights and tones.

Allowing love, she lay seductively
And from the high divan smiled in her ease
At my love—ocean's deep felicity
Mounting to her as tides draw in the seas.

A tiger tamed, her eyes were fixed on mine,
With absent air she posed in novel ways,
Whose candour and lubricity combined
Made charming all her metamorphoses;

Her shoulders and her arms, her legs, her thighs,
Polished with oil, undulent like a swan,
Passed by my tranquil and clairvoyant eyes;
Then belly, breasts, those clusters on my vine,*

Came on, tempting me more than devils could
To break the peace my soul claimed as its own,
And to disturb the crystal rock abode
Where distant, calm, it had assumed its throne.

Je croyais voir unis par un nouveau dessin
Les hanches de l'Antiope au buste d'un imberbe,
Tant sa taille faisait ressortir son bassin.
Sur ce teint fauve et brun le fard était superbe!

— Et la lampe s'étant résignée à mourir,
Comme le foyer seul illuminait la chambre,
Chaque fois qu'il poussait un flamboyant soupir,
Il inondait de sang cette peau couleur d'ambre!

22. Parfum exotique

Quand, les deux yeux fermés, en un soir chaud d'automne,
Je respire l'odeur de ton sein chaleureux,
Je vois se dérouler des rivages heureux
Qu'éblouissent les feux d'un soleil monotone;

Une île paresseuse où la nature donne
Des arbres singuliers et des fruits savoureux;
Des hommes dont le corps est mince et vigoureux,
Et des femmes dont l'œil par sa franchise étonne.

Guidé par ton odeur vers de charmants climats,
Je vois un port rempli de voiles et de mâts
Encor tout fatigués par la vague marine,

Pendant que le parfum des verts tamariniers,
Qui circule dans l'air et m'enfle la narine,
Se mêle dans mon âme au chant des mariniers.

Her waist contrasted with her haunches so
It seemed to me I saw, in new design,
A boy above, Antiope* below.
The painting on her brown skin was sublime!

—And since the lamp resigned itsef to die,
The hearth alone lit up the room within;
Each time it uttered forth a blazing sigh
It washed with tones of blood her amber skin.

22. Exotic Perfume

When, eyes closed, on a pleasant autumn night,
I breathe the warm scent of your breast, I see
Inviting shorelines* spreading out for me
Where steady sunlight dazzles in my sight.

An idle isle, where friendly nature brings
Singular trees, fruit that is savoury,
Men who are lean and vigorous and free,
Women whose frank eyes are astonishing.

Led by your fragrance to these charming shores
I see a bay of sails and masts and oars,
Still wearied from the onslaught of the waves—

While verdant tamarind's enchanting scent,
Filling my nostrils, swirling to the brain,
Blends in my spirit with the boatmen's chant.

23. La Chevelure

Ô toison, moutonnant jusque sur l'encolure!
Ô boucles! Ô parfum chargé de nonchaloir!
Extase! Pour peupler ce soir l'alcôve obscure
Des souvenirs dormant dans cette chevelure,
Je la veux agiter dans l'air comme un mouchoir!

La langoureuse Asie et la brûlante Afrique,
Tout un monde lointain, absent, presque défunt,
Vit dans tes profondeurs, forêt aromatique!
Comme d'autres esprits voguent sur la musique,
Le mien, ô mon amour! nage sur ton parfum.

J'irai là-bas où l'arbre et l'homme, pleins de sève,
Se pâment longuement sous l'ardeur des climats;
Fortes tresses, soyez la houle qui m'enlève!
Tu contiens, mer d'ébène, un éblouissant rêve
De voiles, de rameurs, de flammes et de mâts:

Un port retentissant où mon âme peut boire
A grands flots le parfum, le son et la couleur;
Où les vaisseaux, glissant dans l'or et dans la moire,
Ouvrent leurs vastes bras pour embrasser la gloire
D'un ciel pur où frémit l'éternelle chaleur.

Je plongerai ma tête amoureuse d'ivresse
Dans ce noir océan où l'autre est enfermé;
Et mon esprit subtil que le roulis caresse
Saura vous retrouver, ô féconde paresse!
Infinis bercements du loisir embaumé!

Cheveux bleus, pavillon de ténèbres tendues,
Vous me rendez l'azur du ciel immense et rond;
Sur les bords duvetés de vos mèches tordues
Je m'enivre ardemment des senteurs confondues
De l'huile de coco, du musc et du goudron.

23. Head of Hair

O fleece, billowing even down the neck!
O locks! O perfume charged with nonchalance!
What ecstasy! To people our dark room
With memories that sleep within this mane,
I'll shake it like a kerchief in the air!

Languorous Asia, scorching Africa,
A whole world distant, vacant, nearly dead,
Lives in your depths, o forest of perfume!
While other spirits sail on symphonies
Mine, my beloved, swims along your scent.

I will go down there, where the trees and men,
Both full of sap, swoon in the ardent heat;
Strong swelling tresses, carry me away!
Yours, sea of ebony, a dazzling dream
Of sails, of oarsmen, waving pennants, masts:*

A sounding harbour where my soul can drink
From great floods subtle tones, perfumes and hues;
Where vessels gliding in the moire and gold
Open their wide arms to the glorious sky
Where purely trembles the eternal warmth.

I'll plunge my drunken head, dizzy with love
In this black sea where that one is confined;
My subtle soul that rolls in its caress
Will bring you back, o fertile indolence!
Infinite lulling, leisure steeped in balm!

Blue head of hair, tent of spread shadows, you
Give me the azure of the open sky;
In downy wisps along your twisted locks
I'll gladly drug myself on mingled scents,
Essence of cocoa-oil, pitch and musk.

Longtemps! toujours! ma main dans ta crinière lourde
Sèmera le rubis, la perle et le saphir,
Afin qu'à mon désir tu ne sois jamais sourde!
N'es-tu pas l'oasis où je rêve, et la gourde
Où je hume à longs traits le vin du souvenir?

24. 'Je t'adore à l'égal . . .'

Je t'adore à l'égal de la voûte nocturne,
Ô vase de tristesse, ô grande taciturne,
Et t'aime d'autant plus, belle, que tu me fuis,
Et que tu me parais, ornement de mes nuits,
Plus ironiquement accumuler les lieues
Qui séparent mes bras des immensités bleues.

Je m'avance à l'attaque, et je grimpe aux assauts,
Comme après un cadavre un chœur de vermisseaux,
Et je chéris, ô bête implacable et cruelle!
Jusqu'à cette froideur par où tu m'es plus belle!

25. 'Tu mettrais l'univers entier . . .'

Tu mettrais l'univers entier dans ta ruelle,
Femme impure! L'ennui rend ton âme cruelle.
Pour exercer tes dents à ce jeu singulier,
Il te faut chaque jour un cœur au râtelier.
Tes yeux, illuminés ainsi que des boutiques
Et des ifs flamboyants dans les fêtes publiques,
Usent insolemment d'un pouvoir emprunté,
Sans connaître jamais la loi de leur beauté.

Machine aveugle et sourde, en cruautés féconde!
Salutaire instrument, buveur du sang du monde,
Comment n'as-tu pas honte et comment n'as-tu pas
Devant tous les miroirs vu pâlir tes appas?

For ages! always! in your heavy mane
My hand will scatter ruby, sapphire, pearl
So you will never chill to my desire!
Are you not the oasis where I dream,
My drinking-gourd for memory's fine wine?

24. 'I love you as I love . . .'

I love you as I love the night's high vault
O silent one, o sorrow's lachrymal,*
And love you more because you flee from me,
And temptress of my nights, ironically
You seem to hoard the space, to take to you
What separates my arms from heaven's blue.

I climb to the assault, attack the source,
A choir of wormlets pressing towards a corpse,
And cherish your unbending cruelty,
This iciness so beautiful to me.*

25. 'You'd entertain the universe . . .'

You'd entertain the universe in bed,
Foul woman;* ennui makes you mean of soul.
To exercise your jaws at this strange sport
Each day you work a heart between your teeth.
Your eyes, illuminated like boutiques
Or blazing stanchions at a public fair,
Use haughtily a power not their own,
With no awareness of their beauty's law.

Blind, deaf machine, fertile in cruelties!
Valuable tool, that drinks the whole world's blood,
Why are you not ashamed, how have you not
In mirrors seen your many charms turn pale?

La grandeur de ce mal où tu te crois savante
Ne t'a donc jamais fait reculer d'épouvante,
Quand la nature, grande en ses desseins cachés,
De toi se sert, ô femme, ô reine des péchés,
— De toi, vil animal, — pour pétrir un génie?

Ô fangeuse grandeur! sublime ignominie!

26. *Sed non satiata*

Bizarre déité, brune comme les nuits,
Au parfum mélangé de musc et de havane,
Œuvre de quelque obi, le Faust de la savane,
Sorcière au flanc d'ébène, enfant des noirs minuits,

Je préfère au constance, à l'opium, au nuits,
L'élixir de ta bouche où l'amour se pavane;
Quand vers toi mes désirs partent en caravane,
Tes yeux sont la citerne où boivent mes ennuis.

Par ces deux grands yeux noirs, soupiraux de ton âme,
Ô démon sans pitié! verse-moi moins de flamme;
Je ne suis pas le Styx pour t'embrasser neuf fois,

Hélas! et je ne puis, Mégère libertine,
Pour briser ton courage et te mettre aux abois,
Dans l'enfer de ton lit devenir Proserpine!

27. 'Avec ses vêtements ...'

Avec ses vêtements ondoyants et nacrés,
Même quand elle marche on croirait qu'elle danse,
Comme ces longs serpents que les jongleurs sacrés
Au bout de leurs bâtons agitent en cadence.

The magnitude of all your evil schemes,
Has this, then, never shrunk your heart with fear,
When Nature, mighty in her secret plans,
Makes use of you, o woman! queen of sins!
—Of you, vile beast—to mould a genius?

O filthy grandeur! o sublime disgrace!

26. *Sed non satiata**

Singular goddess, brown as night, and wild,
Perfumed of fine tobacco smoke and musk,
Work of some Faust,* some wizard of the dusk,
Ebony sorceress, black midnight's child,

Rare wines or opium are less a prize
Than your moist lips where love struts its pavane;*
When my lusts move towards you in caravan
My ennuis drink from cisterns of your eyes.

From these black orbits where the soul breathes through,
O heartless demon! pour a drink less hot;
I'm not the Styx,* nine times embracing you,

Alas! and my Megaera,* I can not,
To break your nerve and bring you to your knees,
In your bed's hell become Persephone!*

27. 'The way her silky garments ...'

The way her silky garments undulate
It seems she's dancing as she walks along,
Like serpents that the sacred charmers make
To move in rhythms of their waving wands.

Comme le sable morne et l'azur des déserts,
Insensibles tous deux à l'humaine souffrance,
Comme les longs réseaux de la houle des mers,
Elle se développe avec indifférence.

Ses yeux polis sont faits de minéraux charmants,
Et dans cette nature étrange et symbolique
Où l'ange inviolé se mêle au sphinx antique,

Où tout n'est qu'or, acier, lumière et diamants,
Resplendit à jamais, comme un astre inutile,
La froide majesté de la femme stérile.

28. Le Serpent qui danse

Que j'aime voir, chère indolente,
   De ton corps si beau,
Comme une étoffe vacillante,
   Miroiter la peau!

Sur ta chevelure profonde
   Aux âcres parfums,
Mer odorante et vagabonde
   Aux flots bleus et bruns,

Comme un navire qui s'éveille
   Au vent du matin,
Mon âme rêveuse appareille
   Pour un ciel lointain.

Tes yeux, où rien ne se révèle
   De doux ni d'amer,
Sont deux bijoux froids où se mêle
   L'or avec le fer.

Like desert sands and skies she is as well,
As unconcerned with human misery,
Like the long networks of the ocean's swells
Unfolding with insensibility.

Her polished eyes are made of charming stones,
And in her essence, where the natures mix
Of holy angel and the ancient sphinx,*

Where all is lit with gold, steel, diamonds,
A useless star, it shines eternally,
The sterile woman's frigid majesty.

28. The Dancing Serpent

How I adore, dear indolent,
    Your lovely body, when
Like silken cloth it shimmers—
    Your sleek and glimmering skin!

Within the ocean of your hair,
    All pungent with perfumes,
A fragrant and a wayward sea
    Of waves of browns and blues,

Like a brave ship awakening
    To winds at break of day,
My dreamy soul sets forth on course
    For skies so far away.

Your eyes, where nothing is revealed,
    The bitter nor the sweet,
Are two cold stones, in which the tinctures
    Gold and iron meet.

A te voir marcher en cadence,
   Belle d'abandon,
On dirait un serpent qui danse
   Au bout d'un bâton.

Sous le fardeau de ta paresse
   Ta tête d'enfant
Se balance avec la mollesse
   D'un jeune éléphant,

Et ton corps se penche et s'allonge
   Comme un fin vaisseau
Qui roule bord sur bord et plonge
   Ses vergues dans l'eau.

Comme un flot grossi par la fonte
   Des glaciers grondants,
Quand l'eau de ta bouche remonte
   Au bord de tes dents,

Je crois boire un vin de Bohême,
   Amer et vainqueur,
Un ciel liquide qui parsème
   D'étoiles mon cœur!

29. Une charogne

Rappelez-vous l'objet que nous vîmes, mon âme,
   Ce beau matin d'été si doux:
Au détour d'un sentier une charogne infâme
   Sur un lit semé de cailloux,

Les jambes en l'air, comme une femme lubrique,
   Brûlante et suant les poisons,
Ouvrait d'une façon nonchalante et cynique
   Son ventre plein d'exhalaisons.

Viewing the rhythm of your walk,
    Beautifully dissolute,
One seems to see a serpent dance
    Before a wand and flute.

Your childlike head lolls with the weight
    Of all your idleness,
And sways with all the slackness of
    A baby elephant's,

And your lithe body bends and stretches
    Like a splendid barque
That rolls from side to side and wets
    With seas its tipping yards.

As when the booming glaciers thaw
    They swell the waves beneath,
When your mouth's water floods into
    The borders of your teeth,

I know I drink a gypsy wine,
    Bitter, subduing, tart,
A liquid sky that strews and spangles
    Stars across my heart!

29. A Carcass

Remember, my love, the object we saw
    That beautiful morning in June:
By a bend in the path a carcass reclined
    On a bed sown with pebbles and stones;

Her legs were spread out like a lecherous whore,
    Sweating out poisonous fumes,
Who opened in slick invitational style
    Her stinking and festering womb.

Le soleil rayonnait sur cette pourriture,
    Comme afin de la cuire à point,
Et de rendre au centuple à la grande Nature
    Tout ce qu'ensemble elle avait joint;

Et le ciel regardait la carcasse superbe
    Comme une fleur s'épanouir.
La puanteur était si forte, que sur l'herbe
    Vous crûtes vous évanouir.

Les mouches bourdonnaient sur ce ventre putride,
    D'où sortaient de noirs bataillons
De larves, qui coulaient comme un épais liquide
    Le long de ces vivants haillons.

Tout cela descendait, montait comme une vague,
    Ou s'élançait en petillant;
On eût dit que le corps, enflé d'un souffle vague,
    Vivait en se multipliant.

Et ce monde rendait une étrange musique,
    Comme l'eau courante et le vent,
Ou le grain qu'un vanneur d'un mouvement rythmique
    Agite et tourne dans son van.

Les formes s'effaçaient et n'étaient plus qu'un rêve,
    Une ébauche lente à venir,
Sur la toile oubliée, et que l'artiste achève
    Seulement par le souvenir.

Derrière les rochers une chienne inquiète
    Nous regardait d'un œil fâché,
Épiant le moment de reprendre au squelette
    Le morceau qu'elle avait lâché.

— Et pourtant vous serez semblable à cette ordure,
    A cette horrible infection,
Étoile de mes yeux, soleil de ma nature,
    Vous, mon ange et ma passion!

The sun on this rottenness focused its rays
 To cook the cadaver till done,
And render to Nature a hundredfold gift
 Of all she'd united in one.

And the sky cast an eye on this marvellous meat
 As over the flowers in bloom.
The stench was so wretched that there on the grass
 You nearly collapsed in a swoon.

The flies buzzed and droned on these bowels of filth
 Where an army of maggots arose,
Which flowed with a liquid and thickening stream
 On the animate rags of her clothes.

And it rose and it fell, and pulsed like a wave,
 Rushing and bubbling with health.
One could say that this carcass, blown with vague breath,
 Lived in increasing itself.

And this whole teeming world made a musical sound
 Like babbling brooks and the breeze,
Or the grain that a man with a winnowing-fan
 Turns with a rhythmical ease.

The shapes wore away as if only a dream
 Like a sketch that is left on the page
Which the artist forgot and can only complete
 On the canvas, with memory's aid.

From back in the rocks, a pitiful bitch
 Eyed us with angry distaste,
Awaiting the moment to snatch from the bones
 The morsel she'd dropped in her haste.

—And you, in your turn, will be rotten as this:
 Horrible, filthy, undone,
O sun of my nature and star of my eyes,
 My passion, my angel in one!

Oui! telle vous serez, ô la reine des grâces,
  Après les derniers sacrements,
Quand vous irez, sous l'herbe et les floraisons grasses,
  Moisir parmi les ossements.

Alors, ô ma beauté! dites à la vermine
  Qui vous mangera de baisers,
Qui j'ai gardé la forme et l'essence divine
  De mes amours décomposés!

30. *De profundis clamavi*

J'implore ta pitié, Toi, l'unique que j'aime,
Du fond du gouffre obscur où mon cœur est tombé.
C'est un univers morne à l'horizon plombé,
Où nagent dans la nuit l'horreur et le blasphème;

Un soleil sans chaleur plane au-dessus six mois,
Et les six autres mois la nuit couvre la terre;
C'est un pays plus nu que la terre polaire;
— Ni bêtes, ni ruisseaux, ni verdure, ni bois!

Or il n'est pas d'horreur au monde qui surpasse
La froide cruauté de ce soleil de glace
Et cette immense nuit semblable au vieux Chaos;

Je jalouse le sort des plus vils animaux
Qui peuvent se plonger dans un sommeil stupide,
Tant l'écheveau du temps lentement se dévide!

Yes, such will you be, o regent of grace,
   After the rites have been read,
Under the weeds, under blossoming grass
   As you moulder with bones of the dead.

Ah then, o my beauty, explain to the worms
   Who cherish your body so fine,
That I am the keeper for corpses of love
   Of the form, and the essence divine!*

30. *De profundis clamavi**

I beg your pity, You, my only love;
My fallen heart lies in a deep abyss,
A universe of leaden heaviness,
Where cursing terrors swim the night above!

For six months stands a sun with heatless beams,
The other months are spent in total night;
It is a polar land to human sight
—No greenery, no trees, no running streams!

But there is not a horror to surpass
The cruelty of that blank sun's cold glass,
And that long night, that Chaos come again!

I'm jealous of the meanest of the beasts
Who plunge themselves into a stupid sleep—
So slowly does the time unwind its skein!

31. Le Vampire

Toi qui, comme un coup de couteau,
Dans mon cœur plaintif es entrée;
Toi qui, forte comme un troupeau
De démons, vins, folle et parée,

De mon esprit humilié
Faire ton lit et ton domaine;
— Infâme à qui je suis lié
Comme le forçat à la chaîne,

Comme au jeu le joueur têtu,
Comme à la bouteille l'ivrogne,
Comme aux vermines la charogne,
— Maudite, maudite sois-tu!

J'ai prié le glaive rapide
De conquérir ma liberté,
Et j'ai dit au poison perfide
De secourir ma lâcheté.

Hélas! le poison et le glaive
M'ont pris en dédain et m'ont dit:
'Tu n'es pas digne qu'on t'enlève
A ton esclavage maudit,

Imbécile! — de son empire
Si nos efforts te délivraient,
Tes baisers ressusciteraient
Le cadavre de ton vampire!'

31. The Vampire

You invaded my sorrowful heart
Like the sudden stroke of a blade;
Bold as a lunatic troupe
Of demons in drunken parade,

You in my mortified soul
Made your bed and your domain;
—Abhorrence, to whom I am bound
As the convict is to the chain,

As the drunkard is to the jug,
As the gambler to the game,
As to the vermin the corpse,
—I damn you, out of my shame!

And I prayed to the eager sword
To win my deliverance,
And have asked the perfidious vial
To redeem my cowardice.

Alas! the vial and the sword
Disdainfully said to me;
'You are not worthy to lift
From your wretched slavery,

You fool! — if from her command
Our efforts delivered you forth,
Your kisses would waken again
Your vampire lover's corpse!'

31a. Le Léthé

Viens sur mon cœur, âme cruelle et sourde,
Tigre adoré, monstre aux airs indolents;
Je veux longtemps plonger mes doigts tremblants
Dans l'épaisseur de ta crinière lourde;

Dans tes jupons remplis de ton parfum
Ensevelir ma tête endolorie,
Et respirer, comme une fleur flétrie,
Le doux relent de mon amour défunt.

Je veux dormir! dormir plutôt que vivre!
Dans un sommeil aussi doux que la mort,
J'étalerai mes baisers sans remord
Sur ton beau corps poli comme le cuivre.

Pour engloutir mes sanglots apaisés
Rien ne me vaut l'abîme de ta couche;
L'oubli puissant habite sur ta bouche,
Et le Léthé coule dans tes baisers.

A mon destin, désormais mon délice,
J'obéirai comme un prédestiné;
Martyr docile, innocent condamné,
Dont la ferveur attise le supplice,

Je sucerai, pour noyer ma rancœur,
Le népenthès et la bonne ciguë
Aux bouts charmants de cette gorge aiguë,
Qui n'a jamais emprisonné de cœur.

31a. Lethe*

Come to my heart, you tiger I adore.
You sullen monster, cruel and speechless spirit;
Into the thickness of your heavy mane
I want to plunge my trembling fingers' grip.

I want to hide the throbbing of my head
In your perfume, under those petticoats,
And breathe the musky scent of our old love,
The fading fragrance of the dying rose.

I want to sleep! to sleep and not to live!
And in a sleep as sweet as death, to dream
Of spreading out my kisses without shame
On your smooth body, bright with copper sheen.

If I would swallow down my softened sobs
It must be in your bed's profound abyss—
Forgetfulness is moistening your breath,
Lethe itself runs smoothly in your kiss.

My destiny, from now on my delight,
Is to obey as one who has been sent
To guiltless martyrdom, when all the while
His passion fans the flames of his torment.

My lips will suck the cure for bitterness:
Oblivion, nepenthe* has its start
In the bewitching teats of those hard breasts,
That never have been harbour of a heart.

32. 'Une nuit que j'étais près...'

Une nuit que j'étais près d'une affreuse Juive,
Comme au long d'un cadavre un cadavre étendu,
Je me pris à songer près de ce corps vendu
A la triste beauté dont mon désir se prive.

Je me réprésentai sa majesté native,
Son regard de vigueur et de grâces armé,
Ses cheveux qui lui font un casque parfumé,
Et dont le souvenir pour l'amour me ravive.

Car j'eusse avec ferveur baisé ton noble corps,
Et depuis tes pieds frais jusqu'à tes noires tresses
Déroulé le trésor des profondes caresses,

Si, quelque soir, d'un pleur obtenu sans effort
Tu pouvais seulement, ô reine des cruelles!
Obscurcir la splendeur de tes froides prunelles.

33. Remords posthume

Lorsque tu dormiras, ma belle ténébreuse,
Au fond d'un monument construit en marbre noir,
Et lorsque tu n'auras pour alcôve et manoir
Qu'un caveau pluvieux et qu'une fosse creuse;

Quand la pierre, opprimant ta poitrine peureuse
Et tes flancs qu'assouplit un charmant nonchaloir,
Empêchera ton cœur de battre et de vouloir,
Et tes pieds de courir leur course aventureuse,

32. 'Beside a monstrous Jewish whore ...'

Beside a monstrous Jewish whore* I lay
One night, we were two corpses side by side,
And came to dream beside this hired bride
Of beauty my desire had turned away.*

I saw again her native majesty,
Her gaze empowered with a strength and grace,
Her hair a perfumed casque around her face,
An image that revived the love in me.

For I would fervently have kissed your flesh,
From your sweet feet up to your sable hair
Unrolled the treasure of a deep caress,

If on some evening, with a simple tear,
O queen of cruelty! you had devised
To dim the brilliance of those soulless eyes.

33. Remorse after Death

When, sullen beauty, you will sleep and have
As resting place a fine black marble tomb,
When for a boudoir in your manor-home
You have a hollow pit, a sodden cave,

When stone, now heavy on your fearful breast
And loins once supple in their tempered fire,
Will stop your heart from beating, and desire,
And keep your straying feet from wantonness,

Le tombeau, confident de mon rêve infini
(Car le tombeau toujours comprendra le poëte),
Durant ces grandes nuits d'où le somme est banni,

Te dira: 'Que vous sert, courtisane imparfaite,
De n'avoir pas connu ce que pleurent les morts?'
— Et le ver rongera ta peau comme un remords.

34. Le Chat

Viens, mon beau chat, sur mon cœur amoureux;
    Retiens les griffes de ta patte,
Et laisse-moi plonger dans tes beaux yeux,
    Mêlés de métal et d'agate.

Lorsque mes doigts caressent à loisir
    Ta tête et ton dos élastique,
Et que ma main s'enivre du plaisir
    De palper ton corps électrique,

Je vois ma femme en esprit. Son regard,
    Comme le tien, aimable bête,
Profond et froid, coupe et fend comme un dard,

    Et, des pieds jusques à la tête,
Un air subtil, un dangereux parfum
    Nagent autour de son corps brun.

35. *Duellum*

Deux guerriers ont couru l'un sur l'autre; leurs armes
Ont éclaboussé l'air de lueurs et de sang.
Ces jeux, ces cliquetis du fer sont les vacarmes
D'une jeunesse en proie à l'amour vagissant.

The Tomb, who knows what yearning is about
(The Tomb grasps what the poet has to say)
Will question you these nights you cannot rest,

'Vain courtesan, how could you live that way
And not have known what all the dead cry out?'
—And like remorse the worm will gnaw your flesh.

34. The Cat

Come, my fine cat, to my amorous heart;
    Please let your claws be concealed.
And let me plunge into your beautiful eyes,
    Coalescence of agate and steel.

When my leisurely fingers are stroking your head
    And your body's elasticity,
And my hand becomes drunk with the pleasure it finds
    In the feel of electricity,

My woman comes into my mind. Her regard
    Like your own, my agreeable beast,
Is deep and is cold, and it splits like a spear,

    And, from her head to her feet,
A subtle and dangerous air of perfume
    Floats always around her brown skin.

35. *Duellum**

Two warriors have grappled, and their arms
Have flecked the air with blood and flashing steel.
These frolics, this mad clanking, these alarms
Proceed from childish love's frantic appeal.

Les glaives sont brisés! comme notre jeunesse,
Ma chère! Mais les dents, les ongles acérés,
Vengent bientôt l'épée et la dague traîtresse.
— Ô fureur des cœurs mûrs par l'amour ulcérés!

Dans le ravin hanté des chats-pards et des onces
Nos héros, s'étreignant méchamment, ont roulé,
Et leur peau fleurira l'aridité des ronces.

— Ce gouffre, c'est l'enfer, de nos amis peuplé!
Roulons-y sans remords, amazone inhumaine,
Afin d'éterniser l'ardeur de notre haine!

36. Le Balcon

Mère des souvenirs, maîtresse des maîtresses,
Ô toi, tous mes plaisirs! ô toi, tous mes devoirs!
Tu te rappelleras la beauté des caresses,
La douceur du foyer et le charme des soirs,
Mère des souvenirs, maîtresse des maîtresses!

Les soirs illuminés par l'ardeur du charbon,
Et les soirs au balcon, voilés de vapeurs roses.
Que ton sein m'était doux! que ton cœur m'était bon!
Nous avons dit souvent d'impérissables choses
Les soirs illuminés par l'ardeur du charbon.

Que les soleils sont beaux dans les chaudes soirées!
Que l'espace est profond! que le cœur est puissant!
En me penchant vers toi, reine des adorées,
Je croyais respirer le parfum de ton sang.
Que les soleils sont beaux dans les chaudes soirées!

The swords are broken! like our youthful life
My dear! But tooth and nail, avid and sharp,
Soon fill the place of rapier and knife.
—O bitter heat of love, o cankered hearts!

In a ravine haunted by catlike forms
These two have tumbled, struggling to the end;
Shreds of their skin will bloom on arid thorns.

—This pit is Hell, its denizens our friends!
Amazon,* let us roll there guiltlessly
In spiteful fervour, for eternity!

36. The Balcony

Mother of memories, mistress of mistresses,
O thou of all my pleasures, all my debts of love!
Call to your mind the gentle touch of our caress,
The sweetness of the hearth, the charming sky above,
Mother of memories, mistress of mistresses!

Evenings illumined by the ardour of the coal,
And on the balcony, the pink that vapours bring;
How sweet your bosom to me, and how kind your soul!
We often told ourselves imperishable things,
Evenings illumined by the ardour of the coal.

How beautiful the suns! How warm their evening beams!
How endless is the space! The heart, how strong and good!
On bending towards you, o beloved, o my queen,
I thought that I could breathe the perfume of your blood.
How beautiful the suns! How warm their evening beams!

La nuit s'épaississait ainsi qu'une cloison,
Et mes yeux dans le noir devinaient tes prunelles,
Et je buvais ton souffle, ô douceur! ô poison!
Et tes pieds s'endormaient dans mes mains fraternelles.
La nuit s'épaississait ainsi qu'une cloison.

Je sais l'art d'évoquer les minutes heureuses,
Et revis mon passé blotti dans tes genoux.
Car à quoi bon chercher tes beautés langoureuses
Ailleurs qu'en ton cher corps et qu'en ton cœur si doux?
Je sais l'art d'évoquer les minutes heureuses!

Ces serments, ces parfums, ces baisers infinis,
Renaîtront-ils d'un gouffre interdit à nos sondes,
Comme montent au ciel les soleils rajeunis
Après s'être lavés au fond des mers profondes?
— Ô serments! ô parfums! ô baisers infinis!

37. Le Possédé

Le soleil s'est couvert d'un crêpe. Comme lui,
Ô Lune de ma vie! emmitoufle-toi d'ombre;
Dors ou fume à ton gré; sois muette, sois sombre,
Et plonge tout entière au gouffre de l'Ennui;

Je t'aime ainsi! Pourtant, si tu veux aujourd'hui,
Comme un astre éclipsé qui sort de la pénombre,
Te pavaner aux lieux que la Folie encombre,
C'est bien! Charmant poignard, jaillis de ton étui!

Allume ta prunelle à la flamme des lustres!
Allume le désir dans les regards des rustres!
Tout de toi m'est plaisir, morbide ou pétulant;

Sois ce que tu voudras, nuit noire, rouge aurore;
Il n'est pas une fibre en tout mon corps tremblant
Qui ne crie: *Ô mon cher Belzébuth, je t'adore!*

Then we would be enclosed within the thickening night,
And in the dark my eyes divined your eyes so deep,
And I would drink your breath, o poison, o delight!
In my fraternal hands, your feet would go to sleep,
When we would be enclosed within the thickening night.

I have the art of calling forth the happy times,
Seeing again my past there curled within your knees.
Where should I look for beauty, languorous and sublime,
If not in your dear heart, and body at its ease?
I have the art of calling forth the happy times!

These vows, these sweet perfumes, these kisses infinite,
Will they be reborn from a gulf we cannot sound,
As suns rejuvenated take celestial flight
Having been bathed in oceans, mighty and profound?
—O vows! O sweet perfumes! O kisses infinite!

37. The Possessed

The sun is wrapped within a pall of mist,
Moon of my life! enshroud yourself like him;
Sleep, damp your fires; be silent, dim,
And plunge to ennui's most profound abyss;

I love you this way! But, if you decline,
And choose to move from your eclipse to light,
To strut yourself where Folly throngs tonight,
Spring, charming dagger, from your sheath! That's fine!

Light up your eyes with flames of candle glow!
Light up the lust in yokels at the show!
I love your moods, no one of them the best;

Be night or dawn, do what you want to do;
I cry in every fibre of my flesh:
'O my Beelzebub,* I worship you!'

38. Un fantôme

I

Les Ténèbres

Dans les caveaux d'insondable tristesse
Où le Destin m'a déjà relégué;
Où jamais n'entre un rayon rose et gai;
Où, seul avec la Nuit, maussade hôtesse,

Je suis comme un peintre qu'un Dieu moqueur
Condamne à peindre, hélas! sur les ténèbres;
Où, cuisinier aux appetits funèbres,
Je fais bouillir et je mange mon cœur,

Par instants brille, et s'allonge, et s'étale
Un spectre fait de grâce et de splendeur.
A sa rêveuse allure orientale,

Quand il atteint sa totale grandeur,
Je reconnais ma belle visiteuse:
C'est Elle! noire et pourtant lumineuse.

II

Le Parfum

Lecteur, as-tu quelquefois respiré
Avec ivresse et lente gourmandise
Ce grain d'encens qui remplit une église,
Ou d'un sachet le musc invétéré?

Charme profond, magique, dont nous grise
Dans le présent le passé restauré!
Ainsi l'amant sur un corps adoré
Du souvenir cueille la fleur exquise.

38. A Phantom

I

The Blackness

In vaults of fathomless obscurity
Where Destiny has sentenced me for life;
Where cheerful rosy beams may never shine;
Where, living with that sullen hostess, Night,

I am an artist that a mocking God
Condemns, alas! to paint the gloom itself;
Where like a cook with ghoulish appetite
I boil and devour my own heart,

Sometimes there sprawls, and stretches out, and glows
A splendid ghost, of a surpassing charm,
And when this vision growing in my sight

In oriental languor, like a dream,
Is fully formed, I know the phantom's name:
Yes, it is She! though black, yet full of light.

II

The Perfume

During your lifetime, reader, have you breathed,
Slow-savouring to the point of dizziness,
That grain of incense which fills up a church,
Or the pervasive musk of a sachet?

Magical charm, in which the past restored
Intoxicates us with its presence here!
So from the body of his well-beloved
The lover plucks remembrance's bright bloom.

De ses cheveux élastiques et lourds,
Vivant sachet, encensoir de l'alcôve,
Une senteur montait, sauvage et fauve,

Et des habits, mousseline ou velours,
Tout imprégnés de sa jeunesse pure,
Se dégageait un parfum de fourrure.

III
Le Cadre

Comme un beau cadre ajoute à la peinture,
Bien qu'elle soit d'un pinceau très-vanté,
Je ne sais quoi d'étrange et d'enchanté
En l'isolant de l'immense nature,

Ainsi bijoux, meubles, métaux, dorure,
S'adaptaient juste à sa rare beauté;
Rien n'offusquait sa parfaite clarté,
Et tout semblait lui servir de bordure.

Même on eût dit parfois qu'elle croyait
Que tout voulait l'aimer; elle noyait
Sa nudité voluptueusement

Dans les baisers du satin et du linge,
Et, lente ou brusque, à chaque mouvement
Montrait la grâce enfantine du singe.

IV
Le Portrait

La Maladie et la Mort font des cendres
De tout le feu qui pour nous flamboya.
De ces grands yeux si fervents et si tendres,
De cette bouche où mon cœur se noya,

Out of the phantom's dense, resilient locks,
Living sachet, censer of the alcove,
Would rise an alien and tawny scent,

And all her clothes, of muslin or of plush,
Redolent as they were with her pure youth,
Released the soft perfume of thickest fur.

III

The Frame

Just as the frame adds to the painter's art,
Although the brush itself be highly praised,
A something that is captivating, strange,
Setting it off from all in nature else,

So jewels and metals, gildings, furnishings
Exactly fit her rich and rare appeal;
Nothing offends her perfect clarity,
And all would seem a frame for her display.

And one could say at times that she believed
Everything loved her, in that she would bathe
Freely, voluptuously, her nudity

In kisses of the linen and the silk,
And with each charming movement, slow or quick,
Display a cunning monkey's childlike grace.

IV

The Portrait

Disease and Death make only dust and ash
Of all the fire that blazed so bright for us.
Of those great eyes so tender and so warm,
Of this mouth where my heart has drowned itself,

De ces baisers puissants comme un dictame,
De ces transports plus vifs que des rayons,
Que reste-t-il? C'est affreux, ô mon âme!
Rien qu'un dessin fort pâle, aux trois crayons,

Qui, comme moi, meurt dans la solitude,
Et que le Temps, injurieux vieillard,
Chaque jour frotte avec son aile rude . . .

Noir assassin de la Vie et de l'Art,
Tu ne tueras jamais dans ma mémoire
Celle qui fut mon plaisir et ma gloire!

39. 'Je te donne ces vers . . .'

Je te donne ces vers afin que si mon nom
Aborde heureusement aux époques lointaines,
Et fait rêver un soir les cervelles humaines,
Vaisseau favorisé par un grand aquilon,

Ta mémoire, pareille aux fables incertaines,
Fatigue le lecteur ainsi qu'un tympanon,
Et par un fraternel et mystique chaînon
Reste comme pendue à mes rimes hautaines;

Être maudit à qui, de l'abîme profond
Jusqu'au plus haut du ciel, rien, hors moi, ne répond!
—Ô toi qui, comme une ombre à la trace éphémère,

Foules d'un pied léger et d'un regard serein
Les stupides mortels qui t'ont jugée amère,
Statue aux yeux de jais, grand ange au front d'airain!

Of kisses puissant as a healing balm,
Of transports more intense than flaring light,
What now remains? Appalling, o my soul!
Only a fading sketch in three pale tones,

Like me, dying away in solitude,
And which Time, that maleficent old man,
Each day rubs over with his churlish wing . . .

Time, you black murderer of Life and Art,
You'll never kill her in my memory—
Not She, who was my pleasure and my pride!

39. 'I give to you these verses . . .'

I give to you these verses, that if in
Some future time my name lands happily
To bring brief pleasure to humanity,
The craft supported by a great north wind,

Your memory, like tales from ancient times,
Will bore the reader like a dulcimer,
And by a strange fraternal chain live here
As if suspended in my lofty rhymes.

From deepest pit into the highest sky
Damned being, only I can bear you now.
—O shadow, barely present to the eye,

You lightly step, with a serene regard
On mortal fools who've judged you mean and hard—
Angel with eyes of jet, great burnished brow!

40. *Semper eadem*

'D'où vous vient, disiez-vous, cette tristesse étrange,
Montant comme la mer sur le roc noir et nu?'
— Quand notre cœur a fait une fois sa vendange,
Vivre est un mal. C'est un secret de tous connu,

Une douleur très-simple et non mystérieuse,
Et, comme votre joie, éclatante pour tous.
Cessez donc de chercher, ô belle curieuse!
Et, bien que votre voix soit douce, taisez-vous!

Taisez-vous, ignorante! âme toujours ravie!
Bouche au rire enfantin! Plus encor que la Vie,
La Mort nous tient souvent par des liens subtils.

Laissez, laissez mon cœur s'enivrer d'un *mensonge*,
Plonger dans vos beaux yeux comme dans un beau songe,
Et sommeiller longtemps à l'ombre de vos cils!

41. Tout entière

Le Démon, dans ma chambre haute,
Ce matin est venu me voir,
Et, tâchant à me prendre en faute,
Me dit: 'Je voudrais bien savoir,

Parmi toutes les belles choses
Dont est fait son enchantement,
Parmi les objets noirs ou roses
Qui composent son corps charmant,

40. *Semper eadem**

You said, there grows within you some strange gloom,
A sea rising on rock, why is it so?
—When once your heart has brought its harvest home
Life is an evil! (secret all men know),

A simple sorrow, not mysterious,
And, like your joy, it sparkles for us all.
So, lovely one, be not so curious!
And even though your voice is sweet, be still!

Be quiet silly girl! Soul of delight!
Mouth of the childish laugh! More, still, than Life
Death holds us often in the subtlest ways.

So let my heart be lost within a *lie,**
As in a sweet dream, plunge into your eyes
And sleep a long time in your lashes' shade.

41. Completely One

The Devil and I had a chat
This morning in my snuggery;
Trying to catch me in a lapse,
'Tell me', he said beseechingly,

'Among the many charming things
Of which her body is composed
That make her so enrapturing,
Among the objects, black or rose,**

Quel est le plus doux.' — Ô mon âme!
Tu répondis à l'Abhorré:
'Puisqu'en Elle tout est dictame,
Rien ne peut être préféré.

Lorsque tout me ravit, j'ignore
Si quelque chose me séduit.
Elle éblouit comme l'Aurore
Et console comme la Nuit;

Et l'harmonie est trop exquise,
Qui gouverne tout son beau corps,
Pour que l'impuissante analyse
En note les nombreux accords.

Ô métamorphose mystique
De tous mes sens fondus en un!
Son haleine fait la musique,
Comme sa voix fait le parfum!'

42. 'Que diras-tu ce soir…'

Que diras-tu ce soir, pauvre âme solitaire,
Que diras-tu, mon cœur, cœur autrefois flétri,
A la très-belle, à la très-bonne, à la très-chère,
Dont le regard divin t'a soudain refleuri?

—Nous mettrons notre orgueil à chanter ses louanges:
Rien ne vaut la douceur de son autorité;
Sa chair spirituelle a le parfum des Anges,
Et son œil nous revêt d'un habit de clarté.

Que ce soit dans la nuit et dans la solitude,
Que ce soit dans la rue et dans la multitude,
Son fantôme dans l'air danse comme un flambeau.

Which is the sweetest.'—O my soul!
You foiled the Tempter with these words:
'Since all is solace in the whole
No single thing may be preferred.

I can't, when all is ravishing,
Say some one thing seduces me.
She is the Daybreak's dazzling,
The Night's consoling sympathy.

And the exquisite government
The harmony her grace affords,
Makes analytics impotent
To note its numerous accords.

O mystic metamorphoses
In me, my senses all confused!
She makes a music when she breathes,
Sounds of her voice are sweet perfumes!'

42. 'What will you say tonight . . .'

What will you say tonight, poor lonely soul,
What will you say old withered heart of mine,
To the most beautiful, the best, most dear,
Whose heavenly regard brings back your bloom?

—We will assign our pride to sing her praise:
Nothing excels the sweetness of her will;
Her holy body has an angel's scent,
Her eye invests us with a cloak of light.

Whether it be in night and solitude,
Or in the streets among the multitude,
Her ghost before us dances like a torch.

Parfois il parle et dit: 'Je suis belle, et j'ordonne
Que pour l'amour de moi vous n'aimiez que le Beau;
Je suis l'Ange gardien, la Muse et la Madone!'

43. Le Flambeau vivant

Ils marchent devant moi, ces Yeux pleins de lumières,
Qu'un Ange très-savant a sans doute aimantés;
Ils marchent, ces divins frères qui sont mes frères,
Secouant dans mes yeux leurs feux diamantés.

Me sauvant de tout piége et de tout péché grave,
Ils conduisent mes pas dans la route du Beau;
Ils sont mes serviteurs et je suis leur esclave;
Tout mon être obéit à ce vivant flambeau.

Charmants Yeux, vous brillez de la clarté mystique
Qu'ont les cierges brûlant en plein jour; le soleil
Rougit, mais n'éteint pas leur flamme fantastique;

Ils célèbrent la Mort, vous chantez le Réveil;
Vous marchez en chantant le réveil de mon âme,
Astres dont nul soleil ne peut flétrir la flamme!

43a. A celle qui est trop gaie

Ta tête, ton geste, ton air
Sont beaux comme un beau paysage;
Le rire joue en ton visage
Comme un vent frais dans un ciel clair.

Le passant chagrin que tu frôles
Est ébloui par la santé
Qui jaillit comme une clarté
De tes bras et de tes épaules.

It speaks out: 'I am lovely and command
That you will love only the Beautiful;
I am your Guardian, Madonna, Muse!'

43. The Living Torch

They march ahead, those brilliant Eyes in you
A master Angel doubtless magnetized;
They march, those holy twins, my brothers too,
Raising a gem-like flame within my eyes.

From all the snares and deadly sins they save
Me, and they lead my steps in Beauty's way;
They are my servants, yet I am their slave;
This living torch makes all my heart obey.

Fair eyes, you glimmer with the secret rays
Of tapers lit at noon; in growing red
The sun does not put out their mystic blaze;

You sing Awakening, they praise the Dead;*
You march and wake with song this soul of mine,
Stars of a flame the sun can not outshine!

43a. To One Who Is Too Cheerful

Your head, your air, your every way
Are scenic as the countryside;
The smile plays in your lips and eyes
Like fresh winds on a cloudless day.

The gloomy drudge, brushed by your charms,
Is dazzled by the vibrancy
That flashes forth so brilliantly
Out of your shoulders and your arms.

Les retentissantes couleurs
Dont tu parsèmes tes toilettes
Jettent dans l'esprit des poëtes
L'image d'un ballet de fleurs.

Ces robes folles sont l'emblème
De ton esprit bariolé;
Folle dont je suis affolé,
Je te hais autant que je t'aime!

Quelquefois dans un beau jardin
Où je traînais mon atonie,
J'ai senti comme une ironie,
Le soleil déchirer mon sein;

Et le printemps et la verdure
Ont tant humilié mon cœur,
Que j'ai puni sur une fleur
L'insolence de la Nature.

Ainsi je voudrais, une nuit,
Quand l'heure des voluptés sonne,
Vers les trésors de ta personne,
Comme un lâche, ramper sans bruit,

Pour châtier ta chair joyeuse,
Pour meurtrir ton sein pardonné,
Et faire à ton flanc étonné
Une blessure large et creuse,

Et, vertigineuse douceur!
A travers ces lèvres nouvelles,
Plus éclatantes et plus belles,
T'infuser mon venin, ma sœur!

All vivid colours, and the way
They resonate in how you dress
Have poets in their idleness
Imagining a flower-ballet.

These lavish robes are emblems of
The mad profusion that is you;
Madwoman, I am maddened too,
And hate you even as I love!

Sometimes within a park, at rest,
Where I have dragged my apathy,
I have felt like an irony
The sunshine lacerate my breast.

And then the spring's luxuriance
Humiliated so my heart
That I have pulled a flower apart
To punish Nature's insolence.

So I would wish, when you're asleep,
The time for sensuality,
Towards your body's treasury
Silently, stealthily to creep,

To bruise your ever-tender breast,
And carve in your astonished side
An injury both deep and wide,
To chastize your too-joyous flesh.

And, sweetness that would dizzy me!
In these two lips so red and new
My sister, I have made for you,
To slip my venom,* lovingly!

44. Réversibilité

Ange plein de gaieté, connaissez-vous l'angoisse,
La honte, les remords, les sanglots, les ennuis,
Et les vagues terreurs de ces affreuses nuits
Qui compriment le cœur comme un papier qu'on froisse?
Ange plein de gaieté, connaissez-vous l'angoisse?

Ange plein de bonté, connaissez-vous la haine,
Les poings crispés dans l'ombre et les larmes de fiel,
Quand la Vengeance bat son infernal rappel,
Et de nos facultés se fait le capitaine?
Ange plein de bonté, connaissez-vous la haine?

Ange plein de santé, connaissez-vous les Fièvres,
Qui, le long des grands murs de l'hospice blafard,
Comme des exilés, s'en vont d'un pied traînard,
Cherchant le soleil rare et remuant les lèvres?
Ange plein de santé, connaissez-vous les Fièvres?

Ange plein de beauté, connaissez-vous les rides,
Et la peur de vieillir, et ce hideux tourment
De lire la secrète horreur du dévouement
Dans des yeux où longtemps burent nos yeux avides?
Ange plein de beauté, connaissez-vous les rides?

Ange plein de bonheur, de joie et de lumières,
David mourant aurait demandé la santé
Aux émanations de ton corps enchanté;
Mais de toi je n'implore, ange, que tes prières,
Ange plein de bonheur, de joie et de lumières!

44. Reversibility

Angel of gladness, do you know of anguish,
Shame, of troubles, sobs, and of remorse,
And the vague terrors of those awful nights
That squeeze the heart like paper in a ball?
Angel of gladness, do you know of pain?

Angel of kindness, do you know of hatred,
Clenched fists in the shadow, tears of gall,
When Vengeance beats his hellish call to arms,
And makes himself the captain of our will?
Angel of kindness, do you know revenge?

Angel of health, are you aware of Fevers
Who by pallid hospitals' great walls
Stagger like exiles, with the lagging foot,
Searching for sunlight, mumbling with their lips?
Angel of health, do you know of disease?

Angel of beauty, do you know of wrinkles,
Fear of growing old, the great torment
To read the horror of self-sacrifice
In eyes our avid eyes had drunk for years?
Angel of beauty, do you know these lines?

Angel of fortune, happiness and light,
David in dying might have claimed the health*
That radiates from your enchanted flesh;
But, angel, I implore only your prayers,
Angel of fortune, happiness and light!

45. Confession

Une fois, une seule, aimable et douce femme,
    A mon bras votre bras poli
S'appuya (sur le fond ténébreux de mon âme
    Ce souvenir n'est point pâli);

Il était tard; ainsi qu'une médaille neuve
    La pleine lune s'étalait,
Et la solennité de la nuit, comme un fleuve,
    Sur Paris dormant ruisselait.

Et le long des maisons, sous les portes cochères,
    Des chats passaient furtivement,
L'oreille au guet, ou bien, comme des ombres chères,
    Nous accompagnaient lentement.

Tout à coup, au milieu de l'intimité libre
    Éclose à la pâle clarté,
De vous, riche et sonore instrument où ne vibre
    Que la radieuse gaieté,

De vous, claire et joyeuse ainsi qu'une fanfare
    Dans le matin étincelant,
Une note plaintive, une note bizarre
    S'échappa, tout en chancelant

Comme une enfant chétive, horrible, sombre, immonde,
    Dont sa famille rougirait,
Et qu'elle aurait longtemps, pour la cacher au monde,
    Dans un caveau mise au secret.

Pauvre ange, elle chantait, votre note criarde:
    'Que rien ici-bas n'est certain,
Et que toujours, avec quelque soin qu'il se farde,
    Se trahit l'égoïsme humain;

45. Confession

One special time, my sweet and lovely friend,
   Your smooth arm on my own was laid
(Deep in my spirit where the shadows blend
   That memory will never fade):

Late night, and like a medal in the sky
   The harvest moon was beaming down,
And, like a river, the solemnity
   Of night streamed on the sleeping town.

Along the houses, by the hitching-posts,
   Some silent cats passed furtively
With ears alert, and like familiar ghosts
   They walked with us as company.

Then suddenly, within the confidence
   Born of the pale and limpid night,
From you, that rich, resounding instrument
   Ringing with radiant delight,

From you, as joyous as a trumpet cry
   That greets the sparkling break of day,
A wistful note, a note bizarre, and shy,
   Slipped almost haltingly away

As if it were a soiled, stunted girl,
   Dishonour to her family
Who'd tried for years to hide her from the world
   Down in a cellar, secretly.

She sang, poor dear, your note of plaintive sighs:
   'Nothing is certain here,' she said,
'Always, no matter what its new disguise,
   The human ego rears its head;

Que c'est un dur métier que d'être belle femme,
   Et que c'est le travail banal
De la danseuse folle et froide qui se pâme
   Dans un sourire machinal;

Que bâtir sur les cœurs est une chose sotte;
   Que tout craque, amour et beauté,
Jusqu'à ce que l'Oubli les jette dans sa hotte
   Pour les rendre à l'Éternité!'

J'ai souvent évoqué cette lune enchantée,
   Ce silence et cette langueur,
Et cette confidence horrible chuchotée
   Au confessionnal du cœur.

46. L'Aube spirituelle

Quand chez les débauchés l'aube blanche et vermeille
Entre en société de l'Idéal rongeur,
Par l'opération d'un mystère vengeur
Dans la brute assoupie un ange se réveille.

Des Cieux Spirituels l'inaccessible azur,
Pour l'homme terrassé qui rêve encore et souffre,
S'ouvre et s'enfonce avec l'attirance du gouffre.
Ainsi, chère Déesse, Être lucide et pur,

Sur les débris fumeux des stupides orgies
Ton souvenir plus clair, plus rose, plus charmant,
A mes yeux agrandis voltige incessamment.

Le soleil a noirci la flamme des bougies;
Ainsi, toujours vainqueur, ton fantôme est pareil,
Âme resplendissante, à l'immortel soleil!

Being a beauty is a hard affair,
  A banal business, vanity,
The swoons of mad and frigid dancers, where
  The smiles are done mechanically.

And it is foolishness to trust in hearts,
  For hearts will break and beauty dies,
Till Darkness with his hod picks up the parts,
  To haul them to Eternal skies!'

Often I think about that mystery,
  The moon's enchantment over all,
And of the confidence you breathed to me
  There at the heart's confessional.

46. The Spiritual Dawn

When white and ruby dawn among the rakes
Breaks in, she's with the harrying Ideal,
And by some strange retributive appeal
Within the sleepy brute, an angel wakes.

The perfect blue of Spiritual Skies—
For the lost man who dreams and suffers, this
Pierces him, fascinates like the abyss.
And so, dear Goddess, lucid, pure and wise,

Over debris the orgies leave behind
Your memory, more rosy, more divine
Constantly flickers in my vision's sight.

The sun has blackened candles of the night;
Your phantom does the same, o conquering one,
Resplendent soul, of the immortal sun!

47. Harmonie du soir

Voici venir les temps où vibrant sur sa tige
Chaque fleur s'évapore ainsi qu'un encensoir;
Les sons et les parfums tournent dans l'air du soir;
Valse mélancolique et langoureux vertige!

Chaque fleur s'évapore ainsi qu'un encensoir;
Le violon frémit comme un cœur qu'on afflige;
Valse mélancolique et langoureux vertige!
Le ciel est triste et beau comme un grand reposoir.

Le violon frémit comme un cœur qu'on afflige,
Un cœur tendre, qui hait le néant vaste et noir!
Le ciel est triste et beau comme un grand reposoir;
Le soleil s'est noyé dans son sang qui se fige.

Un cœur tendre qui hait le néant vaste et noir,
Du passé lumineux recueille tout vestige!
Le soleil s'est noyé dans son sang qui se fige...
Ton souvenir en moi luit comme un ostensoir!

48. Le Flacon

Il est de forts parfums pour qui toute matière
Est poreuse. On dirait qu'ils pénètrent le verre.
En ouvrant un coffret venu de l'Orient
Dont la serrure grince et rechigne en criant,

Ou dans une maison déserte quelque armoire
Pleine de l'âcre odeur des temps, poudreuse et noire,
Parfois on trouve un vieux flacon qui se souvient,
D'où jaillit toute vive une âme qui revient.

47. The Harmony of Evening

Now it is nearly time when, quivering on its stem,
Each flower, like a censer, sprinkles out its scent;
Sounds and perfumes are mingling in the evening air;
Waltz of a mournfulness and languid vertigo!

Each flower, like a censer, sprinkles out its scent,
The violin is trembling like a grieving heart,
Waltz of a mournfulness and languid vertigo!
The sad and lovely sky spreads like an altar-cloth;

The violin is trembling like a grieving heart,
A tender heart, that hates non-being, vast and black!
The sad and lovely sky spreads like an altar-cloth;
The sun is drowning in its dark, congealing blood.

A tender heart that hates non-being, vast and black
Assembles every glowing vestige of the past!
The sun is drowning in its dark, congealing blood . . .
In me your memory, as in a monstrance,* shines!

48. The Flask

There are some strong perfumes that cannot be contained,
Which seep through any glass of bottle or of vial.
For instance, taking up an Oriental chest,
Whose stubborn lock will creak and groan in opening,

Or poking through a house, in closets shut for years,
Full of the smell of time—acrid, musty, dank,
One comes, perhaps, upon a flask of memories
In whose escaping scent a soul returns to life.

Mille pensers dormaient, chrysalides funèbres,
Frémissant doucement dans les lourdes ténèbres,
Qui dégagent leur aile et prennent leur essor,
Teintés d'azur, glacés de rose, lamés d'or.

Voilà le souvenir enivrant qui voltige
Dans l'air troublé; les yeux se ferment; le Vertige
Saisit l'âme vaincue et la pousse à deux mains
Vers un gouffre obscurci de miasmes humains;

Il la terrasse au bord d'un gouffre séculaire,
Où, Lazare odorant déchirant son suaire,
Se meut dans son réveil le cadavre spectral
D'un vieil amour ranci, charmant et sépulcral.

Ainsi, quand je serai perdu dans la mémoire
Des hommes, dans le coin d'une sinistre armoire
Quand on m'aura jeté, vieux flacon désolé,
Décrépit, poudreux, sale, abject, visqueux, fêlé,

Je serai ton cercueil, aimable pestilence!
Le témoin de ta force et de ta virulence,
Cher poison préparé par les anges! liqueur
Qui me ronge, ô la vie et la mort de mon cœur!

49. Le Poison

Le vin sait revêtir le plus sordide bouge
　　D'un luxe miraculeux,
Et fait surgir plus d'un portique fabuleux
　　Dans l'or de sa vapeur rouge,
Comme un soleil couchant dans un ciel nébuleux.

A thousand thoughts have slept cocooned within this flask,
But sweetly trembling there, packed closely in the dark;
Now they release their wings and take their gaudy flight,
Tinged with an azure blue, rose-glazed, spangled in gold.

Fluttering to the brain through the unsettled air,
Rapturous memory pervades the atmosphere;
The eyes are forced to close; Vertigo grasps the soul,
And thrusts her with his hands into the mists of mind.

He forces her to lie next to an ancient tomb,
From which with cloying scent—Lazarus* splitting his shroud—
A gaunt cadaver moves to its awakening:
Ghost of a spoiled love, enchanting though impure.

So when I am entombed to mortal memory,
When I am closeted in some deserted house,
When I've been thrown away, an old forgotten flask,
Decrepit, dusty, cracked, rejected, filthy, rank,

I will be tomb for you, beloved pestilence,
The witness of your force and of its virulence,
Dear poison made by angels, drink that eats my soul,
O you who are the life and ruin of my heart!

49. Poison

Wine can invest the most disgusting hole
    With wonders to our eyes,
And make the fabled porticoes arise
    In its red vapour's gold
That show in sunsets seen through hazy skies.

L'opium agrandit ce qui n'a pas de bornes,
    Allonge l'illimité,
Approfondit le temps, creuse la volupté,
    Et de plaisirs noirs et mornes
Remplit l'âme au delà de sa capacité.

Tout cela ne vaut pas le poison qui découle
    De tes yeux, de tes yeux verts,
Lacs où mon âme tremble et se voit à l'envers...
    Mes songes viennent en foule
Pour se désaltérer à ces gouffres amers.

Tout cela ne vaut pas le terrible prodige
    De ta salive qui mord,
Qui plonge dans l'oubli mon âme sans remord,
    Et, charriant le vertige,
La roule défaillante aux rives de la mort!

50. Ciel brouillé

On dirait ton regard d'une vapeur couvert;
Ton œil mystérieux (est-il bleu, gris ou vert?)
Alternativement tendre, rêveur, cruel,
Réfléchit l'indolence et la pâleur du ciel.

Tu rappelles ces jours blancs, tièdes et voilés,
Qui font se fondre en pleurs les cœurs ensorcelés,
Quand, agités d'un mal inconnu qui les tord,
Les nerfs trop éveillés raillent l'esprit qui dort.

Tu ressembles parfois à ces beaux horizons
Qu'allument les soleils des brumeuses saisons...
Comme tu resplendis, paysage mouillé
Qu'enflamment les rayons tombant d'un ciel brouillé!

Opium* will expand beyond all measures,
   Stretch out the limitless,
Will deepen time, make rapture bottomless,
   With dismal pleasures
Surfeit the soul to point of helplessness.

But that is nothing to the poison flow
   Out of your eyes, those round
Green lakes in which my soul turns upside-down ..
   To these my dreams all go
At these most bitter gulfs to drink or drown.

But all that is not worth the prodigy
   Of your saliva, girl,
That bites my soul, and dizzies it, and swirls
   It down remorselessly,
Rolling it, fainting, to the underworld!

50. Misty Sky

A vapour seems to hide your face from view;
Your mystic eye (is it green, grey, or blue?)
Tender by turns, dreamy or merciless,
Reflects the heavens' pallid indolence.

You call to mind white, mild, enshrouded days
That make enchanted hearts dissolve away,
When, agitated by a twisting ache,
The taut nerves call the spirit to awake.

Sometimes you're like horizons set aglow
By suns in rainy seasons here below ...
Like you superb, a watery countryside
That rays enflame out of a misty sky!

Ô femme dangereuse, ô séduisants climats!
Adorerai-je aussi ta neige et vos frimas,
Et saurai-je tirer de l'implacable hiver
Des plaisirs plus aigus que la glace et le fer?

51. Le Chat

I

Dans ma cervelle se promène,
Ainsi qu'en son appartement,
Un beau chat, fort, doux et charmant.
Quand il miaule, on l'entend à peine,

Tant son timbre est tendre et discret;
Mais que sa voix s'apaise ou gronde,
Elle est toujours riche et profonde.
C'est là son charme et son secret.

Cette voix, qui perle et qui filtre
Dans mon fonds le plus ténébreux,
Me remplit comme un vers nombreux
Et me réjouit comme un philtre.

Elle endort les plus cruels maux
Et contient toutes les extases;
Pour dire les plus longues phrases,
Elle n'a pas besoin de mots.

Non, il n'est pas d'archet qui morde
Sur mon cœur, parfait instrument,
Et fasse plus royalement
Chanter sa plus vibrante corde,

O weather! woman!—both seduce me so!
Will I adore as well your frost and snow,
And will I draw from winter's ruthless vice
Pleasures more keen than iron or than ice?

51. The Cat

I

A cat is strolling through my mind
Acting as though he owned the place,
A lovely cat—strong, charming, sweet.
When he meows, one scarcely hears,

So tender and discreet his tone;
But whether he should growl or purr
His voice is always rich and deep.
That is the secret of his charm.

This purling voice that filters down
Into my darkest depths of soul
Fulfils me like a balanced verse,
Delights me as a potion would.

It puts to sleep the cruellest ills
And keeps a rein on ecstasies—
Without the need for any words
It can pronounce the longest phrase.

Oh no, there is no bow that draws
Across my heart, fine instrument,
And makes to sing so royally
The strongest and the purest chord,

Que ta voix, chat mystérieux,
Chat séraphique, chat étrange,
En qui tout est, comme en un ange,
Aussi subtil qu'harmonieux!

II

De sa fourrure blonde et brune
Sort un parfum si doux, qu'un soir
J'en fus embaumé, pour l'avoir
Caressée une fois, rien qu'une.

C'est l'esprit familier du lieu;
Il juge, il préside, il inspire
Toute choses dans son empire;
Peut-être est-il fée, est-il dieu?

Quand mes yeux, vers ce chat que j'aime
Tirés comme par un aimant,
Se retournent docilement
Et que je regarde en moi-même,

Je vois avec étonnement
La feu des ses prunelles pâles,
Clairs fanaux, vivantes opales,
Qui me contemplent fixement.

52. Le Beau Navire

Je veux te raconter, ô molle enchanteresse!
Les diverses beautés qui parent ta jeunesse;
   Je veux te peindre ta beauté,
Où l'enfance s'allie à la maturité.

More than your voice, mysterious cat,
Exotic cat, seraphic* cat,
In whom all is, angelically,
As subtle as harmonious.

II

From his soft fur, golden and brown,
Goes out so sweet a scent, one night
I might have been embalmed in it
By giving him one little pet.

He is my household's guardian soul;
He judges, he presides, inspires
All matters in his royal realm;
Might he be fairy? or a god?

When my eyes, to this cat I love
Drawn as by a magnet's force,
Turn tamely back from that appeal,
And when I look within myself,

I notice with astonishment
The fire of his opal eyes,
Clear beacons glowing, living jewels,
Taking my measure, steadily.

52. The Splendid Ship

O soft enchantress, let me tell the truth
Of all the beauties decking out your youth!
    I'll paint the charms for you to see
Of childhood married with maturity.

Quand tu vas balayant l'air de ta jupe large,
Tu fais l'effet d'un beau vaisseau qui prend le large,
  Chargé de toile, et va roulant
Suivant un rythme doux, et paresseux, et lent.

Sur ton cou large et rond, sur tes épaules grasses,
Ta tête se pavane avec d'étranges grâces;
  D'un air placide et triomphant
Tu passes ton chemin, majestueuse enfant.

Je veux te raconter, ô molle enchanteresse!
Les diverses beautés qui parent ta jeunesse;
  Je veux te peindre ta beauté,
Où l'enfance s'allie à la maturité.

Ta gorge qui s'avance et qui pousse la moire,
Ta gorge triomphante est une belle armoire
  Dont les panneaux bombés et clairs
Comme les boucliers accrochent des éclairs;

Boucliers provoquants, armés de pointes roses!
Armoire à doux secrets, pleine de bonnes choses,
  De vins, de parfums, de liqueurs
Qui feraient délirer les cerveaux et les cœurs!

Quand tu vas balayant l'air de ta jupe large,
Tu fais l'effet d'un beau vaisseau qui prend le large,
  Chargé de toile, et va roulant
Suivant un rythme doux, et paresseux, et lent.

Tes nobles jambes, sous les volants qu'elles chassent,
Tourmentent les désirs obscurs et les agacent,
  Comme deux sorcières qui font
Tourner un philtre noir dans un vase profond.

Tes bras, qui se joueraient des précoces hercules,
Sont des boas luisants les solides émules,
  Faits pour serrer obstinément,
Comme pour l'imprimer dans ton cœur, ton amant.

When you step out, your broad skirt sweeps the breeze
As if you were a ship on easy seas
   Under full sail, that rolls along
In rhythm with a slow and languid song.

On your plump shoulders and your rounded neck
Your head parades itself with rare effect;
   In a composed, triumphant style
You go your stately way, majestic child.

O soft enchantress, let me tell the truth
Of all the beauties decking out your youth!
   I'll paint the charms for you to see
Of childhood married with maturity.

Your jutting bosom stretching out the moire,*
Triumphant bosom, is a fine armoire
   Whose bright and swelling panels might
Like shields reflect the flashing of the light;

Enticing shields, equipped with rosy tips!
Armoire of treasures, full of secret gifts,
   Of perfumes, of liqueurs, of wines
Making delirious men's hearts and minds!

When you step out your broad skirt sweeps the breeze
As if you were a ship on easy seas
   Under full sail, that rolls along
In rhythm with a slow and languid song.

Your noble legs, the flounces they inspire,
Torment and agitate obscure desires.
   They're like two witches who stir up
A black concoction in a lavish cup.

Your arms, that rival infant Hercules',*
Are like two glimmering boas, which with ease
   Can crush their prey against your chest,
As if you'd print your lover on your breast.

Sur ton cou large et rond, sur tes épaules grasses,
Ta tête se pavane avec d'étranges grâces;
   D'un air placide et triomphant
Tu passes ton chemin, majestueuse enfant.

53. L'Invitation au voyage

   Mon enfant, ma sœur,
   Songe à la douceur
D'aller là-bas vivre ensemble!
   Aimer à loisir,
   Aimer et mourir
Au pays qui te ressemble!
   Les soleils mouillés
   De ces ciels brouillés
Pour mon esprit ont les charmes
   Si mystérieux
   De tes traîtres yeux,
Brillant à travers leurs larmes.

Là, tout n'est qu'ordre et beauté,
Luxe, calme et volupté.

   Des meubles luisants,
   Polis par les ans,
Décoreraient notre chambre;
   Les plus rares fleurs
   Mêlant leurs odeurs
Aux vagues senteurs de l'ambre,
   Les riches plafonds,
   Les miroirs profonds,
La splendeur orientale,
   Tout y parlerait
   A l'âme en secret
Sa douce langue natale.

On your plump shoulders and your rounded neck
Your head parades itself with rare effect;
   In a composed, triumphant style
You go your stately way, majestic child.

53. Invitation to the Voyage

   My sister, my child
   Imagine how sweet
To live there as lovers do!
   To kiss as we choose
   To love and to die
In that land resembling you!
   The misty suns
   Of shifting skies
To my spirit are as dear
   As the evasions
   Of your eyes
That shine behind their tears.

There, all is order and leisure,
Luxury, beauty, and pleasure.

   The tables would glow
   With the lustre of years
To ornament our room.
   The rarest of blooms
   Would mingle their scents
With amber's vague perfume.
   The ceilings, rich
   The mirrors, deep—
The splendour of the East—
   All whisper there
   To the silent soul
Her sweet familiar speech.

Là, tout n'est qu'ordre et beauté,
Luxe, calme et volupté.

  Vois sur ces canaux
  Dormir ces vaisseaux
Dont l'humeur est vagabonde;
  C'est pour assouvir
  Ton moindre désir
Qu'ils viennent du bout du monde.
  — Les soleils couchants
  Revêtent les champs,
Les canaux, la ville entière,
  D'hyancinthe et d'or;
  Le monde s'endort
Dans une chaude lumière.

Là, tout n'est qu'ordre et beauté,
Luxe, calme et volupté.

54. L'Irréparable

Pouvons-nous étouffer le vieux, le long Remords,
  Qui vit, s'agite et se tortille,
Et se nourrit de nous comme le ver des morts,
  Comme du chêne la chenille?
Pouvons-nous étouffer l'implacable Remords?

Dans quel philtre, dans quel vin, dans quelle tisane,
  Noierons-nous ce vieil ennemi,
Destructeur et gourmand comme la courtisane,
  Patient comme la fourmi?
Dans quel philtre? — dans quel vin? — dans quel tisane?

There, all is order and leisure,
Luxury, beauty, and pleasure.

And these canals*
Bear ships at rest,
Although in a wandering mood;
To gratify
Your least desire
They have sailed around the world.
The setting suns
Enrobe the fields
The canals, the entire town
With hyacinth, gold;
The world falls asleep
In a warmly glowing gown.

There, all is order and leisure,
Luxury, beauty, and pleasure.

54. The Irreparable

How can we kill the long, the old Remorse
That lives, writhes, twists itself
And mines us as the worm devours the dead,
The cankerworm the oak?
How can we choke the old, the long Remorse?

And what brew, or what philtre, or what wine
Could drown this enemy,
As deadly as the avid courtesan,
And patient as the ant?
In what brew?—in what philtre?—in what wine?

Dis-le, belle sorcière, oh! dis, si tu le sais,
     A cet esprit comblé d'angoisse
Et pareil au mourant qu'écrasent les blessés,
     Que le sabot du cheval froisse,
Dis-le, belle sorcière, oh! dis, si tu le sais,

A cet agonisant que le loup déjà flaire
     Et que surveille le corbeau,
A ce soldat brisé! s'il faut qu'il désespère
     D'avoir sa croix et son tombeau;
Ce pauvre agonisant que déjà le loup flaire!

Peut-on illuminer un ciel bourbeux et noir?
     Peut-on déchirer des ténèbres
Plus denses que la poix, sans matin et sans soir,
     Sans astres, sans éclairs funèbres?
Peut-on illuminer un ciel bourbeux et noir?

L'Espérance qui brille aux carreaux de l'Auberge
     Est soufflée, est morte à jamais!
Sans lune et sans rayons, trouver où l'on héberge
     Les martyrs d'un chemin mauvais!
Le Diable a tout éteint aux carreaux de l'Auberge!

Adorable sorcière, aimes-tu les damnés?
     Dis, connais-tu l'irrémissible?
Connais-tu le Remords, aux traits empoisonnés,
     A qui notre cœur sert de cible?
Adorable sorcière, aimes-tu les damnés?

L'Irréparable ronge, avec sa dent maudite
     Notre âme, piteux monument,
Et souvent il attaque, ainsi que le termite,
     Par la base le bâtiment.
L'Irréparable ronge avec sa dent maudite!

Oh, say it if you know, sweet sorceress!
   To this my anguished soul,
Like one who's dying, crushed by wounded men,
   Stamped, trampled by a horse's hoof.
Oh, say it if you know, sweet sorceress,

To this man whom the wolf already sniffs
   And whom the crow surveys,
This broken soldier! Must he then despair
   Of having cross and tomb,
This dying man the wolf already sniffs!

Can one light up a black and muddy sky?
   Tear through a murkiness
Thicker than pitch, no evening and no dawn,
   No stars, no mournful flares?
Can one light up a black and muddy sky?

The Hope that shines at windows of the Inn
   Is gone, forever gone!
No moon, no rays to light the way to rest
   For martyrs on the road!
Satan has blown the lights out at the Inn!

Enchantress, say it—do you love the damned?
   The irremissible,*
You know it? Know Remorse, whose poisoned shafts
   Find targets in our hearts?
Enchantress, say it—do you love the damned?

The Irreparable with cursed tooth
   Gnaws souls, weak monuments,
And often, like the termite, he invades
   The structures at their base.
The Irreparable gnaws with sharp tooth!

— J'ai vu parfois, au fond d'un théâtre banal
    Qu'enflammait l'orchestre sonore,
Une fée allumer dans un ciel infernal
    Une miraculeuse aurore;
J'ai vu parfois au fond d'un théâtre banal

Un être, qui n'était que lumière, or et gaze,
    Terrasser l'énorme Satan;
Mais mon cœur, que jamais ne visite l'extase,
    Est un théâtre où l'on attend
Toujours, toujours en vain, l'Être aux ailes de gaze!

55. Causerie

Vous êtes un beau ciel d'automne, clair et rose!
Mais la tristesse en moi monte comme la mer,
Et laisse, en refluant, sur ma lèvre morose
Le souvenir cuisant de son limon amer.

— Ta main se glisse en vain sur mon sein qui se pâme;
Ce qu'elle cherche, amie, est un lieu saccagé
Par la griffe et la dent féroce de la femme.
Ne cherchez plus mon cœur; les bêtes l'ont mangé.

Mon cœur est un palais flétri par la cohue;
On s'y soûle, on s'y tue, on s'y prend aux cheveux!
— Un parfum nage autour de votre gorge nue!...

Ô Beauté, dur fléau des âmes, tu le veux!
Avec tes yeux de feu, brillants comme des fêtes,
Calcine ces lambeaux qu'ont épargnés les bêtes!

—I've seen, within a tawdry theatre
  Warmed by a brazen band,
A fairy, from a hellish sky, light up
  The miracle of dawn;
Sometimes I've seen within a theatre*

A Being made of light, and gold, and gauze
  Lay the great Satan low;
But in my heart, no home to ecstasy,
  Sad playhouse, one awaits
Always in vain, the fine and filmy wings!

55. Conversation

You are a pink and lovely autumn sky!
But sadness in me rises like the sea,
And leaves in ebbing only bitter clay
On my sad lip, the smart of memory.

Your hand slides up my fainting breast at will;
But, love, it only finds a ravaged pit
Pillaged by woman's savage tooth and nail.
My heart is lost; the beasts have eaten it.

It is a palace sullied by the rout;
They drink, they pull each other's hair, they kill!
—A perfume swims around your naked throat! ...

O Beauty, scourge of souls, you want it still!*
You with hot eyes that flash in fiery feasts,
Burn up these meagre scraps spared by the beasts!

56. Chant d'automne

I

Bientôt nous plongerons dans les froides ténèbres;
Adieu, vive clarté de nos étés trop courts!
J'entends déjà tomber avec des chocs funèbres
Le bois retentissant sur le pavé des cours.

Tout l'hiver va rentrer dans mon être: colère,
Haine, frissons, horreur, labeur dur et forcé,
Et, comme le soleil dans son enfer polaire,
Mon cœur ne sera plus qu'un bloc rouge et glacé.

J'écoute en frémissant chaque bûche qui tombe;
L'échafaud qu'on bâtit n'a pas d'écho plus sourd.
Mon esprit est pareil à la tour qui succombe
Sous les coups du bélier infatigable et lourd.

Il me semble, bercé par ce choc monotone,
Qu'on cloue en grande hâte un cercueil quelque part.
Pour qui? — C'était hier l'été; voici l'automne!
Ce bruit mystérieux sonne comme un départ.

II

J'aime de vos longs yeux la lumière verdâtre,
Douce beauté, mais tout aujourd'hui m'est amer,
Et rien, ni votre amour, ni le boudoir, ni l'âtre,
Ne me vaut le soleil rayonnant sur la mer.

Et pourtant aimez-moi, tendre cœur! soyez mère,
Même pour un ingrat, même pour un méchant;
Amante ou sœur, soyez la douceur éphémère
D'un glorieux automne ou d'un soleil couchant.

56. Autumn Song

I

Now will we plunge into the frigid dark,
The living light of summer gone too soon!
Already I can hear a dismal sound,
The thump of logs on courtyard paving stones.

All winter comes into my being: wrath,
Hate, chills and horror, forced and plodding work,
And like the sun in polar underground
My heart will be a red and frozen block.

I shudder as I hear each log that drops;
A gallows being built makes no worse sound.
My mind is like the tower that succumbs,
Under a heavy engine battered down.

It seems to me, dull with this constant thud,
That someone nails a coffin, but for whom?
Yesterday summer, now the fall! something
With all this eerie pounding will be gone.

II

I love the greenish light in your long eyes
My sweet! but all is bitterness to me,
And nothing, not the boudoir nor the hearth,
Today is worth the sunlight on the sea.

But love me anyway, o tender heart!
Be mother of this mean, ungrateful one;
O lover, sister, be the fleeting sweetness
Of the autumn, of the setting sun.

Courte tâche! La tombe attend; elle est avide!
Ah! laissez-moi, mon front posé sur vos genoux,
Goûter, en regrettant l'été blanc et torride,
De l'arrière-saison le rayon jaune et doux!

57. A une Madone

Ex-Voto dans le goût espagnol

Je veux bâtir pour toi, Madone, ma maîtresse,
Un autel souterrain au fond de ma détresse,
Et creuser dans le coin le plus noir de mon cœur,
Loin du désir mondain et du regard moqueur,
Une niche, d'azur et d'or tout émaillée,
Où tu te dresseras, Statue émerveillée.
Avec mes Vers polis, treillis d'un pur métal
Savamment constellé de rimes de cristal,
Je ferai pour ta tête une énorme Couronne;
Et dans ma Jalousie, ô mortelle Madone,
Je saurai te tailler un Manteau, de façon
Barbare, roide et lourd, et doublé de soupçon,
Qui, comme une guérite, enfermera tes charmes;
Non de Perles brodé, mais de toutes mes Larmes!
Ta Robe, ce sera mon Désir, frémissant,
Onduleux, mon Désir qui monte et qui descend,
Aux pointes se balance, aux vallons se repose,
Et revêt d'un baiser tout ton corps blanc et rose.
Je te ferai de mon Respect de beaux Souliers
De satin, par tes pieds divins humiliés,
Qui, les emprisonnant dans une molle étreinte,
Comme un moule fidèle en garderont l'empreinte.
Si je ne puis, malgré tout mon art diligent,
Pour Marchepied tailler une Lune d'argent,
Je mettrai le Serpent qui me mord les entrailles
Sous tes talons, afin que tu foules et railles,
Reine victorieuse et féconde en rachats,

Brief task! The Tomb is waiting in its greed!
Kneeling before you, let me taste and hold,
While I lament the summer, fierce and white,
A ray of the late fall, mellow and gold.

57. To a Madonna

Votive in the Spanish Style*

Madonna, mistress, out of my distress
I'd like to raise an altar in the depths,
And in the blackest corner of my heart,
From earthly joys and mockeries apart,
Hollow a niche, enamelled gold and blue,
Astonished Statue, sanctified for you.
With polished Verses, metal deftly twined,
Learnedly spangled with my crystal rhymes,
I'll weave a Crown for your celebrity;
And, mortal Mary, in my Jealousy
I'll cut your Cloak in the barbaric mode,
Lined with Distrust, a heavy, stiff abode
Emprisoning those charms I hold so dear;
Brocaded not of Pearls, but of my Tears!
My trembling Lust will do me for your Gown,
Surging Desire that rises or sinks down,
Poises on peaks, or in your valleys rests,
Clothing with kisses all your rosy flesh.
From my Respect I'll make some lovely Shoes
Of satin, for your holy feet to use,
Which, holding them within a soft embrace,
Will take the faithful imprint of their shapes.
If I, with all the craft at my command,
Can not cut out a Moon where you may stand,*
Under your heels I'll place that gnawing Snake,
That monster puffed with venom and with hate
That eats my entrails—bruise him with your tread*

Ce monstre tout gonflé de haine et de crachats.
Tu verras mes Pensers, rangés comme les Cierges
Devant l'autel fleuri de la Reine des Vierges,
Étoilant de reflets le plafond peint en bleu,
Te regarder toujours avec des yeux de feu;
Et comme tout en moi te chérit et t'admire,
Tout se fera Benjoin, Encens, Oliban, Myrrhe,
Et sans cesse vers toi, sommet blanc et neigeux,
En Vapeurs montera mon Esprit orageux.

Enfin, pour compléter ton rôle de Marie,
Et pour mêler l'amour avec la barbarie,
Volupté noire! des sept Péchés capitaux,
Bourreau plein de remords, je ferai sept Couteaux
Bien affilés, et comme un jongleur insensible,
Prenant le plus profond de ton amour pour cible,
Je les planterai tous dans ton Cœur pantelant,
Dans ton Cœur sanglotant, dans ton Cœur ruisselant!

58. Chanson d'après-midi

Quoique tes sourcils méchants
Te donnent un air étrange
Qui n'est pas celui d'un ange,
Sorcière aux yeux alléchants,

Je t'adore, ô ma frivole,
Ma terrible passion!
Avec la dévotion
Du prêtre pour son idole.

Le désert et la forêt
Embaument tes tresses rudes,
Ta tête a les attitudes
De l'énigme et du secret.

Victorious Queen, redemption's fountainhead.
My thoughts, set out like Tapers, will be seen
Before your flowery altar, Virgin Queen,
Spangling the deep blue ceiling with their rays,
Always to look at you with fiery gaze;
And since I worship you in every sense
All become Benjamin, or Frankincense,
And, white and snowy peak, around your slopes
My stormy Soul will rise in fragrant Smoke.

At last, so you're my Mary perfectly,
And mixing love with pagan cruelty,
Full of a dark, remorseful joy, I'll take
The seven deadly sins,* and of them make
Seven bright Daggers; with a juggler's lore
Target your love within its deepest core,
And plant them all within your panting Heart,
Within your sobbing Heart, your streaming Heart!

58. Song of the Afternoon

Although your wayward brows
Give you a curious air
Angelic not at all,
Witch of the tempting stare,

I love you with a passion
Terrible and odd,
With the obeisance
Of priest to golden god.

The desert and the woods
Embalm your heavy hair;
Your head takes attitudes
Mysterious and rare.

Sur ta chair le parfum rôde
Comme autour d'un encensoir;
Tu charmes comme le soir,
Nymphe ténébreuse et chaude.

Ah! les philtres les plus forts
Ne valent pas ta paresse,
Et tu connais la caresse
Qui fait revivre les morts!

Tes hanches sont amoureuses
De ton dos et de tes seins,
Et tu ravis les coussins
Par tes poses langoureuses.

Quelquefois, pour apaiser
Ta rage mystérieuse,
Tu prodigues, sérieuse,
La morsure et le baiser;

Tu me déchires, ma brune,
Avec un rire moqueur,
Et puis tu mets sur mon cœur
Ton œil doux comme la lune.

Sous tes souliers de satin,
Sous tes charmants pieds de soie,
Moi, je mets ma grande joie,
Mon génie et mon destin,

Mon âme par toi guérie,
Par toi, lumière et couleur!
Explosion de chaleur
Dans ma noire Sibérie!

A censer's faint perfume
Prowls along your skin;
You charm as evening charms,
Warm and shadowy Nymph.

Ah! strongest potions stir me
Less than your idleness,
And you can make the dead
Revive with your caress!

Your hips are amorous
Of back and breasts and thighs,
And ravished by your pose
Are cushions where you lie.

Sometimes to appease
A rage that comes in fits,
Serious one, you squander
Bites within the kiss;

You wound me, my brunette,
With ever-mocking smile,
Then sweetly, like the moon,
Gaze on my heart a while.

Under your satin shoes,
Your charming silken feet,
I place myself, my joy,
My genius and my fate,

My soul, mended by you,
By you, colour and light,
Explosion of heat
In my Siberian night!*

59. Sisina

Imaginez Diane en galant équipage,
Parcourant les forêts ou battant les halliers,
Cheveux et gorge au vent, s'enivrant de tapage,
Superbe et défiant les meilleurs cavaliers!

Avez-vous vu Théroigne, amante du carnage,
Excitant à l'assaut un peuple sans souliers,
La joue et l'œil en feu, jouant son personnage,
Et montant, sabre au poing, les royaux escaliers?

Telle la Sisina! Mais la douce guerrière
A l'âme charitable autant que meurtrière;
Son courage, affolé de poudre et de tambours,

Devant les suppliants sait mettre bas les armes,
Et son cœur, ravagé par la flamme, a toujours,
Pour qui s'en montre digne, un réservoir de larmes.

60. *Franciscae meae laudes*

Novis te cantabo chordis,
O novelletum quod ludis
In solitudine cordis.

Esto sertis implicata,
O femina delicata
Per quam solvuntur peccata!

Sicut beneficum Lethe,
Hauriam oscula de te,
Quæ imbuta es magnete.

59. Sisina*

Picture Diana* decked out for the chase,
Charging through forests, beating brush aside,
Drunk with the action, wind around her face,
Breast bare, her finest horsemen left behind!

You've seen Théroigne,* carnage in her heart,
Rousing the shoeless masses to resist,
Cheek and eye blazing, playing out her part,
Mounting the royal stair, sabre in fist?

Such is Sisina, but the gentle knight
Within her heart can love as well as fight;
Though spurred by powder and by drums, her nerve

Before her suppliants lays arms to earth,
And her flame-ravaged heart keeps in reserve
A well of tears, for those who've proved their worth.

60. Praises for My Francisca

With new chords I'll sing your praises,
Little shoot, because you dally
In the heart's sweet solitude.

Be into a garland woven,
O my captivating woman
Through whom sins are all absolved!

As I would obliging Lethe,*
Let me freely sip your kisses,
So magnetically imbued.

Quum vitiorum tempestas
Turbabat omnes semitas,
Apparuisti, Deitas,

Velut stella salutaris
In naufragiis amaris . . .
Suspendam cor tuis aris!

Piscina plena virtutis,
Fons æternæ juventutis,
Labris vocem redde mutis!

Quod erat spurcum, cremasti;
Quod rudius, exæquasti;
Quod debile, confirmasti.

In fame mea taberna,
In nocte mea lucerna,
Recte me semper guberna.

Adde nunc vires viribus,
Dulce balneum suavibus
Unguentatem odoribus!

Meos circa lumbos mica,
O castitatis lorica,
Aqua tincta seraphica;

Patera gemmis corusca,
Panis salsus, mollis esca,
Divinum vinum, Francisca!

When the storm of all my vices
Put in peril all my pathways,
You, Divinity, appeared,

As redeeming as the Lodestar,*
Saviour in our bitter shipwrecks...
On your altar hangs my heart!

Lovely pool that fills with virtue,
Of eternal youth the fountain,
Bring my silent lips to speech!

You have purified the filthy
And have smoothed out all the rudeness,
What was weak, you have made strong.

In my hunger, you're the tavern,
In the darkness, you're my lantern—
Guide me always in the right.

Now add potency to mankind,
Wholesome bath that is anointed
With the most entrancing scents!

Gleam around my loins and guard them
O thou corselet of virtue
Made of water angel-dyed;

Drinking bowl that gleams with gemstones,
Salted bread and tender morsel,
My Francisca, heaven's wine!

61. A une dame créole

Au pays parfumé que le soleil caresse,
J'ai connu, sous un dais d'arbres tout empourprés
Et de palmiers d'où pleut sur les yeux la paresse,
Une dame créole aux charmes ignorés.

Son teint est pâle et chaud; la brune enchanteresse
A dans le cou des airs noblement maniérés;
Grande et svelte en marchant comme une chasseresse,
Son sourire est tranquille et ses yeux assurés.

Si vous alliez, Madame, au vrai pays de gloire,
Sur les bords de la Seine ou de la verte Loire,
Belle digne d'orner les antiques manoirs,

Vous feriez, à l'abri des ombreuses retraites,
Germer mille sonnets dans le cœur des poëtes,
Que vos grands yeux rendraient plus soumis que vos noirs.

62. *Mœsta et errabunda*

Dis-moi, ton cœur parfois s'envole-t-il, Agathe,
Loin du noir océan de l'immonde cité,
Vers un autre océan où la splendeur éclate,
Bleu, clair, profond, ainsi que la virginité?
Dis-moi, ton cœur parfois s'envole-t-il, Agathe?

La mer, la vaste mer, console nos labeurs!
Quel démon a doté la mer, rauque chanteuse
Qu'accompagne l'immense orgue des vents grondeurs,
De cette fonction sublime de berceuse?
La mer, la vaste mer, console nos labeurs!

61. For a Creole Lady*

Off in a perfumed land bathed gently by the sun,
Under a palm tree's shade tinged with a crimson trace,
A place where indolence drops on the eyes like rain,
I met a Creole lady of unstudied grace.

This brown enchantress' skin is warm and light in tone;
Her neck is noble, proud, her manner dignified;
Slender and tall, she goes with huntress' easy stride;
Her smile is tranquil, and her eyes are confident.

Madame, if you should come to place of pride and praise—
Beside the green Loire, or by the pleasant Seine,
Adorning ancient mansions with your stately ways—

There in the shelter of the shady groves, you'd start
A thousand sonnets blooming in the poets' hearts,
Whom your great eyes would turn to sycophants and slaves.

62. *Mœsta et errabunda**

Agatha,* tell me, could your heart take flight
From this black city, from this filthy sea
Off to some other sea, where splendour might
Burst blue and clear—a new virginity?
Agatha, tell me, could your heart take flight?

The vast sea offers comfort in our pain!
What demon lets the ocean's raucous cry
Above the great wind-organ's grumbling strain
Perform the holy rite of lullaby?
The vast sea offers comfort in our pain!

Emporte-moi, wagon! enlève-moi, frégate!
Loin! loin! ici la boue est faite de nos pleurs!
— Est-il vrai que parfois le triste cœur d'Agathe
Dise: Loin des remords, des crimes, des douleurs,
Emporte-moi, wagon, enlève-moi, frégate?

Comme vous êtes loin, paradis parfumé,
Où sous un clair azur tout n'est qu'amour et joie,
Où tout ce que l'on aime est digne d'être aimé,
Où dans la volupté pure le cœur se noie!
Comme vous êtes loin, paradis parfumé!

Mais le vert paradis des amours enfantines,
Les courses, les chansons, les baisers, les bouquets,
Les violons vibrant derrière les collines,
Avec les brocs de vin, le soir, dans les bosquets,
— Mais le vert paradis des amours enfantines,

L'innocent paradis, plein de plaisirs furtifs,
Est-il déjà plus loin que l'Inde et que la Chine?
Peut-on le rappeler avec des cris plaintifs,
Et l'animer encor d'une voix argentine,
L'innocent paradis plein de plaisirs furtifs?

63. Le Revenant

Comme les anges à l'œil fauve,
Je reviendrai dans ton alcôve
Et vers toi glisserai sans bruit
Avec les ombres de la nuit;

Et je te donnerai, ma brune,
Des baisers froids comme la lune
Et des caresses de serpent
Autour d'une fosse rampant.

Frigate or wagon, carry me away!
Away from where the mud is made of tears!
—Agatha, can your sad heart sometimes say:
Far from the crimes, remorse, the grief of years,
Frigate or wagon, carry me away!

How distant are you, perfumed paradise,
Where lovers play beneath the blue above,
Where hearts may drown themselves in pure delights,
Where what one loves is worthy to be loved!
How distant are you, perfumed paradise!

But the green paradise of youthful loves,
The games and songs, the kisses, the bouquets,
The violins that sing in hilly groves,
The evening cups of wine in shady ways,
—But the green paradise of youthful loves,

The sinless paradise of stolen joys,
Is it already far beyond the seas?
Can we recall it with our plaintive voice,
And give it life with silver melodies,
The sinless paradise of stolen joys?

63. The Ghost

Like angels who have bestial eyes
I'll come again to your alcove
And glide in silence to your side
In shadows of the night, my love;

And I will give to my dark mate
Cold kisses, frigid as the moon,
And I'll caress you like a snake
That slides and writhes around a tomb.

Quand viendra le matin livide,
Tu trouveras ma place vide,
Où jusqu'au soir il fera froid.

Comme d'autres par la tendresse,
Sur ta vie et sur ta jeunesse,
Moi, je veux régner par l'effroi.

64. Sonnet d'automne

Ils me disent, tes yeux, clairs comme le cristal:
'Pour toi, bizarre amant, quel est donc mon mérite?'
— Sois charmante et tais-toi! Mon cœur, que tout irrite,
Excepté la candeur de l'antique animal,

Ne veut pas te montrer son secret infernal,
Berceuse dont la main aux longs sommeils m'invite,
Ni sa noire légende avec la flamme écrite.
Je hais la passion et l'esprit me fait mal!

Aimons-nous doucement. L'Amour dans sa guérite,
Ténébreux, embusqué, bande son arc fatal.
Je connais les engins de son vieil arsenal:

Crime, horreur et folie! — Ô pâle marguerite!
Comme moi n'es-tu pas un soleil automnal,
Ô ma si blanche, ô ma si froide Marguerite?

65. Tristesses de la lune

Ce soir, la lune rêve avec plus de paresse;
Ainsi qu'une beauté, sur de nombreux coussins,
Qui d'une main distraite et légère caresse
Avant de s'endormir le contour de ses seins,

When the livid morning breaks
You will find no one in my place,
And feel a chill till night is near.

Some others by their tenderness
May try to guide your youthfulness,
Myself, I want to rule by fear.

64. Autumn Sonnet

I hear them say to me, your crystal eyes,
'Strange love, what merit do you find in me?'
—Be charming and be still! My heart, disturbed
By all except the candour of the flesh

Prefers to hide the secret of its hell
From you whose hand would rock me into sleep,
Nor will it show the legend writ with flame.
Passion I hate, and spirit plays me false!

Let us love gently. Eros in his den,*
Hiding in sombre ambush, bends his bow.
I know his arsenal, his worn-out bolts,

Crime, madness, horror—oh pale marguerite,
Are we not both like the autumnal sun,
My o so cool, my fading Marguerite?*

65. Sorrows of the Moon

The moon tonight dreams vacantly, as if
She were a beauty cushioned at her rest
Who strokes with wandering hand her lifting
Nipples, and the contour of her breasts;

Sur le dos satiné des molles avalanches,
Mourante, elle se livre aux longues pâmoisons,
Et promène ses yeux sur les visions blanches
Qui montent dans l'azur comme des floraisons.

Quand parfois sur ce globe, en sa langueur oisive,
Elle laisse filer une larme furtive,
Un poëte pieux, ennemi du sommeil,

Dans le creux de sa main prend cette larme pâle,
Aux reflets irisés comme un fragment d'opale,
Et la met dans son cœur loin des yeux du soleil.

66. Les Chats

Les amoureux fervents et les savants austères
Aiment également, dans leur mûre saison,
Les chats puissants et doux, orgueil de la maison,
Qui comme eux sont frileux et comme eux sédentaires.

Amis de la science et de la volupté,
Ils cherchent le silence et l'horreur des ténèbres;
L'Érèbe les eût pris pour ses coursiers funèbres,
S'ils pouvaient au servage incliner leur fierté.

Ils prennent en songeant les nobles attitudes
Des grands sphinx allongés au fond des solitudes,
Qui semblent s'endormir dans un rêve sans fin;

Leurs reins féconds sont pleins d'étincelles magiques,
Et des parcelles d'or, ainsi qu'un sable fin,
Étoilent vaguement leurs prunelles mystiques.

Lying as if for love, glazed by the soft
Luxurious avalanche, dying in swoons,
She turns her eyes to visions—clouds aloft
Billowing hugely, blossoming in blue.

When sometimes from her stupefying calm
On to this earth she drops a furtive tear
Pale as an opal, iridescent, rare,

The poet, sleepless watchman, is the one
To take it up within his hollowed palm
And in his heart to hide it from the sun.

66. Cats

Stiff scholars and the hotly amorous
Will in their ripeness equally admire
Powerful, gentle cats, pride of the house,
Who, like them, love to sit around the fire.

Friends both of sciences and of l'amour,
They seek the silent horror of the night;
Erebus* wants them for his funeral corps,
But in their pride they'd never choose that fate.

They take in sleeping noble attitudes—
Great sphinxes in the desert solitudes,*
Who seem to be entranced by endless dreams;

Within their potent loins are magic sparks,
And flakes of gold, fine sand, are vaguely seen
Behind their mystic eyes, gleaming like stars.

67. Les Hiboux

Sous les ifs noirs qui les abritent,
Les hiboux se tiennent rangés,
Ainsi que les dieux étrangers,
Dardant leur œil rouge. Ils méditent

Sans remuer ils se tiendront
Jusqu'à l'heure mélancolique
Où, poussant le soleil oblique,
Les ténèbres s'établiront.

Leur attitude au sage enseigne
Qu'il faut en ce monde qu'il craigne
Le tumulte et le mouvement;

L'homme ivre d'une ombre qui passe
Porte toujours le châtiment
D'avoir voulu changer de place.

68. La Pipe

Je suis la pipe d'un auteur;
On voit, à contempler ma mine
D'Abyssinienne ou de Cafrine,
Que mon maître est un grand fumeur

Quand il est comblé de douleur,
Je fume comme la chaumine
Où se prépare la cuisine
Pour le retour du laboureur.

J'enlace et je berce son âme
Dans le réseau mobile et bleu
Qui monte de ma bouche en feu,

67. Owls

Under black yew-trees, in the shade,
The owls have kept themselves apart;
Like strange divinities, they dart
The red eye, as they meditate.

They stand like statues, silent, straight
Up to the melancholy time
When, shouldering the sun aside,
Darkness establishes his state.

They teach the sage a lesson here,
That in the world he ought to fear
All movement, uproar, turbulence;

But, drunk on shadows, our strange race
Carries within the punishment
Of having yearned for change of place.*

68. The Pipe

I am a writer's pipe; you see
In looking at my dusky face,
Complexion of the Kaffir race,*
My master makes good use of me.

When he is full of grief and gloom
I smoke as if I were a shack
With supper stewing in the back
To feed the ploughman coming home.

I cradle and enwrap his soul
Within the blue and moving net
That from my fiery mouth uncoils,

Et je roule un puissant dictame
Qui charme son cœur et guérit
De ses fatigues son esprit.

69. La Musique

La musique souvent me prend comme une mer!
    Vers ma pâle étoile,
Sous un plafond de brume ou dans un vaste éther,
    Je mets à la voile;

La poitrine en avant et les poumons gonflés
    Comme de la toile,
J'escalade le dos des flots amoncelés
    Que la nuit me voile;

Je sens vibrer en moi toutes les passions
    D'un vaisseau qui souffre;
Le bon vent, la tempête et ses convulsions

    Sur l'immense gouffre
Me bercent. D'autres fois, calme plat, grand miroir
    De mon désespoir!

70. Sépulture

Si par une nuit lourde et sombre
Un bon chrétien, par charité,
Derrière quelque vieux décombre
Enterre votre corps vanté,

A l'heure où les chastes étoiles
Ferment leurs yeux appesantis,
L'araignée y fera ses toiles,
Et la vipère ses petits;

And is a healing balm that rolls
To charm his weary heart, and let
His spirit rest from heavy toils.

69. Music

Music will often take me like the sea!
  When clouds are low
Or in clear ether, I, towards my pale star,
  Set sail and go;

With chest thrust forward and with lungs puffed out
  My sails are tight;
I climb the backs of all the heaped-up waves
  As day turns night;

Throbbing within me are the passions of
  A suffering ship;
The mild breeze, or the tempest and its throes

  On the abyss
Rock me. At other times, dead calm, the glass
  Of hopelessness.

70. Burial

If on some woebegone night
A generous Christian soul
Behind an old garbage-dump, might
Drop your proud corpse in a hole,

When the chaste stars are nodding their heads
And closing their eyes to the earth,
There the spider will weave her web,
While the viper is giving birth;

Vous entendrez toute l'année
Sur votre tête condamnée
Les cris lamentables des loups
Et des sorcières faméliques,
Les ébats des vieillards lubriques
Et les complots des noirs filous.

71. Une gravure fantastique

Ce spectre singulier n'a pour toute toilette,
Grotesquement campé sur son front de squelette,
Qu'un diadème affreux sentant le carnaval.
Sans éperons, sans fouet, il essouffle un cheval,
Fantôme comme lui, rosse apocalyptique,
Qui bave des naseaux comme un épileptique.
Au travers de l'espace ils s'enfoncent tous deux,
Et foulent l'infini d'un sabot hasardeux.
Le cavalier promène un sabre qui flamboie
Sur les foules sans nom que sa monture broie,
Et parcourt, comme un prince inspectant sa maison,
Le cimetière immense et froid, sans horizon,
Où gisent, aux lueurs d'un soleil blanc et terne,
Les peuples de l'histoire ancienne et moderne.

72. Le Mort joyeux

Dans une terre grasse et pleine d'escargots
Je veux creuser moi-même une fosse profonde,
Où je puisse à loisir étaler mes vieux os
Et dormir dans l'oubli comme un requin dans l'onde.

You will listen the whole long year
Above your cursed bones
To wolvish howls, and then
To starving witches' moans,
Frolics of dirty old men,
Plottings of black racketeers.

71. A Fantastical Engraving

This freakish ghost has nothing else to wear
But some cheap crown he picked up at a fair
Grotesquely perched atop his bony corpse.
Without a whip or spur he drives his horse—
Ghostly as he, hack of apocalypse—
To pant and drool like someone in a fit.
This duo makes its charge through endless space,
Trampling the infinite with reckless pace.
The horseman waves a blazing sword around
The nameless crowds he's trampled to the ground,
And like a prince inspecting his domain
He travels to a graveyard's empty plain
Where lie, with pallid sunshine overhead,
From old and modern times, the storied dead.

72. The Happy Corpse

In a rich land, fertile, replete with snails
I'd like to dig myself a spacious pit
Where I might spread at leisure my old bones
And sleep unnoticed, like a shark at sea.

Je hais les testaments et je hais les tombeaux;
Plutôt que d'implorer une larme du monde,
Vivant, j'aimerais mieux inviter les corbeaux
A saigner tous les bouts de ma carcasse immonde.

Ô vers! noirs compagnons sans oreille et sans yeux,
Voyez venir à vous un mort libre et joyeux;
Philosophes viveurs, fils de la pourriture,

A travers ma ruine allez donc sans remords,
Et dites-moi s'il est encor quelque torture
Pour ce vieux corps sans âme et mort parmi les morts!

73. Le Tonneau de la Haine

La Haine est le tonneau des pâles Danaïdes;
La Vengeance éperdue aux bras rouges et forts
A beau précipiter dans ses ténèbres vides
De grands seaux pleins du sang et des larmes des morts.

Le Démon fait des trous secrets à ces abîmes,
Par où fuiraient mille ans de sueurs et d'efforts,
Quand même elle saurait ranimer ses victimes,
Et pour les pressurer ressusciter leurs corps.

La Haine est un ivrogne au fond d'une taverne,
Qui sent toujours la soif naître de la liqueur
Et se multiplier comme l'hydre de Lerne.

— Mais les buveurs heureux connaissent leur vainqueur,
Et la Haine est vouée à ce sort lamentable
De ne pouvoir jamais s'endormir sous la table.

I hate both testaments and epitaphs;
Sooner than beg remembrance from the world
I would, alive, invite the hungry crows
To bleed my tainted carcass inch by inch.

O worms! dark playmates minus ear or eye,
Prepare to meet a free and happy corpse;
Droll *philosophes*,* children of rottenness,

Go then along my ruin guiltlessly,
And say if any torture still exists
For this old soulless corpse, dead with the dead!

73. The Cask of Hate

Hate is the cask of the Danaïdes;*
Vengeance, distraught, has red and brawny arms,
With which she hurls into her empty dark
Buckets of blood and tears from dead men's eyes.

Satan makes secret holes through which will fly
Out of these depths a thousand years of pain,
Though Hate will use her victims once again,
Resuscitating them to squeeze them dry.

Hate is a drunkard in a tavern's depths
Who feels a constant thirst, from drinking born,
That thrives and multiplies like Hydra's heads.*

But happy drinkers know their conqueror,
And Hate is dealt a bitter fate, unable
Ever to fall asleep under the table.

74. La Cloche fêlée

Il est amer et doux, pendant les nuits d'hiver,
D'écouter, près du feu qui palpite et qui fume,
Les souvenirs lointains lentement s'élever
Au bruit des carillons qui chantent dans la brume.

Bienheureuse la cloche au gosier vigoureux
Qui, malgré sa vieillesse, alerte et bien portante,
Jette fidèlement son cri religieux,
Ainsi qu'un vieux soldat qui veille sous la tente!

Moi, mon âme est fêlée, et lorsqu'en ses ennuis
Elle veut de ses chants peupler l'air froid des nuits,
Il arrive souvent que sa voix affaiblie

Semble le râle épais d'un blessé qu'on oublie
Au bord d'un lac de sang, sous un grand tas de morts,
Et qui meurt, sans bouger, dans d'immenses efforts.

75. Spleen (I)

Pluviôse, irrité contre la ville entière,
De son urne à grands flots verse un froid ténébreux
Aux pâles habitants du voisin cimetière
Et la mortalité sur les faubourgs brumeux.

Mon chat sur le carreau cherchant une litière
Agite sans repos son corps maigre et galeux;
L'âme d'un vieux poëte erre dans la gouttière
Avec la triste voix d'un fantôme frileux.

Le bourdon se lamente, et la bûche enfumée
Accompagne en fausset la pendule enrhumée,
Cependant qu'en un jeu plein de sales parfums,

74. The Cracked Bell

How bittersweet it is on winter nights
To hear old recollections raise themselves
Around the flickering fire's wisps of light
And through the mist, in voices of the bells.

Blessed is the bell of clear and virile throat
Alert and dignified despite his rust,
Who faithfully repeats religion's notes
As an old soldier keeps a watchman's trust.

My spirit, though, is cracked; when as she can
She chants to fill the cool night's emptiness,
Too often can her weakening voice be said

To sound the rattle of a wounded man
Beside a bloody pool, stacked with the dead,
Who cannot budge, and dies in fierce distress!

75. Spleen (I)

Pluvius,* this whole city on his nerves,
Spills from his urn great waves of chilling rain
On graveyards' pallid inmates, and he pours
Mortality in gloomy district streets.

My restless cat goes scratching on the tiles
To make a litter for his scabby hide.
Some poet's phantom roams the gutter-spouts,
Moaning and whimpering like a freezing soul.

A great bell wails—within, the smoking log
Pipes in falsetto to a wheezing clock,
And meanwhile, in a reeking deck of cards—

Héritage fatal d'une vieille hydropique,
Le beau valet de cœur et la dame de pique
Causent sinistrement de leurs amours défunts.

76. Spleen (II)

J'ai plus de souvenirs que si j'avais mille ans.

Un gros meuble à tiroirs encombré de bilans,
De vers, de billets doux, de procès, de romances,
Avec de lourds cheveux roulés dans des quittances,
Cache moins de secrets que mon triste cerveau.
C'est une pyramide, un immense caveau,
Qui contient plus de morts que la fosse commune.
— Je suis un cimetière abhorré de la lune,
Où comme des remords se traînent de longs vers
Qui s'acharnent toujours sur mes morts les plus chers.
Je suis un vieux boudoir plein de roses fanées,
Où gît tout un fouillis de modes surannées,
Où les pastels plaintifs et les pâles Boucher,
Seuls, respirent l'odeur d'un flacon débouché.

Rien n'égale en longueur les boiteuses journées,
Quand sous les lourds flocons des neigeuses années,
L'ennui, fruit de la morne incuriosité,
Prend les proportions de l'immortalité.
— Désormais tu n'es plus, ô matière vivante!
Qu'un granit entouré d'une vague épouvante,
Assoupi dans le fond d'un Saharah brumeux;
Un vieux sphinx ignoré du monde insoucieux,
Oublié sur la carte, et dont l'humeur farouche
Ne chante qu'aux rayons du soleil qui se couche.

Some dropsied crone's foreboding legacy—
The dandy Jack of Hearts and Queen of Spades
Trade sinister accounts of wasted love.

76. Spleen (II)

More memories than if I'd lived a thousand years!

A giant chest of drawers, stuffed to the full
With balance sheets, love letters, lawsuits, verse
Romances, locks of hair rolled in receipts,
Hides fewer secrets than my sullen skull.
It is a pyramid, a giant vault
Holding more corpses than a common grave.
—I am a graveyard hated by the moon
Where like remorse the long worms crawl, and turn
Attention to the dearest of my dead.
I am a dusty boudoir where are heaped
Yesterday's fashions, and where withered roses,
Pale pastels, and faded old Bouchers,*
Alone, breathe perfume from an opened flask.

Nothing is longer than the limping days
When under heavy snowflakes of the years,
Ennui, the fruit of dulling lassitude,
Takes on the size of immortality.*
—Henceforth, o living flesh, you are no more!
You are of granite, wrapped in a vague dread,
Slumbering in some Sahara's hazy sands,
An ancient sphinx lost to a careless world,
Forgotten on the map, whose haughty mood
Sings only in the glow of setting sun.*

77. Spleen (III)

Je suis comme le roi d'un pays pluvieux,
Riche, mais impuissant, jeune et pourtant très-vieux,
Qui, de ses précepteurs méprisant les courbettes,
S'ennuie avec ses chiens comme avec d'autres bêtes.
Rien ne peut l'égayer, ni gibier, ni faucon,
Ni son peuple mourant en face du balcon.
Du bouffon favori la grotesque ballade
Ne distrait plus le front de ce cruel malade;
Son lit fleurdelisé se transforme en tombeau,
Et les dames d'atour, pour qui tout prince est beau,
Ne savent plus trouver d'impudique toilette
Pour tirer un souris de ce jeune squelette.
Le savant qui lui fait de l'or n'a jamais pu
De son être extirper l'élément corrompu,
Et dans ces bains de sang qui des Romains nous viennent,
Et dont sur leurs vieux jours les puissants se souviennent,
Il n'a su réchauffer ce cadavre hébété
Où coule au lieu de sang l'eau verte du Léthé.

78. Spleen (IV)

Quand le ciel bas et lourd pèse comme un couvercle
Sur l'esprit gémissant en proie aux longs ennuis,
Et que de l'horizon embrassant tout le cercle
Il nous verse un jour noir plus triste que les nuits;

Quand la terre est changée en un cachot humide,
Où l'Espérance, comme une chauve-souris,
S'en va battant les murs de son aile timide
Et se cognant la tête à des plafonds pourris;

77. Spleen (III)

I might as well be king of rainy lands—
Wealthy and young, but impotent and old,
Who scorns the troupe of tutors at his feet
And dallies with his dogs and other beasts.
Nothing can cheer him*—game or falconry—
Not even subjects dying at his door.
The comic jingles of the court buffoon
Do not amuse this twisted invalid.
His regal bed is nothing but a tomb,
And courtesans, who dote on any prince,
No longer have the antics or the clothes
To get a smile from this young rack of bones.
The alchemist who made him gold cannot
Attend his soul and extirpate the flaw;
Nor in those baths of blood* the Romans claimed
Would bring an old man's body youthful force,
Can scholar's knowledge bring to life a corpse
With Lethe's* putrid water in its veins.

78. Spleen (IV)

When low and heavy sky weighs like a lid
Upon the spirit moaning in ennui,
And when, spanning the circle of the world,
It pours a black day sadder than our nights;

When earth is changed into a sweaty cell,
In which Hope, captured, like a frantic bat,
Batters the walls with her enfeebled wing,
Striking her head against the rotting beams;

Quand la pluie étalant ses immenses traînées
D'une vaste prison imite les barreaux,
Et qu'un peuple muet d'infâmes araignées
Vient tendre ses filets au fond de nos cerveaux,

Des cloches tout à coup sautent avec furie
Et lancent vers le ciel un affreux hurlement,
Ainsi que des esprits errants et sans patrie
Qui se mettent à geindre opiniâtrement.

— Et de longs corbillards, sans tambours ni musique,
Défilent lentement dans mon âme; l'Espoir,
Vaincu, pleure, et l'Angoisse atroce, despotique,
Sur mon crâne incliné plante son drapeau noir.

79. Obsession

Grands bois, vous m'effrayez comme des cathédrales;
Vous hurlez comme l'orgue; et dans nos cœurs maudits,
Chambres d'éternel deuil où vibrent de vieux râles,
Répondent les échos de vos *De profundis*.

Je te hais, Océan! tes bonds et tes tumultes,
Mon esprit les retrouve en lui; ce rire amer
De l'homme vaincu, plein de sanglots et d'insultes,
Je l'entends dans le rire énorme de la mer.

Comme tu me plairais, ô nuit! sans ces étoiles
Dont la lumière parle un langage connu!
Car je cherche le vide, et le noir, et le nu!

Mais les ténèbres sont elles-mêmes des toiles
Où vivent, jaillissant de mon œil par milliers,
Des êtres disparus aux regards familiers.

When steady rain trailing its giant train
Descends on us like heavy prison bars,
And when a silent multitude of spiders
Spins its disgusting threads deep in our brains,

Bells all at once jump out with all their force,
And hurl about a mad cacophony
As if they were those lost and homeless souls
Who send a dogged whining to the skies.

—And long cortèges minus drum or tone
Deploy morosely through my being: Hope
The conquered, moans, and tyrant Anguish gloats—
In my bowed skull he fixed his black flag.

79. Obsession

You scare me, forests, as cathedrals do!
You howl like organs; and in your damned hearts,
Those mourning-chambers where old death-rales ring,
Your *De Profundis** echoes in response.

Ocean, I hate you! Your great crests and troughs,
I see them in my soul; the conquered man's
Mad laughter, full of insults and of sobs,
I hear it in the roaring of the sea.

But how you'd please me, night! without those stars
Whose light speaks in a language I have known!
Since I seek for the black, the blank, the bare!

Ah, but the darkness is itself a screen
Where thousands are projected from my eyes—
Those vanished beings whom I recognize.

80. Le Goût du néant

Morne esprit, autrefois amoureux de la lutte,
L'Espoir, dont l'éperon attisait ton ardeur,
Ne veut plus t'enfourcher! Couche-toi sans pudeur,
Vieux cheval dont le pied à chaque obstacle bute.

Résigne-toi, mon cœur; dons ton sommeil de brute.

Esprit vaincu, fourbu! Pour toi, vieux maraudeur,
L'amour n'a plus de goût, non plus que la dispute;
Adieu donc, chants du cuivre et soupirs de la flûte!
Plaisirs, ne tentez plus un cœur sombre et boudeur!

Le Printemps adorable a perdu son odeur!

Et le Temps m'engloutit minute par minute,
Comme la neige immense un corps pris de roideur;
Je contemple d'en haut le globe en sa rondeur
Et je n'y cherche plus l'abri d'une cahute.

Avalanche, veux-tu m'emporter dans ta chute?

81. Alchimie de la douleur

L'un t'éclaire avec son ardeur,
L'autre en toi met son deuil, Nature!
Ce qui dit à l'un: Sépulture!
Dit à l'autre: Vie et splendeur!

Hermès inconnu qui m'assistes
Et qui toujours m'intimidas,
Tu me rends l'égal de Midas,
Le plus triste des alchimistes;

80. The Taste for Nothingness

Dull soul, to whom the battle once was sweet,
Hope, who had spurred your ardour and your fame
Will no more ride you! Lie down without shame
Old horse, who makes his way on stumbling feet.

Give up, my heart, and sleep your stolid sleep.

For you old rover, spirit sadly spent,
Love is no longer fair, nor is dispute;
Farewell to brass alarms, sighs of the flute!
Pleasures, give up a heart grown impotent!

The Spring, once wonderful, has lost its scent!

And Time engulfs me in its steady tide,
As blizzards cover corpses with their snow;
And poised on high I watch the world below,
No longer looking for a place to hide.

Avalanche, sweep me off within your slide!

81. Alchemy of Suffering

One's ardour, Nature, makes you bright,
One finds within you mourning, grief!
What speaks to one of tombs and death
Says to the other, Splendour! Life!

Mystical Hermes,* help to me,
Intimidating though you are,
You make me Midas' counterpart,*
No sadder alchemist than he;

Par toi je change l'or en fer
Et le paradis en enfer;
Dans le suaire des nuages

Je découvre un cadavre cher,
Et sur les célestes rivages
Je bâtis de grands sarcophages.

82. Horreur sympathique

De ce ciel bizarre et livide,
Tourmenté comme ton destin,
Quels pensers dans ton âme vide
Descendent? réponds, libertin.

— Insatiablement avide
De l'obscur et de l'incertain,
Je ne geindrai pas comme Ovide
Chassé du paradis latin.

Cieux déchirés comme des grèves,
En vous se mire mon orgueil;
Vos vastes nuages en deuil

Sont les corbillards de mes rêves,
Et vos lueurs sont le reflet
De l'Enfer où mon cœur se plaît.

83. *L'Héautontimorouménos*
A J.G.F.

Je te frapperai sans colère
Et sans haine, comme un boucher,
Comme Moïse le rocher!
Et je ferai de ta paupière,

My gold is iron by your spell,
And paradise turns into hell;
I see in winding-sheets of clouds

A dear cadaver in its shroud,
And there upon celestial strands
I raise huge tombs above the sands.

82. Congenial Horror

From this bizarre and livid sky
Tormented by your destiny,
Into your vacant spirit fly
What thoughts? respond, you libertine.

—Voracious in my appetite
For the uncertain and unknown,
I do not whine for paradise
As Ovid did, expelled from Rome.*

Skies torn apart like wind-swept sands,
You are the mirrors of my pride;
Your mourning clouds, so black and wide,

Are hearses that my dreams command,
And you reflect in flashing light
The Hell in which my heart delights.

83. *Heautontimoroumenos**
*for J.G.F.**

I'll strike you without rage or hate
The way a butcher strikes his block,
The way that Moses smote the rock!*
So that your eyes may irrigate

Pour abreuver mon Saharah,
Jaillir les eaux de la souffrance
Mon désir gonflé d'espérance
Sur tes pleurs salés nagera

Comme un vaisseau qui prend le large,
Et dans mon cœur qu'ils soûleront
Tes chers sanglots retentiront
Comme un tambour qui bat la charge!

Ne suis-je pas un faux accord
Dans la divine symphonie,
Grâce à la vorace Ironie
Qui me secoue et qui me mord?

Elle est dans ma voix, la criarde!
C'est tout mon sang, ce poison noir!
Je suis le sinistre miroir
Où la mégère se regarde!

Je suis la plaie et le couteau!
Je suis le soufflet et la joue!
Je suis les membres et la roue,
Et la victime et le bourreau!

Je suis de mon cœur le vampire,
— Un de ces grands abandonnés
Au rire éternel condamnés
Et qui ne peuvent plus sourire!

My dry Sahara, I'll allow
The tears to flow of your distress.
Desire, that hope embellishes,
Will swim along the overflow

As ships set out for voyaging,
And like a drum that beats the charge
In my infatuated heart
The echoes of your sobs will ring!

But am I not a false accord
Within the holy symphony,
Thanks to voracious Irony
Who gnaws on me and shakes me hard?

She's in my voice, in all I do!
Her poison flows in all my veins!
I am the looking-glass of pain
Where she regards herself, the shrew!

I am the wound, and rapier!
I am the cheek, I am the slap!
I am the limbs, I am the rack,
The prisoner, the torturer!

I am my own blood's epicure
—One of those great abandoned men
Who are eternally condemned
To laugh, but who can smile no more!*

84. L'Irrémédiable

I

Une Idée, une Forme, un Être
Parti de l'azur et tombé
Dans un Styx bourbeux et plombé
Où nul œil du Ciel ne pénètre;

Un Ange, imprudent voyageur
Qu'a tenté l'amour du difforme,
Au fond d'un cauchemar énorme
Se débattant comme un nageur,

Et luttant, angoisses funèbres!
Contre un gigantesque remous
Qui va chantant comme les fous
Et pirouettant dans les ténèbres;

Un malheureux ensorcelé
Dans ses tâtonnements futiles,
Pour fuir d'un lieu plein de reptiles,
Cherchant la lumière et la clé;

Un damné descendant sans lampe,
Au bord d'un gouffre dont l'odeur
Trahit l'humide profondeur,
D'éternels escaliers sans rampe,

Où veillent des monstres visqueux
Dont les larges yeux de phospore
Font une nuit plus noire encore
Et ne rendent visibles qu'eux;

84. The Irremediable

I

A Being, a Form, an Idea
Having fallen from out of the blue
Into the Stygian slough*
Where no eye of the sky ever sees;

An impetuous Angel, allured
By the love of the twisted and mean,
In the depths of a nightmarish dream
Like a swimmer who struggles for shore,

Contending in wretched distress
With a whirlpool that swivels along
Singing a madman's song,
Performing its dark pirouettes;

A bewildered man, miserably
Attempting a groping escape
Out of a place full of snakes,
Lacking the lamp and the key;

A damned soul fumbling down steps
Of an infinite stair without rails
At the edge of a gulf, with a smell
Betraying the clammy depths,

Where monsters watch below,
Whose eyeballs' glowing light
Makes blacker still the night—
Themselves are all they show;

Un navire pris dans le pôle,
Comme en un piége de cristal,
Cherchant par quel détroit fatal
Il est tombé dans cette geôle;

— Emblèmes nets, tableau parfait
D'une fortune irrémédiable,
Qui donne à penser que le Diable
Fait toujours bien tout ce qu'il fait!

II

Tête-à-tête sombre et limpide
Qu'un cœur devenu son miroir!
Puits de Vérité, clair et noir,
Où tremble une étoile livide,

Un phare ironique, infernal,
Flambeau des grâces sataniques,
Soulagement et gloire uniques,
— La conscience dans le Mal!

85. L'Horloge

Horloge! dieu sinistre, effrayant, impassible,
Dont le doigt nous menace et nous dit: 'Souviens-toi!
Les vibrantes Douleurs dans ton cœur plein d'effroi
Se planteront bientôt comme dans une cible;

Le Plaisir vaporeux fuira vers l'horizon
Ainsi qu'une sylphide au fond de la coulisse;
Chaque instant te dévore un morceau de délice
A chaque homme accordé pour toute sa saison.

An iced-in polar ship
Seized in a vice of glass,
Searching the fatal path
Of this imprisoning trip;

Pure emblems, a perfect tableau
Of an irremediable evil,
Which makes us think that the Devil
Does well what he chooses to do!

II

It's a face-to-face sombre and clear
When a heart gives its own image back!
Well of Verity, limpid and black,
Where trembles a ghastly star,

An ironic beacon, from Hell,
Torch of Satanical graces,
And a glory in consolation,
—Evil aware of itself!

85. The Clock

The Clock! a sinister, impassive god
Whose threatening finger says to us: 'Remember!
Soon in your anguished heart, as in a target,
Quivering shafts of Grief will plant themselves;

Vaporous Joy glides over the horizon
The way a sylphid flits into the wings;*
Each instant eats a piece of the delight
A man is granted for his earthly season.

Trois mille six cents fois par heure, la Seconde
Chuchote: *Souviens-toi!* — Rapide, avec sa voix
D'insecte, Maintenant dit: Je suis Autrefois,
Et j'ai pompé ta vie avec ma trompe immonde!

Remember! Souviens-toi! prodigue! *Esto memor!*
(Mon gosier de métal parle toutes les langues.)
Les minutes, mortel folâtre, sont des gangues
Qu'il ne faut pas lâcher sans en extraire l'or!

Souviens-toi que le Temps est un joueur avide
Qui gagne sans tricher, à tout coup! c'est la loi.
Le jour décroît; la nuit augmente; *souviens-toi!*
Le gouffre a toujours soif; la clepsydre se vide.

Tantôt sonnera l'heure où le divin Hasard,
Où l'auguste Vertu, ton épouse encor vierge,
Où le Repentir même (oh! la dernière auberge!),
Où tout te dira: Meurs, vieux lâche! il est trop tard!'

Three thousand and six hundred times an hour
The Second sighs, *Remember!*–Suddenly
That droning insect Now says: I am Past
And I have sucked your life into my nostril!

Esto memor! Remember! Souviens-toi!
(My metal throat speaks out in a every language)
Don't let the minutes, prodigal, be wasted—
They are the ore you must refine for gold!

Remember, Time is greedy at the game
And wins on every roll! perfectly legal.
The day runs down; the night comes on; *remember!*
The water-clock bleeds into the abyss.

Soon sounds the hour when Chance the heavenly,
When Virtue the august, eternal virgin,
When even (oh! your last retreat) Repentance,
Will tell you: Die old coward! it's too late!'

Tableaux parisiens

Parisian Scenes

86. Paysage

Je veux, pour composer chastement mes églogues,
Coucher auprès du ciel, comme les astrologues,
Et, voisin des clochers, écouter en rêvant
Leurs hymnes solennels emportés par le vent.
Les deux mains au menton, du haut de ma mansarde,
Je verrai l'atelier qui chante et qui bavarde;
Les tuyaux, les clochers, ces mâts de la cité,
Et les grands ciels qui font rêver d'éternité.

Il est doux, à travers les brumes, de voir naître
L'étoile dans l'azur, la lampe à la fenêtre,
Les fleuves de charbon monter au firmament
Et la lune verser son pâle enchantement.
Je verrai les printemps, les étés, les automnes,
Et quand viendra l'hiver aux neiges monotones,
Je fermerai partout portières et volets
Pour bâtir dans la nuit mes féeriques palais.
Alors je rêverai des horizons bleuâtres,
Des jardins, des jets d'eau pleurant dans les albâtres,
Des baisers, des oiseaux chantant soir et matin,
Et tout ce que l'Idylle a de plus enfantin.
L'Émeute, tempêtant vainement à ma vitre,
Ne fera pas lever mon front de mon pupitre;
Car je serai plongé dans cette volupté
D'évoquer le Printemps avec ma volonté,
De tirer un soleil de mon cœur, et de faire
De mes pensers brûlants une tiède atmosphère.

86. Landscape

So as to write my eclogues* in the purest verse
I wish to lay me down, like the astrologers,
Next to the sky, and hear in reverie the hymns
Of all the neighbouring belfries, carried on the wind
My two hands to my chin, up in my attic room,
I'll see the atelier singing a babbled tune;
The chimney-pipes, the steeples, all the city's masts,
The great, inspiring skies, magnificent and vast.

How sweet it is to see, across the misty gloom,
A star born in the blue, a lamp lit in a room,
Rivers of chimney smoke, rising in purplish streams,
The pale of glow of the moon, transfiguring the scene.
I will look out on springs and summers, autumn's show,
And when the winter comes, in monotone of snow,
I'll lock up all the doors and shutters neat and tight,
And build a fairy palace for myself at night.
So I will dream of bright horizons in the blue
Where fountains weep in pools of alabaster hue,
Of kisses in the glades, where birds sing night and day,
Of all to make an idyll in a childish way.
Riot,* that rages vainly at my window glass,
Will never make me raise my forehead from my task,
Since I am plunged in this voluptuous delight—
Of conjuring the spring with all the poet's might,
Of hauling forth a sun out of my heart, with care
Transmuting furious thoughts to gently breathing air.

87. Le Soleil

Le long du vieux faubourg, où pendent aux masures
Les persiennes, abri des secrètes luxures,
Quand le soleil cruel frappe à traits redoublés
Sur la ville et les champs, sur les toits et les blés,
Je vais m'exercer seul à ma fantasque escrime,
Flairant dans tous les coins les hasards de la rime,
Trébuchant sur les mots comme sur les pavés,
Heurtant parfois des vers depuis longtemps rêvés.

Ce père nourricier, ennemi des chloroses,
Éveille dans les champs les vers comme les roses;
Il fait s'évaporer les soucis vers le ciel,
Et remplit les cerveaux et les ruches de miel.
C'est lui qui rajeunit les porteurs de béquilles
Et les rend gais et doux comme des jeunes filles,
Et commande aux moissons de croître et de mûrir
Dans le cœur immortel qui toujours veut fleurir!

Quand, ainsi qu'un poëte, il descend dans les villes,
Il ennoblit le sort des choses les plus viles,
Et s'introduit en roi, sans bruit et sans valets,
Dans tous les hôpitaux et dans tous les palais.

88. A une mendiante rousse

Blanche fille aux cheveux roux,
Dont la robe par se trous
Laisse voir la pauvreté
  Et la beauté,

87. The Sun

Through all the district's length, where from the shacks
Hang shutters for concealing secret acts,
When shafts of sunlight strike with doubled heat
On towns and fields, on rooftops, on the wheat,
I practise my quaint swordsmanship alone,*
Stumbling on words as over paving stones,
Sniffing in corners all the risks of rhyme,
To find a verse I'd dreamt of a long time.

This foster-father, fighter of chlorosis,*
Wakes in the fields the worms as well as roses;
He sends our cares in vapour to the skies,
And fills our minds, with honey fills the hives,
Gives crippled men a new view of the world,
And makes them gay and gentle as young girls,
Commands the crops to grow, and nourishes
Them, in that heart that always flourishes!

When, poet-like, he comes to town awhile,
He lends a grace to things that are most vile,
And simply, like a king, he makes the rounds
Of all the hospitals, the palace grounds.

88. To a Red-Haired Beggar Girl

Pale girl with russet hair,*
Tatters in what you wear
Show us your poverty
    And your beauty,

Pour moi, poète chétif,
Ton jeune corps maladif,
Plein de taches de rousseur.
  A sa douceur.

Tu portes plus galamment
Qu'une reine de roman
Ses cothurnes de velours
  Tes sabots lourds.

Au lieu d'un haillon trop court,
Qu'un superbe habit de cour
Traîne à plis bruyants et longs
  Sur tes talons;

En place de bas troués,
Que pour les yeux des roués
Sur ta jambe un poignard d'or
  Reluise encor;

Que des nœuds mal attachés
Dévoilent pour nos péchés
Tes deux beaux seins, radieux
  Comme des yeux;

Que pour te déshabiller
Tes bras se fassent prier
Et chassent à coups mutins
  Les doigts lutins;

Perles de la plus belle eau,
Sonnets de maître Belleau
Par tes galants mis aux fers
  Sans cesse offerts,

Valetaille de rimeurs
Te dédiant leurs primeurs
Et contemplant ton soulier
  Sous l'escalier,

For me, poor poet, in
The frail and freckled skin
Of your young flesh
    Is a sweetness.

You move in shoes of wood
More gallantly than could
A velvet-buskined Queen
    Playing a scene;

In place of rags for clothes
Let a majestic robe
Trail in its bustling pleats
    Down to your feet;

Behind the holes in seams
Let a gold dagger gleam
Laid for the roué's eye
    Along your thigh;

Let loosened ribbons, then,
Unveil us for our sins
Two breasts as undisguised
    And bright as eyes;

As for your other charms,
Let your resistant arms
Frustrate with saucy blows
    The groping rogues;

Pearls of a lustrous glow,
Sonnets penned by Belleau,*
Suitors at your command
    Constantly send,

Menial rhymsters, too,
Dedicate works to you;
Seeing your slipper there
    Under the stair,

Maint page épris du hasard,
Maint seigneur et maint Ronsard
Épieraient pour le déduit
   Ton frais réduit!

Tu compterais dans tes lits
Plus de baisers que de lis
Et rangerais sous tes lois
   Plus d'un Valois!

— Cependant tu vas gueusant
Quelque vieux débris gisant
Au seuil de quelque Véfour
   De carrefour;

Tu vas lorgnant en dessous
Des bijoux de vingt-neuf sous
Dont je ne puis, oh! pardon!
   Te faire don.

Va donc, sans autre ornement,
Parfum, perles, diamant,
Que ta maigre nudité,
   Ô ma beauté!

89. Le Cygne

A Victor Hugo

I

Andromaque, je pense à vous! Ce petit fleuve,
Pauvre et triste miroir où jadis resplendit
L'immense majesté de vos douleurs de veuve,
Ce Simoïs menteur qui par vos pleurs grandit,

Pages and noble lords,
Would-be Ronsards* galore,
Spy for the secret sweets
    Of your retreat!

Lilies, in your alcove,
Count less than making love—
You'd hold to lovers' law
    Several Valois!*

—Meanwhile, you beg to eat
Stale bread and tainted meat
Thrown from an alley door—
    Backstreet Véfour—*

And covet secretly
The cheapest jewellery
Which I (forgive me!) can't
    Place in your hand.

Go then, a starveling girl
With no perfume or pearls,
Only your nudity
    O my beauty!

89. The Swan

for Victor Hugo*

I

Andromache,* I think of you—this meagre stream,
This melancholy mirror where had once shone forth
The giant majesty of all your widowhood,
This fraudulent Simois,* fed by bitter tears,

A fécondé soudain ma mémoire fertile,
Comme je traversais le nouveau Carrousel.
Le vieux Paris n'est plus (la forme d'une ville
Change plus vite, hélas! que le cœur d'un mortel);

Je ne vois qu'en esprit tout ce camp de baraques,
Ces tas de chapiteaux ébauchés et de fûts,
Les herbes, les gros blocs verdis par l'eau des flaques,
Et, brillant aux carreaux, le bric-à-brac confus.

Là s'étalait jadis une ménagerie;
Là je vis, un matin, à l'heure où sous les cieux
Froids et clairs le Travail s'éveille, où la voirie
Pousse un sombre ouragan dans l'air silencieux,

Un cygne qui s'était évadé de sa cage,
Et, de ses pieds palmés frottant le pavé sec,
Sur le sol raboteux traînait son blanc plumage.
Près d'un ruisseau sans eau la bête ouvrant le bec

Baignait nerveusement ses ailes dans la poudre,
Et disait, le cœur plein de son beau lac natal:
'Eau, quand donc pleuvras-tu? quand tonneras-tu, foudre?'
Je vois ce malheureux, mythe étrange et fatal,

Vers le ciel quelquefois, comme l'homme d'Ovide,
Vers le ciel ironique et cruellement bleu,
Sur son cou convulsif tendant sa tête avide,
Comme s'il adressait des reproches à Dieu!

II

Paris change! mais rien dans ma mélancolie
N'a bougé! palais neufs, échafaudages, blocs,
Vieux faubourgs, tout pour moi devient allégorie,
Et mes chers souvenirs sont plus lourds que des rocs.

Has quickened suddenly my fertile memory
As I was walking through the modern Carrousel.*
The old Paris is gone* (the form a city takes
More quickly shifts, alas, than does the mortal heart);

I picture in my head the busy camp of huts,
And heaps of rough-hewn columns, capitals and shafts,
The grass, the giant blocks made green by puddle-stain,
Reflected in the glaze, the jumbled bric-à-brac.

Once nearby was displayed a great menagerie,
And there I saw one day—the time when under skies
Cold and newly bright, Labour stirs awake
And sweepers push their storms into the silent air—

A swan, who had escaped from his captivity,
And scuffing his splayed feet along the paving stones,
He trailed his white array of feathers in the dirt.
Close by a dried out ditch the bird opened his beak,

Flapping excitedly, bathing his wings in dust,
And said, with heart possessed by lakes he once had loved:
'Water, when will you rain? Thunder, when will you roar?'
I see this hapless creature, sad and fatal myth,

Stretching the hungry head on his convulsive neck,
Sometimes towards the sky, like the man in Ovid's book—*
Towards the ironic sky, the sky of cruel blue,
As if he were a soul contesting with his God!

II

Paris may change, but in my melancholy mood
Nothing has budged! New palaces, blocks, scaffoldings,
Old neighbourhoods, are allegorical for me,
And my dear memories are heavier than stone.

Aussi devant ce Louvre une image m'opprime:
Je pense à mon grand cygne, avec ses gestes fous,
Comme les exilés, ridicule et sublime,
Et rongé d'un désir sans trêve! et puis à vous,

Andromaque, des bras d'un grand époux tombée,
Vil bétail, sous la main du superbe Pyrrhus,
Auprès d'un tombeau vide en extase courbée;
Veuve d'Hector, hélas! et femme d'Hélénus!

Je pense à la négresse, amaigrie et phthisique,
Piétinant dans la boue, et cherchant, l'œil hagard,
Les cocotiers absents de la superbe Afrique
Derrière la muraille immense du brouillard;

A quiconque a perdu ce qui ne ce retrouve
Jamais, jamais! à ceux qui s'abreuvent de pleurs
Et tettent la Douleur comme une bonne louve!
Aux maigres orphelins séchant comme des fleurs!

Ainsi dans la forêt où mon esprit s'exile
Un vieux Souvenir sonne à plein souffle du cor!
Je pense aux matelots oubliés dans une île,
Aux captifs, aux vaincus! . . . à bien d'autres encor!

90. Les Sept Vieillards

A Victor Hugo

Fourmillante cité, cité pleine de rêves,
Où le spectre en plein jour raccroche le passant!
Les mystères partout coulent comme des sèves
Dans les canaux étroits du colosse puissant.

Un matin, cependant que dans la triste rue
Les maisons, dont la brume allongeait la hauteur,
Simulaient les deux quais d'une rivière accrue,
Et que, décor semblable à l'âme de l'acteur,

And so outside the Louvre an image gives me pause:
I think of my great swan, his gestures pained and mad,
Like other exiles, both ridiculous and sublime,
Gnawed by his endless longing! Then I think of you,

Fallen Andromache, torn from a husband's arms,
Vile property beneath the haughty Pyrrhus' hand,
Next to an empty tomb, head bowed in ecstasy,
Widow of Hector! O! and wife of Helenus!*

I think of a negress, thin and tubercular,
Treading in the mire, searching with haggard eye
For palm trees she recalls from splendid Africa,
Somewhere behind a giant barrier of fog;

Of all those who have lost something they may not find
Ever, ever again! who steep themselves in tears
And suck a bitter milk from that good she-wolf, grief!
Of orphans, skin and bones, dry and wasted blooms!

And likewise in the forest of my exiled soul
Old Memory sings out a full note of the horn!
I think of sailors left forgotten on an isle,
Of captives, the defeated ... many others more!

90. The Seven Old Men
for Victor Hugo

City of swarming, city full of dreams
Where ghosts in daylight tug the stroller's sleeve!
Mysteries everywhere run like the sap
That fills this great colossus' conduits.

One morning, while along the sombre street
The houses, rendered taller by the mist,
Seemed to be towering wharves at riverside,
And while (our stage-set like the actor's soul)

Un brouillard sale et jaune inondait tout l'espace,
Je suivais, roidissant mes nerfs comme un héros
Et discutant avec mon âme déjà lasse,
Le faubourg secoué par les lourds tombereaux.

Tout à coup, un vieillard dont les guenilles jaunes
Imitaient la couleur de ce ciel pluvieux,
Et dont l'aspect aurait fait pleuvoir les aumônes,
Sans la méchanceté qui luisait dans ses yeux,

M'apparut. On eût dit sa prunelle trempée
Dans le fiel; son regard aiguisait les frimas,
Et sa barbe à longs poils, roide comme une épée,
Se projetait, pareille à celle de Judas.

Il n'était pas voûté, mais cassé, son échine
Faisant avec sa jambe un parfait angle droit,
Si bien que son bâton, parachevant sa mine,
Lui donnait la tournure et le pas maladroit

D'un quadrupède infirme ou d'un juif à trois pattes
Dans la neige et la boue il allait s'empêtrant,
Comme s'il écrasait des morts sous ses savates,
Hostile à l'univers plutôt qu'indifférent.

Son pareil le suivait: barbe, œil, dos, bâton, loques,
Nul trait ne distinguait, du même enfer venu,
Ce jumeau centenaire, et ces spectres baroques
Marchaient du même pas vers un but inconnu.

A quel complot infâme étais-je donc en butte,
Ou quel méchant hasard ainsi m'humiliait?
Car je comptai sept fois, de minute en minute,
Ce sinistre vieillard qui se multipliait!

Que celui-là qui rit de mon inquiétude,
Et qui n'est pas saisi d'un frisson fraternel,
Songe bien que malgré tant de décrépitude
Ces sept monstres hideux avaient l'air éternel!

A dirty yellow steam filled all the space,
I followed, with a hero's iron nerve
To set against my spirit's lassitude,
The district streets shaken by rumbling carts.

Then, an old man whose yellowed rags
Were imitations of the rainy sky,
At whose sight charity might have poured down,
Without the evil glitter in his eyes,

Appeared quite suddenly to me. I'd say
His eye was steeped in gall; his glance was sharp
As frost, his shaggy beard, stiff as a sword,
Stood out, and Judas* came into my mind.

You would not call him bent, but cut in two—
His spine made a right angle with his legs
So neatly that his cane, the final touch,
Gave him the figure and the clumsy step

Of some sick beast, or a three-legged Jew.
In snow and filth he made his heavy way,
As if his old shoes trampled on the dead
In hatred, not indifference to life.

His double followed: beard, eye, back, stick, rags,
No separate traits, and come from the same hell.
This second ancient man, baroque, grotesque,
Trod with the same step towards their unknown goal.

To what conspiracy was I exposed,
What wicked chance humiliated me?
For one by one I counted seven times
Multiples of this sinister old man!

Those who would laugh at my frenetic state,
Who are not seized by a fraternal chill,
Must ponder that, despite their feebleness,
These monsters smacked of all eternity!

Aurais-je, sans mourir, contemplé le huitième,
Sosie inexorable, ironique et fatal,
Dégoûtant Phénix, fils et père de lui-même?
— Mais je tournai le dos au cortège infernal.

Exaspéré comme un ivrogne qui voit double,
Je rentrai, je fermai ma porte, épouvanté,
Malade et morfondu, l'esprit fiévreux et trouble,
Blessé par le mystère et par l'absurdité!

Vainement ma raison voulait prendre la barre;
La tempête en jouant déroutait ses efforts,
Et mon âme dansait, dansait, vieille gabarre
Sans mâts, sur une mer monstrueuse et sans bords!

91. Les Petites Vieilles

A Victor Hugo

I

Dans les plis sinueux des vieilles capitales,
Où tout, même l'horreur, tourne aux enchantements,
Je guette, obéissant à mes humeurs fatales,
Des êtres singuliers, décrépits et charmants.

Ces monstres disloqués furent jadis des femmes,
Éponine ou Laïs! Monstres brisés, bossus
Ou tordus, aimons-les! ce sont encor des âmes.
Sous des jupons troués ou sous de froids tissus

Ils rampent, flagellés par les bises iniques,
Frémissant au fracas roulant des omnibus,
Et serrant sur leur flanc, ainsi que des reliques,
Un petit sac brodé de fleurs ou de rébus;

Could I still live and look upon the eighth
Relentless twin, fatal, disgusting freak,
Trick Phoenix,* son and father of himself?
—I turned my back on this parade from Hell.

Bedazzled, like a double-visioned drunk,
I staggered home and shut the door, aghast,
Shaking and sick, the spirit feverous,
Struck by this mystery, this absurdity!

Vainly my reason reached to clutch the helm;
The giddy tempest baffled every grasp,
And my soul danced in circles like a hull
Dismasted, on a monstrous shoreless sea!

91. The Little Old Women

for Victor Hugo

I

In sinuous coils of the old capitals
Where even horror weaves a magic spell,
Gripped by my fatal humours, I observe
Singular beings with appalling charms.

These dislocated wrecks were women once,
Were Eponine or Laïs!* hunchbacked freaks,
Though broken let us love them! they are souls.
Under cold rags, their shredded petticoats,

They creep, lashed by the merciless north wind,
Quake from the riot of an omnibus,
Clasp by their sides like relics of a saint
Embroidered bags of flowery design;

Ils trottent, tout pareils à des marionnettes;
Se traînent, comme font les animaux blessés,
Ou dansent, sans vouloir danser, pauvres sonnettes
Où se pend un Démon sans pitié! Tout cassés

Qu'ils sont, ils ont des yeux perçants comme une vrille,
Luisants comme ces trous où l'eau dort dans la nuit;
Ils ont les yeux divins de la petite fille
Qui s'étonne et qui rit à tout ce qui reluit.

— Avez-vous observé que maints cercueils de vieilles
Sont presque aussi petits que celui d'un enfant?
La Mort savante met dans ces bières pareilles
Un symbole d'un goût bizarre et captivant,

Et lorsque j'entrevois un fantôme débile
Traversant de Paris le fourmillant tableau,
Il me semble toujours que cet être fragile
S'en va tout doucement vers un nouveau berceau;

A moins que, méditant sur la géométrie,
Je ne cherche, à l'aspect de ces membres discords,
Combien de fois il faut que l'ouvrier varie
La forme de la boîte où l'on met tous ces corps.

— Ces yeux sont des puits faits d'un million de larmes,
Des creusets qu'un métal refroidi pailleta . . .
Ces yeux mystérieux ont d'invincibles charmes
Pour celui que l'austère Infortune allaita!

II

De Frascati défunt Vestale enamourée;
Prêtresse de Thalie, hélas! dont le souffleur
Enterré sait le nom; célèbre évaporée
Que Tivoli jadis ombragea dans sa fleur,

They toddle, every bit like marionettes,
Or drag themselves like wounded animals,
Or dance against their will, poor little bells
That a remorseless demon rings! Worn out

They are, yet they have eyes piercing like drills,
Shining like pot-holes where the water sleeps;
Heavenly eyes, as of a little girl
Who laughs with joy at anything that shines.

—Have you observed that coffins of the old
Are nearly small enough to fit a child?
Death, in this similarity, sets up
An eerie symbol with a strange appeal,

And when I glimpse some feeble phantom there,
Part of the swarming tableau of the town,
It always seems to me this fragile soul
Is moving gently to her cradle bed;

Unless geometry occurs to me
In shapes of these contorted limbs, and I
Think how the workmen have to modify
The boxes where these bodies will be lain.

—These eyes are wells, made of a million tears,
Or crucibles where spangled metal cools . . .
These eyes of mystery have deathless charms
For those who suckle Tribulation's breast!

II

Vestal of love,* from old Frascati's rooms;*
Priestess of Thalia,* whose name only
The buried prompter knows; celebrity
Whom Tivoli* once shaded in its blooms,

Toutes m'enivrent! mais parmi ces êtres frêles
Il en est qui, faisant de la douleur un miel,
Ont dit au Dévouement qui leur prêtait ses ailes:
Hippogriffe puissant, mène-moi jusqu'au ciel!

L'une, par sa patrie au malheur exercée,
L'autre, que son époux surchargea de douleurs,
L'autre, par son enfant Madone transpercée,
Toutes auraient pu faire un fleuve avec leurs pleurs!

III

Ah! que j'en ai suivi de ces petites vieilles!
Une, entre autres, à l'heure où le soleil tombant
Ensanglante le ciel de blessures vermeilles,
Pensive, s'asseyait à l'écart sur un banc,

Pour entendre un de ces concerts, riches de cuivre,
Dont les soldats parfois inondent nos jardins,
Et qui, dans ces soirs d'or où l'on se sent revivre,
Versent quelque héroïsme au cœur des citadins.

Celle-là, droite encor, fière et sentant la règle,
Humait avidement ce chant vif et guerrier;
Son œil parfois s'ouvrait comme l'œil d'un vieil aigle;
Son front de marbre avait l'air fait pour le laurier!

IV

Telles vous cheminez, stoïques et sans plaintes.
A travers le chaos des vivantes cités,
Mères au cœur saignant, courtisanes ou saintes
Dont autrefois les noms par tous étaient cités.

Vous qui fûtes la grâce ou qui fûtes la gloire,
Nul ne vous reconnaît! un ivrogne incivil
Vous insulte en passant d'un amour dérisoire;
Sur vos talons gambade un enfant lâche et vil.

All make me drunk! but with these weaker souls
Are those, making a honey of their grief,
Who've said to Sacrifice, who lent them wings,
Lift me into the sky, great Hippogriffe!*

One by her homeland trained in misery,
Another whom her husband overtaxed,
One a Madonna martyred by her child—
Oh, each could make a river with her tears!

III

So many of these women I have stalked!
One among others, when the sun would fall
Steeping the sky in blood from ruby wounds,
Pensive, would settle on a bench alone

To listen to a concert, rich with brass,
With which the soldiers sometimes flood our parks
And pour, in evenings that revive the soul,
Such heroism in the townsmen's hearts.

She, then, upright and proud, stirred by the cause,
Vigorously inhaled this warlike song;
Sometimes her eye gleamed like an eagle's eye;
Fit for the laurel was her marble brow!

IV

So you trudge on, stoic, without complaint,
Through the chaotic city's teeming waste,
Saints, courtesans, mothers of bleeding hearts,
Whose names, in times past, everyone had known.

You glorious ones, you who were full of grace,
Not one remembers you! some rowdy drunk
Insults you on the street with crude remarks;
A taunting child cuts capers at your heels.

Honteuses d'exister, ombres ratatinées,
Peureuses, le dos bas, vous côtoyez les murs;
Et nul ne vous salue, étranges destinées!
Débris d'humanité pour l'éternité mûrs!

Mais moi, moi qui de loin tendrement vous surveille,
L'œil inquiet, fixé sur vos pas incertains,
Tout comme si j'étais votre père, ô merveille!
Je goûte à votre insu des plaisirs clandestins:

Je vois s'épanouir vos passions novices;
Sombres ou lumineux, je vis vos jours perdus;
Mon cœur multiplié jouit de tous vos vices!
Mon âme resplendit de toutes vos vertus!

Ruines! ma famille! ô cerveaux congénères!
Je vous fais chaque soir un solennel adieu!
Où serez-vous demain, Èves octogénaires,
Sur qui pèse la griffe effroyable de Dieu?

92. Les Aveugles

Contemple-les, mon âme; ils sont vraiment affreux!
Pareils aux mannequins; vaguement ridicules;
Terribles, singuliers, comme les somnambules;
Dardant on ne sait où leurs globes ténébreux.

Leurs yeux, d'où la divine étincelle est partie,
Comme s'ils regardaient au loin, restent levés
Au ciel; on ne les voit jamais vers les pavés
Pencher rêveusement leur tête appesantie.

Ils traversent ainsi le noir illimité,
Ce frère du silence éternel. Ô cité!
Pendant qu'autour de nous tu chantes, ris et beugles,

O you ashamed of living, shrunken shades,
Fearful, with backs bent, how you hug the walls;
And no one greets you, strange and fated souls!
Debris of man, ripe for eternity!

But I, who from a distance mark your steps
With tenderness, and restless eye intent
As though I were your father, wondrous thought!
Unknown to you I taste a secret joy:

I see your novice passions blossoming;
Sombre or sunny, I see your lost days;
Heart multiplied, I share in all your vice!
With all your virtue shines my glowing soul!

Ruins! my family! my fellow-minds!
Each evening I will bid a grave adieu!
What of tomorrow, Eves of eighty years,
Pressed by the dreadful talon of the Lord?

92. The Blind

Consider them, my soul, they are a fright!
Like mannequins, vaguely ridiculous,
Peculiar, terrible somnambulists,
Beaming—who can say where—their eyes of night.

These orbs, in which a spark is never seen,
As if in looking far and wide stay raised
On high; they never seem to cast their gaze
Down to the street, head hung, as in a dream.

Thus they traverse the blackness of their days,
Kin to the silence of eternity.
O city! while you laugh and roar and play,

Éprise du plaisir jusqu'à l'atrocité,
Vois! je me traîne aussi! mais, plus qu'eux hébété,
Je dis: Que cherchent-ils au Ciel, tous ces aveugles?

93. A une passante

La rue assourdissante autour de moi hurlait.
Longue, mince, en grand deuil, douleur majestueuse,
Une femme passa, d'une main fastueuse
Soulevant, balançant le feston et l'ourlet;

Agile et noble, avec sa jambe de statue.
Moi, je buvais, crispé comme un extravagant,
Dans son œil, ciel livide où germe l'ouragan,
La douceur qui fascine et le plaisir qui tue.

Un éclair... puis la nuit! — Fugitive beauté
Dont le regard m'a fait soudainement renaître,
Ne te verrai-je plus que dans l'éternité?

Ailleurs, bien loin d'ici! trop tard! *jamais* peut-être!
Car j'ignore où tu fuis, tu ne sais où je vais,
Ô toi que j'eusse aimée, ô toi qui le savais!

94. Le Squelette laboureur

I

Dans les planches d'anatomie
Qui traînent sur ces quais poudreux
Où maint livre cadavéreux
Dort comme une antique momie,

Mad with your lusts to point of cruelty,
Look at me! dragging, dazed more than their kind.
What in the Skies can these men hope to find?

93. To a Woman Passing By

Around me roared the nearly deafening street.
Tall, slim, in mourning,* in majestic grief,
A woman passed me, with a splendid hand
Lifting and swinging her festoon and hem;

Nimble and stately, statuesque of leg.
I, shaking like an addict, from her eye,
Black sky, spawner of hurricanes, drank in
Sweetness that fascinates, pleasure that kills.

One lightning flash . . . then night! Sweet fugitive
Whose glance has made me suddenly reborn,
Will we not meet again this side of death?

Far from this place! too late! *never* perhaps!
Neither one knowing where the other goes,
O you I might have loved, as well you know!

94. Skeletons Digging

I

In anatomical designs*
That hang about these dusty quays
Where books' cadavers lie and sleep
Like mummies of the ancient times,

Dessins auxquels la gravité
Et le savoir d'un vieil artiste,
Bien que le sujet en soit triste,
Ont communiqué la Beauté,

On voit, ce qui rend plus complètes
Ces mystérieuses horreurs,
Bêchant comme des laboureurs,
Des Écorchés et des Squelettes.

II

De ce terrain que vous fouillez,
Manants résignés et funèbres,
De tout l'effort de vos vertèbres,
Ou de vos muscles dépouillés,

Dites, quelle moisson étrange,
Forçats arrachés au charnier,
Tirez-vous, et de quel fermier
Avez-vous à remplir la grange?

Voulez-vous (d'un destin trop dur
Épouvantable et clair emblème!)
Montrer que dans la fosse même
Le sommeil promis n'est pas sûr;

Qu'envers nous le Néant est traître;
Que tout, même la Mort, nous ment,
Et que sempiternellement,
Hélas! il nous faudra peut-être

Dans quelque pays inconnu
Écorcher la terre revêche
Et pousser une lourde bêche
Sous notre pied sanglant et nu?

Drawings of which the gravity
And the engraver's knowing hand,
Although the theme be less than grand,
Communicate an artistry,

One sees, which renders more intense
The horror and the mystery,
Like field-hands working wearily
Some skeletons and skinless men.

II

Out of the land you're digging there,
Obedient and woeful drones,
With all the effort of your bones,
Of all your muscles, stripped and bare,

Say, what strange harvest do you farm,
Convicts from the charnel house,
And what contractor hired you out
To fill what farmer's empty barn?

Do you (our dreadful fate seems clear
In your design) intend to show
That in the pit we may not know
The sleep we have been promised there,

Non-being will not keep its faith;
That even Death can tell a lie,
And that, Alas! eternally
It falls to us, perhaps, at death

In some anonymous retreat
To see the stubborn land is flayed
By pushing the reluctant spade
Under our bare and bleeding feet?

95. Le Crépuscule du soir

Voici le soir charmant, ami du criminel;
Il vient comme un complice, à pas de loup; le ciel
Se ferme lentement comme une grande alcôve,
Et l'homme impatient se change en bête fauve.

Ô soir, aimable soir, désiré par celui
Dont les bras, sans mentir, peuvent dire: Aujourd'hui
Nous avons travaillé! — C'est le soir qui soulage
Les esprits que dévore une douleur sauvage,
Le savant obstiné dont le front s'alourdit,
Et l'ouvrier courbé qui regagne son lit.
Cependant des démons malsains dans l'atmosphère
S'éveillent lourdement, comme des gens d'affaire,
Et cognent en volant les volets et l'auvent.
A travers les lueurs que tourmente le vent
La Prostitution s'allume dans les rues;
Comme une fourmilière elle ouvre ses issues;
Partout elle se fraye un occulte chemin,
Ainsi que l'ennemi qui tente un coup de main;
Elle remue au sein de la cité de fange
Comme un ver qui dérobe à l'Homme ce qu'il mange.
On entend çà et là les cuisines siffler,
Les théâtres glapir, les orchestres ronfler;
Les tables d'hôte, dont le jeu fait les délices,
S'emplissent de catins et d'escrocs, leurs complices,
Et les voleurs, qui n'ont ni trêve ni merci,
Vont bientôt commencer leur travail, eux aussi,
Et forcer doucement les portes et les caisses
Pour vivre quelques jours et vêtir leurs maîtresses.

Recueille-toi, mon âme, en ce grave moment,
Et ferme ton oreille â ce rugissement.
C'est l'heure où les douleurs des malades s'aigrissent!
La sombre Nuit les prend à la gorge; ils finissent

95. Dusk

Sweet evening comes, friend of the criminal,
Like an accomplice with a light footfall;
The sky shuts on itself as though a tomb,
And man turns beast within his restless room.

O evening, night, so wished for by the one
Whose honest, weary arms can say: We've done
Our work today!—The night will bring relief
To spirits who consume themselves with grief,
The scholar who is bowed with heavy head,
The broken worker falling into bed.
Meanwhile, corrupting demons of the air
Slowly wake up like men of great affairs,
And, flying, bump our shutters and our eaves.
Against the glimmerings teased by the breeze
Old Prostitution blazes in the streets;
She opens out her nest-of-ants retreat;
Everywhere she clears the secret routes,
A stealthy force preparing for a coup;
She moves within this city made of mud,
A worm who steals from man his daily food.
One hears the hissing kitchens close at hand,
The playhouse screech, the blaring of a band.
The tables at the inns where gamesmen sport
Are full of swindlers, sluts, and all their sort.
Robbers who show no pity to their prey
Get ready for their nightly work-a-day
Of cracking safes and deftly forcing doors,
To live a few days more and dress their whores.

Collect yourself, my soul, in this grave time,
And shut out all this clamour from the slime.
This the time of sick men's sharpest pain!
Black night will grab their throats; they cry in vain,

Leur destinée et vont vers le gouffre commun;
L'hôpital se remplit de leurs soupirs.—Plus d'un
Ne viendra plus chercher la soupe parfumée,
Au coin du feu, le soir, auprès d'une âme aimée.

Encore la plupart n'ont-ils jamais connu
La douceur du foyer et n'ont jamais vécu!

96. Le Jeu

Dans les fauteuils fanés des courtisanes vieilles,
Pâles, le sourcil peint, l'œil câlin et fatal,
Minaudant, et faisant de leurs maigres oreilles
Tomber un cliquetis de pierre et de métal;

Autour des verts tapis des visages sans lèvre,
Des lèvres sans couleur, des mâchoires sans dent,
Et des doigts convulsés d'une infernale fièvre,
Fouillant la poche vide ou le sein palpitant;

Sous de sales plafonds un rang de pâles lustres
Et d'énormes quinquets projetant leurs lueurs
Sur des fronts ténébreux de poëtes illustres
Qui viennent gaspiller leurs sanglantes sueurs;

Voilà le noir tableau qu'en un rêve nocturne
Je vis se dérouler sous mon œil clairvoyant.
Moi-même, dans un coin de l'antre taciturne,
Je me vis accoudé, froid, muet, enviant,

Enviant de ces gens la passion tenace,
De ces vieilles putains la funèbre gaieté,
Et tous gaillardement trafiquant à ma face,
L'un de son vieil honneur, l'autre de sa beauté!

And finish out their fate in common grave;
The hospital is filled with gasps. They have
No further need to think of evenings spent
At fireside—the fragrant soup, the friend.

But most of them have never known the call
Of friendly hearth, have never lived at all!

96. Gaming

In faded chairs, the pale old courtesans,
Eyebrows painted, eye of fatal calm,
Smirking, and letting drop from skinny ears
Those jingling sounds of metal and of stone;

Around green cloth, the faces without lips,
Lips without colour over toothless jaws,
And fingers twisted by infernal fires,
Digging in pockets, or in panting breast;

Under the filthy ceilings, chandeliers
And lamps of oil doling out their glow
Over the brilliant poets' gloomy brows,
Who come to squander here their bloody sweat;

This is the black tableau that in my dream
I see unroll before my prescient eye.
There in an idle corner of that den
I see myself—cold, mute, and envying,

Envious of these men's tenacious lust,
The morbid gaiety of these old whores,
Trafficking gallantly before my face
In honour and in beauty, as of old!

Et mon cœur s'effraya d'envier maint pauvre homme
Courant avec ferveur à l'abîme béant,
Et qui, soûl de son sang, préférerait en somme
La douleur à la mort et l'enfer au néant!

97. Danse macabre

A Ernest Christophe

Fière, autant qu'un vivant, de sa noble stature,
Avec son gros bouquet, son mouchoir et ses gants,
Elle a la nonchalance et la désinvolture
D'une coquette maigre aux airs extravagants.

Vit-on jamais au bal une taille plus mince?
Sa robe exagérée, en sa royale ampleur,
S'écroule abondamment sur un pied sec que pince
Un soulier pomponné, joli comme une fleur.

La ruche qui se joue au bord des clavicules,
Comme un ruisseau lascif qui se frotte au rocher,
Défend pudiquement des lazzi ridicules
Les funèbres appas qu'elle tient à cacher.

Ses yeux profonds sont faits de vide et de ténèbres,
Et son crâne, de fleurs artistement coiffé,
Oscille mollement sur ses frêles vertèbres.
Ô charme d'un néant follement attifé!

Aucuns t'appelleront une caricature,
Qui ne comprennent pas, amants ivres de chair,
L'élégance sans nom de l'humaine armature.
Tu réponds, grand squelette, à mon goût le plus cher!

Viens-tu troubler, avec ta puissante grimace,
La fête de la Vie? ou quelque vieux désir,
Éperonnant encor ta vivante carcasse,
Te pousse-t-il, crédule, au sabbat du Plaisir?

My heart takes fright to envy this poor lot
Who rush so fervently to the abyss,
And who, drunk on their blood, prefer, in sum,
Suffering to death, and Hell to nothingness!

97. *Danse macabre**

for Ernest Christophe

Proud, like one living, of her noble height,
With handkerchief and gloves, her great bouquet,
She has the graceful nonchalance that might
Befit a gaunt coquette with lavish ways.

At any ball does one see waist so slim?
In all their regal amplitude, her clothes
Unfurl down to a dry foot, pinched within
A pomponned shoe as lovely as a rose.

The frill that plays along her clavicles,
As a lewd streamlet rubs its stony shores,
Modestly shields from jeering ridicule
Enticements her revealing gown obscures.

Her eyes, made of the void, are deep and black;
Her skull, coiffured in flowers down her neck,
Sways slackly on the column of her back,
O charm of nothingness so madly decked!

You will be called by some, 'caricature',
Who do not know, lovers obsessed with flesh,
The grandeur of the human armature.
You please me, skeleton, above the rest!

Do you display your grimace to upset
Our festival of life? Some ancient fire,
Does it ignite your living carcass yet,
And push you to the sabbath of Desire?

Au chant des violons, aux flammes des bougies,
Espères-tu chasser ton cauchemar moqueur,
Et viens-tu demander au torrent des orgies
De rafraîchir l'enfer allumé dans ton cœur?

Inépuisable puits de sottise et de fautes!
De l'antique douleur éternel alambic!
A travers le treillis recourbé de tes côtes
Je vois, errant encor, l'insatiable aspic.

Pour dire vrai, je crains que ta coquetterie
Ne trouve pas un prix digne de ses efforts;
Qui, de ces cœurs mortels, entend la raillerie?
Les charmes de l'horreur n'enivrent que les forts!

Le gouffre de tes yeux, plein d'horribles pensées,
Exhale le vertige, et les danseurs prudents
Ne contempleront pas sans d'amères nausées
Le sourire éternel de tes trente-deux dents.

Pourtant, qui n'a serré dans ses bras un squelette,
Et qui ne s'est nourri des choses du tombeau?
Qu'importe le parfum, l'habit ou la toilette?
Qui fait le dégoûté montre qu'il se croit beau.

Bayadère sans nez, irrésistible gouge,
Dis donc à ces danseurs qui font les offusqués:
'Fiers mignons, malgré l'art des poudres et du rouge,
Vous sentez tous la mort! Ô squelettes musqués,

Antinoüs flétris, dandys à face glabre,
Cadavres vernissés, lovelaces chenus,
Le branle universel de la danse macabre
Vous entraîne en des lieux qui ne sont pas connus!

Des quais froids de la Seine aux bords brûlants du Gange,
Le troupeau mortel saute et se pâme, sans voir
Dans un trou du plafond la trompette de l'Ange
Sinistrement béante ainsi qu'un tromblon noir.

Can you dismiss the nightmare mocking you,
With candle glow and songs of violins,
And will you try what floods of lust can do
To cool the hell that brands the heart within?

Eternal well of folly and of fault!
Alembic* of the old and constant griefs!
I notice how, along the latticed vault
Of ribs, the all-consuming serpent creeps.

Truly, your coquetry will not evoke
Any award that does not do it wrong;
Who of these mortal hearts can grasp the joke?
The charms of horror only suit the strong!

Full of atrocious thoughts, your eyes' abyss
Breathes vertigo—no dancer could begin
Without a bitter nausea to kiss
Two rows of teeth locked in a steady grin.

But who has not embraced a skeleton?
Who has not fed himself on carrion meat?
What matter clothes, or how you put them on?
The priggish dandy shows his self-deceit.

Noseless hetaera,* captivating quean,
Tell all those hypocrites what you know best:
'Proud darlings though you powder and you preen,
O perfumed skeletons, you reek of death!

Favourites faded, withered—in the mob
Antinous,* and many a lovelace—*
The ceaseless swirling of the *danse macabre*
Sweeps you along to some unheard-of place!

From steamy Ganges to the freezing Seine
The troop of mortals leaps and swoons, and does
Not see the Angel's trumpet aimed at them
Down through the ceiling, that black blunderbuss.

En tout climat, sous tout soleil, la Mort t'admire
En tes contorsions, risible Humanité,
Et souvent, comme toi, se parfumant de myrrhe,
Mêle son ironie à ton insanité!'

98. L'Amour du mensonge

Quand je te vois passer, ô ma chère indolente,
Au chant des instruments qui se brise au plafond
Suspendant ton allure harmonieuse et lente,
Et promenant l'ennui de ton regard profond;

Quand je contemple, aux feux du gaz qui le colore,
Ton front pâle, embelli par un morbide attrait,
Où les torches du soir allument une aurore,
Et tes yeux attirants comme ceux d'un portrait,

Je me dis: Qu'elle est belle! et bizarrement fraîche!
Le souvenir massif, royale et lourde tour,
La couronne, et son cœur, meurtri comme une pêche,
Est mûr, comme son corps, pour le savant amour.

Es-tu le fruit d'automne aux saveurs souveraines?
Es-tu vase funèbre attendant quelques pleurs,
Parfum qui fait rêver aux oasis lointaines,
Oreiller caressant, ou corbeille de fleurs?

Je sais qu'il est des yeux, des plus mélancoliques,
Qui ne recèlent point de secrets précieux;
Beaux écrins sans joyaux, médaillons sans reliques,
Plus vides, plus profonds que vous-mêmes, ô Cieux!

Mais ne suffit-il pas que tu sois l'apparence,
Pour réjouir un cœur qui fuit la vérité?
Qu'importe ta bêtise ou ton indifférence?
Masque ou décor, salut! J'adore ta beauté.

In every climate Death admires you
In your contortions, o Humanity,
And perfuming herself as you would do,
Into your madness blends her irony!'

98. The Love of Illusion

When I watch you go by, in all your indolence,
To sound of instruments within the echoing hall
Suspending your appeal of lingering harmony,
And showing in your glance the ennui of your soul;

And when I contemplate, in colouring flames of gas,
Your pallid brow enhanced with a morbidity,
Where torches of the evening light a promised dawn,
And your alluring eyes, a master's artistry,

I think, how lovely! and how oddly innocent!
Massive remembrance, that great tower raised above,
Crowns her, and oh, her heart, bruised like a softened peach,
·Is mellow, like her body, ripe for skilful love.

Are you the fruit of fall, when flavour is supreme?
Funeral vase, that waits for tears in darkened rooms,
Perfume that brings the far oases to our dreams,
Caressing pillow, or a basket of fresh blooms?

I know that there are eyes, the finest and most sad,
That hide no precious secrets, neither truths nor lies;
Handsome, like empty lockets, caskets without jewels,
More empty, more profound, than you yourselves, o skies!

But is it not enough that your appearance can
Restore to joy a heart that flees from what is true?
What if you are inane, what if indifferent!
Mask, decoration, hail! Beauty, I worship you!

99. 'Je n'ai pas oublié...'

Je n'ai pas oublié, voisine de la ville,
Notre blanche maison, petite mais tranquille;
Sa Pomone de plâtre et sa vieille Vénus
Dans un bosquet chétif cachant leurs membres nus,
Et le soleil, le soir, ruisselant et superbe,
Qui, derrière la vitre où se brisait sa gerbe,
Semblait, grand œil ouvert dans le ciel curieux,
Contempler nos dîners longs et silencieux,
Répandant largement ses beaux reflets de cierge
Sur la nappe frugale et les rideaux de serge.

100. 'La servante au grand cœur...'

La servante au grand cœur dont vous étiez jalouse,
Et qui dort son sommeil sous un humble pelouse,
Nous devrions pourtant lui porter quelques fleurs.
Les morts, les pauvres morts, ont de grandes douleurs,
Et quand Octobre souffle, émondeur des vieux arbres,
Son vent mélancolique à l'entour de leurs marbres,
Certe, ils doivent trouver les vivants bien ingrats,
A dormir, comme ils font, chaudement dans leurs draps,
Tandis que, dévorés de noires songeries,
Sans compagnon de lit, sans bonnes causeries,
Vieux squelettes gelés travaillés par le ver,
Ils sentent s'égoutter les neiges de l'hiver
Et le siècle couler, sans qu'amis ni famille
Remplacent les lambeaux que pendent à leur grille.

Lorsque la bûche siffle et chante, si le soir,
Calme, dans le fauteuil, je la voyais s'asseoir,
Si, par une nuit bleue et froide de Décembre,
Je la trouvais tapie en un coin de ma chambre,

99. 'I have not forgotten...'

I have not forgotten our little white retreat
Where we were neighbours to the town of busy streets;
Our plaster Venus and Pomona* barely could
Conceal their nakedness within our meagre wood.
Evenings, the sun would stream superbly, and would splash
Prismatic colours through the simple window glass;
He seemed a curious eye in overarching space
Who watched us as we dined in silence, without haste,
And spread throughout the room a mellow candle-glow
On frugal drapes of serge, the tablecloth below.

100. 'That kind heart you were jealous of...'

That kind heart you were jealous of, my nurse*
Who sleeps her sleep beneath the humble turf,
I'd like to give her flowers, wouldn't you?
The dead, the poor dead, have their sorrows too,
And when October trims the branches down,
Blowing its sombre wind around their stones,
The living seem ungrateful to the dead,
For sleeping as they do, warm in their beds;
Meanwhile, devoured by black imaginings,
No bedmate, and without good gossiping,
Worked by the worm, cold skeletons below
Seem to be filtering the winter's snows,
And time flows by, no family who will
Tend to the scraps that hang from iron grills.

If in the dusk, while logs would smoke and sing,
I'd see her in the armchair, pondering,
Or find her in a night of wintry gloom
Abiding in a corner of my room,

Grave, et venant du fond de son lit éternel,
Couver l'enfant grandi de son œil maternel,
Que pourrais-je répondre à cette âme pieuse,
Voyant tomber des pleurs de sa paupière creuse?

101. Brumes et pluies

Ô fins d'automne, hivers, printemps trempés de boue,
Endormeuses saisons! je vous aime et vous loue
D'envelopper ainsi mon cœur et mon cerveau
D'un linceul vaporeux et d'un vague tombeau.

Dans cette grande plaine où l'autan froid se joue,
Où par les longues nuits la girouette s'enroue,
Mon âme mieux qu'au temps du tiède renouveau
Ouvrira largement ses ailes de corbeau.

Rien n'est plus doux au cœur plein de choses funèbres,
Et sur qui dès longtemps descendent les frimas,
Ô blafardes saisons, reines de nos climats,

Que l'aspect permanent de vos pâles ténèbres,
— Si ce n'est, par un soir sans lune, deux à deux,
D'endormir la douleur sur un lit hasardeux.

102. Rêve parisien

*A Constantin Guys**

I

De ce terrible paysage,
Tel que jamais mortel n'en vit,
Ce matin encore l'image,
Vague et lointaine, me ravit.

Grave spirit, who'd ascended from her pain
To watch with love her grown-up child again,
What could I offer this most pious soul,
Watching her tears fall from their hollow holes?

101. Mists and Rains

Autumn's last days, winters and mud-soaked spring
I praise the stupefaction that you bring
By so enveloping my heart and brain
In shroud of vapours, tomb of mist and rain.

In this great flatness where the chill winds course,
Where through the nights the weather-cock grows hoarse,
My soul, more than in springtime's tepid sky,
Will open out her raven's wings to fly.

O blankest seasons, queens of all my praise,
Nothing is sweet to the funereal breast
That has been steeped in frost and wintriness

But the continuous face of your pale shades
—Except we two, where moonlight never creeps
Daring in bed to put our griefs to sleep.

102. Parisian Dream

for Constantin Guys*

I

Of this strange, awe-inspiring scene
Such as on earth one never sees,
Today the image once again,
Obscure and distant, captures me.

Le sommeil est plein de miracles!
Par un caprice singulier,
J'avais banni de ces spectacles
Le végétal irrégulier,

Et, peintre fier de mon génie,
Je savourais dans mon tableau
L'enivrante monotonie
Du métal, du marbre et de l'eau.

Babel d'escaliers et d'arcades,
C'était un palais infini,
Plein de bassins et de cascades
Tombant dans l'or mat ou bruni;

Et des cataractes pesantes,
Comme des rideaux de cristal,
Se suspendaient, éblouissantes,
A des murailles de métal.

Non d'arbres, mais de colonnades
Les étangs dormants s'entouraient,
Où de gigantesques naïades,
Comme des femmes, se miraient.

Des nappes d'eau s'épanchaient, bleues,
Entre des quais roses et verts,
Pendant des millions de lieues,
Vers les confins de l'univers;

C'étaient des pierres inouïes
Et des flots magiques; c'étaient
D'immenses glaces éblouies
Par tout ce qu'elles reflétaient!

Insouciants et taciturnes,
Des Ganges, dans le firmament,
Versaient le trésor de leurs urnes
Dans des gouffres de diamant.

Sleep is so full of miracles!
By whimsy odd and singular
I've banished from these spectacles
Nature and the irregular.*

And, happy with my artistry,
I painted into my tableau
The ravishing monotony
Of marble, metal, water-flow.

Babel of endless stairs, arcades,
It was a palace multifold
Replete with pools and bright cascades
Falling in dull or burnished gold;

And the more weighty waterfalls
Like crystal screens resplendent there
Along the metal rampart walls
Seemed to suspend themselves in air;

The sleeping pools—there were no trees—
Gathered around them colonnades,
And in them naïads* at their ease
Could cast the narcissistic gaze.*

Sheets of blue water, emptying
Between the green and rosy quays
From multitudes of openings,
Poured to the world's last boundaries;

Magical waves, to please the eye,
Splashed on unheard-of stones, and vast
Reflectors stood there, dazzled by
The world they mirrored in their glass!

Insouciant and taciturn,
Some Ganges, in the firmament,
Poured out the treasure of their urns
Into the gulfs of diamond.

Architecte de mes féeries,
Je faisais, à ma volonté,
Sous un tunnel de pierreries
Passer un océan dompté;

Et tout, même la couleur noire,
Semblait fourbi, clair, irisé;
Le liquide enchâssait sa gloire
Dans le rayon cristallisé.

Nul astre d'ailleurs, nuls vestiges
De soleil, même au bas du ciel,
Pour illuminer ces prodiges,
Qui brillaient d'un feu personnel!

Et sur ces mouvantes merveilles
Planait (terrible nouveauté!
Tout pour l'œil, rien pour les oreilles!)
Un silence d'éternité.

II

En rouvrant mes yeux pleins de flamme
J'ai vu l'horreur de mon taudis,
Et senti, rentrant dans mon âme,
La pointe des soucis maudits;

La pendule aux accents funèbres
Sonnait brutalement midi,
Et le ciel versait des ténèbres
Sur le triste monde engourdi.

Architect of my magic show,
I then required, for my mood,
Through a jewelled conduit to flow
An ocean I had first subdued.

And all, even the colour black,
Seemed polished, sparkling, clear and clean;
The liquid kept its glow intact
Within the solid crystal beam.

No star from anywhere, no sign
Of moon or sunshine, bright or dim,
Illuminate this scene of mine
Glowing with fire from within!

Over the pageantry appears
To hover (awful novelty
For eyes, but nothing for the ear!)
A silence of eternity.

II

Open, my ardent eyes could see
The horror of my wretched hole;
I felt my cursed cares to be
A needle entering my soul;

The clock proclaimed the time was noon
In accents brutal and perverse,
And from the misty sky a gloom
Poured through the torpid universe.

103. Le Crépuscule du matin

La diane chantait dans les cours des casernes,
Et le vent du matin soufflait sur les lanternes.

C'était l'heure où l'essaim des rêves malfaisants
Tord sur leurs oreillers les bruns adolescents;
Où, comme un œil sanglant qui palpite et qui bouge,
La lampe sur le jour fait une tache rouge;
Où l'âme, sous le poids du corps revêche et lourd,
Imite les combats de la lampe et du jour.
Comme un visage en pleurs que les brises essuient,
L'air est plein du frisson des choses qui s'enfuient,
Et l'homme est las d'écrire et la femme d'aimer.

Les maisons çà et là commençait à fumer.
Les femmes de plaisir, la paupière livide,
Bouche ouverte, dormaient de leur sommeil stupide;
Les pauvresses, traînant leurs seins maigres et froids,
Soufflaient sur leurs tisons et soufflaient sur leurs doigts.
C'était l'heure où parmi le froid et la lésine
S'aggravent les douleurs des femmes en gésine;
Comme un sanglot coupé par un sang écumeux
Le chant du coq au loin déchirait l'air brumeux;
Une mer de brouillards baignait les édifices,
Et les agonisants dans le fond des hospices
Poussaient leur dernier râle en hoquets inégaux.
Les débauchés rentraient, brisés par leurs travaux.

L'aurore grelottante en robe rose et verte
S'avançait lentement sur la Seine déserte,
Et le sombre Paris, en se frottant les yeux,
Empoignait ses outils, vieillard laborieux.

103. Dawn

Reveille sang its call among the barracks' paths,
And moving air disturbed the tall, commanding lamps.

It was the time when dreams of lust and swarming heat
Set brown young adolescents twisting in their sheets;
When, like a bloody eye that pulses as it stares,
The lamp will cast a stain of red throughout the air;
When spirits, in the burden of the body's sway,
Mimic the struggles of the lamplight and the day.
The air, a face in tears that breeezes will wipe dry,
Is full of tremors of escaping things that fly,
And he is tired of writing, she of making love.

This house and that began to send their smoke above.
With ghastly painted eyes, the women of the streets,
Mouths gaping open, lay within their stupid sleep.
Poor women, slack breasts dangling, cold and lean as rails,
Blew on their smouldering logs, or on their purple nails.
It was the hour when, among the bare and poor,
Unfortunates in childbed suffered all the more;
Like a wild sob cut short by foaming blood, somewhere
A distant rooster's cry tore through the misty air,
A sea of fogs that bathed the buildings and the streets,
And dying poorhouse wretches from their sad retreats
Rattled away their lives in strangulated coughs.
Love's veterans came home, broken by labours lost.

Aurora,* trembling in her gown of rose and green,
Made her way slowly on the still-deserted Seine.
Old Paris rubbed his eyes, woke to the day again,
And gathered up his tools, that honest working man.

Le Vin

Wine

104. L'Âme du vin

Un soir, l'âme du vin chantait dans les bouteilles:
'Homme, vers toi je pousse, ô cher déshérité,
Sous ma prison de verre et mes cires vermeilles,
Un chant plein de lumière et de fraternité!

Je sais combien il faut, sur la colline en flamme,
De peine, de sueur et de soleil cuisant
Pour engendrer ma vie et pour me donner l'âme;
Mais je ne serai point ingrat ni malfaisant,

Car j'éprouve une joie immense quand je tombe
Dans le gosier d'un homme usé par ses travaux,
Et sa chaude poitrine est une douce tombe
Où je me plais bien mieux que dans mes froids caveaux.

Entends-tu retentir les refrains des dimanches
Et l'espoir qui gazouille en mon sein palpitant?
Les coudes sur la table et retroussant tes manches,
Tu me glorifieras et tu seras content;

J'allumerai les yeux de ta femme ravie;
A ton fils je rendrai sa force et ses couleurs
Et serai pour ce frêle athlète de la vie
L'huile qui raffermit les muscles des lutteurs.

En toi je tomberai, végétale ambroisie,
Grain précieux jeté par l'éternel Semeur,
Pour que de notre amour naisse la poésie
Qui jaillira vers Dieu comme une rare fleur!'

104. The Soul of Wine

One night, from bottles, sang the soul of wine:
'O misfit man, I send you for your good
Out of the glass and wax where I'm confined,
A melody of light and brotherhood!

I know you must, out on the blazing hill,
Suffer and sweat beneath the piercing rays
To grow my life in me, my soul and will;
I'm grateful to you, and I will not play

You false, since I feel joy when I can fall
Into the throat of some old working man,
And his warm belly suits me overall
As resting place more than cold cellars can.

And do you hear the songs that hope believes,
The Sunday music, throbbing from my breast?
Elbows on table, rolling up your sleeves
You praise me, and I'll put your cares to rest;

I'll fire the eyes of your enraptured wife;
I'll grant a force and colour to your son,
And will for this frail athlete of life
Be oil that makes the straining muscles run.

My nectar falls in your fertility,
A precious seed whose Sower is divine,
So from our love is born rare poetry,
Thrusting towards God the blossom on its vine!'

105. Le Vin des chiffonniers

Souvent, à la clarté rouge d'un réverbère
Dont le vent bat la flamme et tourmente le verre,
Au cœur d'un vieux faubourg, labyrinthe fangeux
Où l'humanité grouille en ferments orageux,

On voit un chiffonnier qui vient, hochant la tête,
Butant, et se cognant aux murs comme un poëte,
Et, sans prendre souci des mouchards, ses sujets,
Épanche tout son cœur en glorieux projets.

Il prête des serments, dicte des lois sublimes,
Terrasse les méchants, relève les victimes,
Et sous le firmament comme un dais suspendu
S'enivre des splendeurs de sa propre vertu.

Oui, ces gens harcelés de chagrins de ménage,
Moulus par le travail et tourmentés par l'âge,
Éreintés et pliant sous un tas de débris,
Vomissement confus de l'énorme Paris,

Reviennent, parfumés d'une odeur de futailles,
Suivis de compagnons, blanchis dans les batailles,
Dont la moustache pend comme les vieux drapeaux.
Les bannières, les fleurs et les arcs triomphaux

Se dressent devant eux, solennelle magie!
Et dans l'étourdissante et lumineuse orgie
Des clairons, du soleil, des cris et du tambour,
Ils apportent la gloire au peuple ivre d'amour!

C'est ainsi qu'à travers l'Humanité frivole
Le vin roule de l'or, éblouissant Pactole;
Par le gosier de l'homme il chante ses exploits
Et règne par ses dons ainsi que les vrais rois.

105. The Ragman's Wine

Often, beneath a street lamp's reddish light,
Where wind torments the glass and flame by night,
Where mankind swarms in stormy turbulence
Within a suburb's muddy labyrinth,

One comes upon a shaking ragman, who
Staggers against the walls, as poets do,
And disregardful of policemen's spies,
Pours from his heart some glorious enterprise.

Swearing his oaths, he dictates laws he's made
To vanquish evil, bring the victims aid,
And there beneath the sky, a canopy,
Grows drunk upon his own sublimity.

Yes, and these men harassed by household strife,
Tortured by age, bruised by the blows of life,
Under their heaps of rubbish burdened down,
The dregs, the vomit of this teeming town,

Appear again, redolent of the jar,
With their companions, bleached and battle-scarred,
Moustaches like the rags of bannerets.
Arches of triumph rise before their steps,

A solemn magic! flags and flowers too!
And in this orgy, dazzling to the view,
Of cheers, of bugles, drums, the sun above,
They glorify a people drunk with love!

And so it is, like Pactolus* of old,
For fickle Humankind, wine rolls with gold;
By human throat wine finds a voice to sing,
And reigns by all its gifts, a proper king.

Pour noyer la rancœur et bercer l'indolence
De tous ces vieux maudits qui meurent en silence,
Dieu, touché de remords, avait fait le sommeil;
L'Homme ajouta le Vin, fils sacré du Soleil!

106. Le Vin de l'assassin

Ma femme est morte, je suis libre!
Je puis donc boire tout mon soûl.
Lorsque je rentrais sans un sou,
Ses cris me déchiraient la fibre.

Autant qu'un roi je suis heureux;
L'air est pur, le ciel admirable . . .
Nous avions un été semblable
Lorsque j'en devins amoureux!

L'horrible soif qui me déchire
Aurait besoin pour s'assouvir
D'autant de vin qu'en peut tenir
Son tombeau; — ce n'est pas peu dire:

Je l'ai jetée au fond d'un puits,
Et j'ai même poussé sur elle
Tous les pavés de la margelle.
— Je l'oublierai si je le puis!

Au nom des serments de tendresse,
Dont rien ne peut nous délier,
Et pour nous réconcilier
Comme au beau temps de notre ivresse,

J'implorai d'elle un rendez-vous,
Le soir, sur une route obscure.
Elle y vint!—folle créature!
Nous sommes tous plus ou moins fous!

To drown the spite and dull the lethargy
Of damned old men who die in secrecy,
Remorseful God gave sleep to every one;
Man added wine, true scion of the Sun!

106. The Murderer's Wine

My wife is dead and I am free!
And I can guzzle all I want.
When I came home without a cent
Her crying knifed the heart in me.

I am as happy as a king;
The air is pure, the sky divine . . .
We had such sky another time
When first our love was blossoming!

The awful thirst I feel today
Would need, to get it rightly slaked,
All of the wine that it would take
To fill her tomb;—a lot to say:

I threw her in a well, and then
I even pitched some heavy stones
Out of the well-curb on her bones.
O, I'll forget her, if I can!

Naming those vows of tenderness
From which no power can set us free,
To reconcile us, as when we
Loved with a drunken happiness,

One night, along a road I named,
I begged her for a rendezvous.
She came!—a crazy thing to do!
But more or less we're all insane!

Elle était encore jolie,
Quoique bien fatiguée! et moi,
Je l'aimais trop! voilà pourquoi
Je lui dis: Sors de cette vie!

Nul ne peut me comprendre. Un seul
Parmi ces ivrognes stupides
Songea-t-il dans ses nuits morbides
A faire du vin un linceul?

Cette crapule invulnérable
Comme les machines de fer
Jamais, ni l'été ni l'hiver,
N'a connu l'amour véritable,

Avec ses noirs enchantements,
Son cortége infernal d'alarmes,
Ses fioles de poison, ses larmes,
Ses bruits de chaîne et d'ossements!

— Me voilà libre et solitaire!
Je serai ce soir ivre mort;
Alors, sans peur et sans remord,
Je me coucherai sur la terre,

Et je dormirai comme un chien!
Le chariot aux lourdes roues
Chargé de pierres et de boues,
Le wagon enragé peut bien

Écraser ma tête coupable
Ou me couper par la milieu,
Je m'en moque comme de Dieu,
Du Diable ou de la Sainte Table!

She was still pretty, though a sight—
Tired with age and troubles. I,
I loved her too much. That is why
I said to her: you die tonight!

No one can understand me. Crowds
Of loutish drunks, not one could think
In his most morbid nights of drink
Of turning wine into a shroud.

Scum of the earth, this doltish crew,
Like iron mechanisms all,
Never, in winter, spring or fall
Have understood what love can do.

Love with its dark, enchanting pains,
Troupe of anxieties from hell,
Its flasks of poison, tears as well,
Its rattlings of bones and chains!

—Now I am free and stand alone!
Dead drunk is what I'll get right here
And then, without remorse or fear,
I'll make my bed on dirt and stone

And sleep as any dog would do!
That cart with heavy wheels, the truck
Loaded with rocks and city muck,
That runaway I welcome to

Come crush my head, or it might well
Cut me in half right where I am,
And I don't give a good god-damn
For God, Communion, or for Hell!

107. Le Vin du solitaire

Le regard singulier d'une femme galante
Qui se glisse vers nous comme le rayon blanc
Que la lune onduleuse envoie au lac tremblant,
Quand elle y veut baigner sa beauté nonchalante;

Le dernier sac d'écus dans les doigts d'un joueur;
Un baiser libertin de la maigre Adeline;
Les sons d'une musique énervante et câline,
Semblable au cri lointain de l'humaine douleur,

Tout cela ne vaut pas, ô bouteille profonde,
Les baumes pénétrants que ta panse féconde
Garde au cœur altéré du poëte pieux;

Tu lui verses l'espoir, la jeunesse et la vie,
— Et l'orgueil, ce trésor de toute gueuserie,
Qui nous rend triomphants et semblables aux Dieux!

107. The Solitary's Wine

A handsome woman's tantalizing gaze
Gliding our way as softly as the beam
The sinuous moon sends out in silver sheen
Across the lake to bathe her careless rays;

His purse of cash, the gambler's last relief;
A flaming kiss from slender Adeline;*
Music, which sounds a faint, unnerving whine
That seems the distant cry of human grief,

Great jug, all these together are not worth
The penetrating balms within your girth
Saved for the pious poet's thirsting soul;

You pour out for him youth, and life, and hope
—And pride, the treasure of the beggar folk,
Which makes us like the Gods, triumphant, whole!

108. Le Vin des amants

Aujourd'hui l'espace est splendide!
Sans mors, sans éperons, sans bride,
Partons à cheval sur le vin
Pour un ciel féerique et divin!

Comme deux anges que torture
Une implacable calenture,
Dans le bleu cristal du matin
Suivons le mirage lointain!

Mollement balancés sur l'aile
Du tourbillon intelligent,
Dans un délire parallèle,

Ma sœur, côte à côte nageant,
Nous fuirons sans repos ni trêves
Vers le paradis de mes rêves!

108. The Lovers' Wine

This morning how grand is the space!
Without bridle or spurs, in our haste
Let us set out by horseback on wine,
For the heavens—enchanted, divine!

Like two angels gone insane
With delirium of the brain,
In the crystal blue of the sky
To the distant mirage we will fly!

Gently swinging within the wing
Of the whirlwind who gives us a ride,
My sister who swims by my side,

In a parallel ecstasy,
Without truce or repose we are bound
For the heaven my dreaming has found!

Fleurs du Mal

Flowers of Evil

109. La Destruction

Sans cesse à mes côtés s'agite le Démon;
Il nage autour de moi comme un air impalpable;
Je l'avale et le sens qui brûle mon poumon
Et l'emplit d'un désir éternel et coupable.

Parfois il prend, sachant mon grand amour de l'Art,
La forme de la plus séduisante des femmes,
Et, sous de spécieux prétextes de cafard,
Accoutume ma lèvre à des philtres infâmes.

Il me conduit ainsi, loin du regard de Dieu,
Haletant et brisé de fatigue, au milieu
Des plaines de l'Ennui, profondes et désertes.

Et jette dans mes yeux pleins de confusion
Des vêtements souillés, des blessures ouvertes,
Et l'appareil sanglant de la Destruction!

110. Une martyre

Dessin d'un maître inconnu

Au milieu des flacons, des étoffes lamées
    Et des meubles voluptueux,
Des marbres, des tableaux, des robes parfumées
    Qui traînent à plis somptueux,

Dans une chambre tiède où, comme en une serre,
    L'air est dangereux et fatal,
Où des bouquets mourants dans leurs cercueils de verre
    Exhalent leur soupir final,

109. Destruction

The Fiend* is at my side without a rest;
He swirls around me like a subtle breeze;
I swallow him, and burning fills my breast,
And calls me to desire's shameful needs.

Knowing my love of Art, he may select
A woman's form—most perfect, most corrupt—
And under sanctimonious pretext
Bring to my lips the potion of her lust.

Thus does he lead me, far from sight of God,
Broken and gasping, out into the broad
And wasted plains of Ennui, deep and still,

Then throws before my staring eyes some gowns
And bloody garments stained by open wounds,
And dripping engines of Destruction's will!

110. A Martyr

Drawing by an Unknown Master*

Surrounded by flasks, and by spangled lamés,
    All matter of sumptuous goods,
Marble sculptures, fine paintings, and perfumed peignoirs
    That trail in voluptuous folds,

In a room like a greenhouse, both stuffy and warm,
    An atmosphere heavy with death,
Where arrangements of flowers encoffined in glass
    Exhale their ultimate breath,

Un cadavre sans tête épanche, comme un fleuve,
    Sur l'oreiller désaltéré
Un sang rouge et vivant, dont la toile s'abreuve
    Avec l'avidité d'un pré.

Semblable aux visions pâles qu'enfante l'ombre
    Et qui nous enchaînent les yeux,
La tête, avec l'amas de sa crinière sombre
    Et de ses bijoux précieux,

Sur la table de nuit, comme une renoncule,
    Repose; et, vide de pensers,
Un regard vague et blanc comme le crépuscule
    S'échappe des yeux révulsés.

Sur le lit, le tronc nu sans scrupules étale
    Dans le plus complet abandon
La secrète splendeur et la beauté fatale
    Dont la nature lui fit don;

Un bas rosâtre, orné de coins d'or, à la jambe,
    Comme un souvenir est resté;
La jarretière, ainsi qu'un œil secret qui flambe,
    Darde un regard diamanté.

Le singulier aspect de cette solitude
    Et d'un grand portrait langoureux,
Aux yeux provocateurs comme son attitude,
    Révèle un amour ténébreux,

Une coupable joie et des fêtes étranges
    Pleines de baisers infernaux,
Dont se réjouissait l'essaim de mauvais anges
    Nageant dans les plis des rideaux;

Et cependant, à voir la maigreur élégante
    De l'épaule au contour heurté,
La hanche un peu pointue et la taille fringante
    Ainsi qu'un reptile irrité,

A headless cadaver spills out like a stream
    On a pillow adorning the bed,
A flow of red blood, which the linen drinks up
    With a thirsty meadow's greed.

Like pale apprehensions born in the dark,
    And that enchain the eyes,
The head—the pile of its ebony mane
    With precious jewels entwined—

On the night table, like a ranunculus
    Reposes; and a gaze,
Mindless and vague and as black as the dusk
    Escapes from the pallid face.

On the bed the nude torso displays without shame
    And most lasciviously,
The secret magnificence, fatal allure,
    Of its nature's artistry;

On the leg, a pink stocking adorned with gold clocks
    Remains like a souvenir;
The garter, a diamond-blazing eye,
    Hurls a glance that is cold and severe.

The singular aspect of this solitude,
    Like the portrait hung above
With eyes as enticing as languorous pose,
    Reveals an unspeakable love,

Perverse entertainments and culpable joys
    Full of devilish intimacies,
Which would make the dark angels swarm with delight
    In the folds of the draperies;

And yet, to notice the elegant lines
    Of the shoulder lean and lithe,
The haunch a bit pointed, the turn of the waist,
    Like a snake aroused to strike,

Elle est bien jeune encor! — Son âme exaspérée
    Et ses sens par l'ennui mordus
S'étaient-ils entr'ouverts à la meute altérée
    Des désirs errants et perdus?

L'homme vindicatif que tu n'as pu, vivante,
    Malgré tant d'amour, assouvir,
Combla-t-il sur ta chair inerte et complaisante
    L'immensité de son désir?

Réponds, cadavre impur! et par tes tresses roides
    Te soulevant d'un bras fiévreux,
Dis-moi, tête effrayante, a-t-il sur tes dents froides
    Collé les suprêmes adieux?

— Loin du monde railleur, loin de la foule impure,
    Loin des magistrats curieux,
Dors en paix, dors en paix, étrange créature,
    Dans ton tombeau mystérieux;

Ton époux court le monde, et ta forme immortelle
    Veille prés de lui quand il dort;
Autant que toi sans doute il te sera fidèle,
    Et constant jusques à la mort.

110a. Lesbos

Mère des jeux latins et des voluptés grecques,
Lesbos, où les baisers, languissants ou joyeux,
Chauds comme les soleils, frais comme les pastèques,
Font l'ornement des nuits et des jours glorieux;
Mère des jeux latins et des voluptés grecques,

She is still in her youth!—Did her sickness of soul
  And her senses gnawed by ennui
Open to her that depraved pack of lusts
  And encourage them willingly?

That intractable man whom alive you could not,
  Despite so much love, satisfy,
Did he there, on your still and amenable corpse,
  His appetite gratify?*

Tell me, cadaver! and by your stiff hair
  Raising with feverous hand,
Terrible head, did he paste on your teeth
  His kisses again and again?

—Far away from the world, from the taunts of the mob,
  Far from the prying police,
Strange creature, within your mysterious tomb
  I bid you to sleep in peace.

Your bridegroom may roam, but the image of you
  Stands by him wherever he rests;
As much as you, doubtless, the man will be true,
  And faithful even till death.

110a. Lesbos

Mother of Roman games and Greek delights,
Lesbos,* where kisses languorous or glad,
As hot as suns, or watermelon-fresh,
Make festivals of days and glorious nights;
Mother of Roman games and Greek delights,

Lesbos, où les baisers sont comme les cascades
Qui se jettent sans peur les gouffres sans fonds,
Et courent, sanglotant et gloussant par saccades,
Orageux et secrets, fourmillants et profonds;
Lesbos, où les baisers sont comme les cascades!

Lesbos, où les Phrynés l'une l'autre s'attirent,
Où jamais un soupir ne resta sans écho,
A l'égal de Paphos les étoiles t'admirent,
Et Vénus à bon droit peut jalouser Sapho!
Lesbos, où les Phrynés l'une l'autre s'attirent,

Lesbos, terre des nuits chaudes et langoureuses,
Qui font qu'à leurs miroirs, stérile volupté!
Les filles aux yeux creux, de leurs corps amoureuses,
Caressent les fruits mûrs de leur nubilité;
Lesbos, terre des nuits chaudes et langoureuses,

Laisse du vieux Platon se froncer l'œil austère;
Tu tires ton pardon de l'excès des baisers,
Reine du doux empire, aimable et noble terre,
Et des raffinements toujours inépuisés.
Laisse du vieux Platon se froncer l'œil austère.

Tu tires ton pardon de l'éternel martyre,
Infligé sans relâche aux cœurs ambitieux,
Qu'attire loin de nous le radieux sourire
Entrevu vaguement au bord des autres cieux!
Tu tires ton pardon de l'éternel martyre!

Qui des Dieux osera, Lesbos, être ton juge
Et condamner ton front pâli dans les travaux,
Si ses balances d'or n'ont pesé le déluge
De larmes qu'à la mer ont versé tes ruisseaux?
Qui des Dieux osera, Lesbos, être ton juge?

Lesbos, where love is like the wild cascades
That throw themselves into the deepest gulfs,
And twist and run with gurglings and with sobs,
Stormy and secret, swarming underground;
Lesbos, where love is like the wild cascades!

Lesbos, where Phrynes* seek each other out,
Where no sigh ever went without response,
Lovely as Paphos* in the sight of stars,
Where Venus envies Sappho,* with good cause!
Lesbos, where Phrynes seek each other out.

Lesbos, land of the warm and languid nights
That draw in mirrors sterile fantasies,
So girls with hollow eyes make love alone,
Fondling their avid bodies' mellow fruit;
Lesbos, land of the warm and languid nights,

Let some dry Plato* frown with narrowed eye;
Queen of sweet empire—pleasant, noble land—
You're pardoned by the excess of your kisses,
And by your endless subtleties in love.
Let some dry Plato frown with narrowed eye.

You're pardoned by eternal martyrdom
Lived constantly in those with hungering hearts
Who glimpse that radiant smile beyond our grasp
That beckons from the brink of other skies!
You're pardoned by eternal martyrdom!

What God would dare to act as Lesbos' judge
And to condemn your pale and wasted brow,
Without the weighing in those golden scales
Of floods of tears your brooks have swept to sea?
What God would dare to act as Lesbos' judge?

Que nous veulent les lois du juste et de l'injuste?
Vierges au cœur sublime, honneur de l'archipel,
Votre religion comme une autre est auguste,
Et l'amour se rira de l'Enfer et du Ciel!
Que nous veulent les lois du juste et de l'injuste?

Car Lesbos entre tous m'a choisi sur la terre
Pour chanter le secret de ses vierges en fleurs,
Et je fus dès l'enfance admis au noir mystère
Des rires effrénés mêlés aux sombres pleurs;
Car Lesbos entre tous m'a choisi sur la terre.

Et depuis lors je veille au sommet de Leucate,
Comme une sentinelle à l'œil perçant et sûr,
Qui guette nuit et jour brick, tartane ou frégate,
Dont les formes au loin frissonnent dans l'azur;
Et depuis lors je veille au sommet de Leucate

Pour savoir si la mer est indulgente et bonne,
Et parmi les sanglots dont le roc retentit
Un soir ramènera vers Lesbos, qui pardonne,
Le cadavre adoré de Sapho, qui partit
Pour savoir si la mer est indulgente et bonne!

De la mâle Sapho, l'amante et le poëte,
Plus belle que Vénus par ses mornes pâleurs!
— L'œil d'azur est vaincu par l'œil noir que tachète
Le cercle ténébreux tracé par les douleurs
De la mâle Sapho, l'amante et le poëte!

— Plus belle que Vénus se dressant sur le monde
Et versant les trésors de sa sérénité
Et le rayonnement de sa jeunesse blonde
Sur le vieil Océan de sa fille enchanté;
Plus belle que Vénus se dressant sur le monde!

What do we care for laws of right and wrong?
Maidens of highest heart, pride of the land,
As worthy as another's is your creed,
And love will laugh at Heaven and at Hell!
What do we care for laws of right and wrong!

Since I am Lesbos' choice from all on earth
To sing the secret of her flowering maids,
And I from childhood worshipped in the cult
Of frenzied laughter mixed with sombre tears—
Since I am Lesbos' choice from all on earth,

I spend my time on watch from Leucas' peak,*
A sentinel with sure and piercing eye,
Who searches night and day for sail or hull,
The distant forms that tremble in the blue;
I spend my time on watch from Leucas' peak

To find out if the sea is ever kind,
And to the land where sobbing lives in stones
Will carry home, to Lesbos who forgives,
The worshipped corpse of Sappho, who made trial
To find out if the sea is ever kind!

Of Sappho, male in poetry and love,
Fairer than Venus, though her face be pale!
—The azure eye is conquered by the black
Shadowed by circles drawn by all the grief
Of Sappho, male in poetry and love!

—Fairer than Venus rising on the world
Who spreads out treasures of serenity
And all the radiance of her blonde youth
On father Ocean, dazzled by his child;
Fairer than Venus rising on the world!

— De Sapho qui mourut le jour de son blasphème,
Quand, insultant le rite et le culte inventé,
Elle fit son beau corps la pâture suprême
D'un brutal dont l'orgueil punit l'impiété
De celle qui mourut le jour de son blasphème.

Et c'est depuis ce temps que Lesbos se lamente,
Et, malgré les honneurs que lui rend l'univers,
S'enivre chaque nuit du cri de la tourmente
Que poussent vers les cieux ses rivages déserts!
Et c'est depuis ce temps que Lesbos se lament!

110b. Femmes damnées: Delphine et Hippolyte

A la pâle clarté des lampes languissantes,
Sur de profonds coussins tout imprégnés d'odeur,
Hippolyte rêvait aux caresses puissantes
Qui levaient le rideau de sa jeune candeur.

Elle cherchait, d'un œil troublé par la tempête,
De sa naïveté le ciel déjà lointain,
Ainsi qu'un voyageur qui retourne la tête
Vers les horizons bleus dépassés le matin.

De ses yeux amortis les paresseuses larmes,
L'air brisé, la stupeur, la morne volupté,
Ses bras vaincus, jetés comme de vaines armes,
Tout servait, tout parait sa fragile beauté.

Étendue à ses pieds, calme et pleine de joie,
Delphine la couvait avec des yeux ardents,
Comme un animal fort qui surveille une proie,
Après l'avoir d'abord marquée avec les dents.

—Of Sappho who that day blasphemed and died,
When she, against the rite the cult devised,
Let her sweet body be the rutting-ground
For a brute whose pride condemned the heresy
Of one who on that day blasphemed and died.

And since that time Lesbos has lived with tears;
Neglecting honours that the world holds forth,
She stupefies herself each night with cries
That beat her barren shores against the skies!
And since that time Lesbos has lived with tears!

110b. Condemned Women: Delphine and Hippolyta

Within the dwindling glow of light from languid lamps,
Sunk in the softest cushions soaked with heady scent,
Hippolyta lay dreaming of the thrilling touch
That spread apart the veil of her young innocence.

She searched with troubled eye, afflicted by the storm,
For the once-distant sky of her naïvety,
A voyager who turns and looks beyond the wake
To blue horizons which had once been overhead.

The heavy tears that fell from dull and weary eyes,
The broken look, the stupor, the voluptuousness,
Her conquered arms thrown down, surrendered in the field,
All strangely served her still, to show her fragile charm.

Stretched calmly at her feet, joyfully satisfied,
Delphine looked up at her with those compelling eyes
Like a strong animal that oversees her prey,
First having taken care to mark it with her teeth.

Beauté forte à genoux devant la beauté frêle,
Superbe, elle humait voluptueusement
Le vin de son triomphe, et s'allongeait vers elle,
Comme pour recueillir un doux remercîment.

Elle cherchait dans l'œil de sa pâle victime
Le cantique muet que chante le plaisir,
Et cete gratitude infinie et sublime
Qui sort de la paupière ainsi qu'un long soupir.

— 'Hippolyte, cher cœur, que dis-tu de ces choses?
Comprends-tu maintenant qu'il ne faut pas offrir
L'holocauste sacré de tes premières roses
Aux souffles violents qui pourraient les flétrir?

Mes baisers sont légers comme ces éphémères
Qui caressent le soir les grands lacs transparents,
Et ceux de ton amant creuseront leurs ornières
Comme des chariots ou des socs déchirants;

Ils passeront sur toi comme un lourd attelage
De chevaux et de bœufs aux sabots sans pitié . . .
Hippolyte, ô ma sœur! tourne donc ton visage,
Toi, mon âme et mon cœur, mon tout et ma moitié,

Tourne vers moi tes yeux pleins d'azur et d'étoiles!
Pour un de ces regards charmants, baume divin,
Des plaisirs plus obscurs je lèverai les voiles
Et je t'endormirai dans un rêve sans fin!'

Mais Hippolyte alors, levant sa jeune tête:
— 'Je ne suis point ingrate et ne me repens pas,
Ma Delphine, je souffre et je suis inquiète,
Comme après un nocturne et terrible repas.

Je sens fondre sur moi de lourdes épouvantes
Et de noirs bataillons de fantômes épars,
Qui veulent me conduire en des routes mouvantes
Qu'un horizon sanglant ferme de toutes parts.

Strong beauty on her knees before frail beauty's couch,
Superb, luxurious, she breathed completely in
The wine of triumph, and she stretched out towards her love
As if to gather in a kiss of recompense.

She looked within the eye of that pale conquered soul
For silent canticles, chanting of love's delight
And of that gratitude, sublime and infinite,
Which from the eyelids spreads like a soft-breathing sigh.

—'Hippolyta, dear heart, what do you have to say?
Now do you understand you do not need to give
The sacred offering of roses of your youth
To one who'd wither them with his tempestuous breath?

My kisses are as light as mayflies on the wing
Caressing in the dusk the great transparent lakes.
But those your lover gives dig out their cruel ruts
Like chariots, or like the farmer's biting plough;

They pass across you like a heavy, coupled team—
Pitiless horses' tread, or oxen's brutal hooves . . .
Sister Hippolyta! then turn your face to me.
My darling, heart and soul, my better self, my all,

Turn down to me your eyes, so blue and full of stars!
For just one charming glance, divinely healing balm,
I'll raise the veil for you of pleasure's secret depths,
And lull you fast asleep within an endless dream!'

But then Hippolyta, lifting her troubled head:
—'My Delphine, do not think that I repent our love;
I'm not ungrateful, but I suffer in distress
As if I'd been a part of some strange feast at night.

I feel such heavy dread dissolving over me,
And black battalions of a scattered troop of ghosts
Who wish to lead me off on roads that shift and move
Beneath a bloody sky that closes all around.

Avons-nous donc commis une action étrange?
Explique, si tu peux, mon trouble et mon effroi:
Je frissonne de peur quand tu me dis: "Mon ange!"
Et cependant je sens ma bouche aller vers toi.

Ne me regarde pas ainsi, toi, ma pensée!
Toi que j'aime à jamais, ma sœur d'élection,
Quand même tu serais une embûche dressée
Et le commencement de ma perdition!'

Delphine, secouant sa crinière tragique,
Et comme trépignant sur le trépied de fer,
L'œil fatal, répondit d'une voix despotique:
— 'Qui donc devant l'amour ose parler d'enfer?

Maudit soit à jamais le rêveur inutile
Qui voulut le premier, dans sa stupidité,
S'éprenant d'un problème insoluble et stérile,
Aux choses de l'amour mêler l'honnêteté!

Celui qui veut unir dans un accord mystique
L'ombre avec la chaleur, la nuit avec le jour,
Ne chauffera jamais son corps paralytique
A ce rouge soleil que l'on nomme l'amour!

Va, si tu veux, chercher un fiancé stupide;
Cours offrir un cœur vierge à ses cruels baisers;
Et, pleine de remords et d'horreur, et livide,
Tu me rapporteras tes seins stigmatisés . . .

On ne peut ici-bas contenter qu'un seul maître!'
Mais l'enfant, épanchant une immense douleur,
Cria soudain: — 'Je sens s'élargir dans mon être
Un abîme béant; cet abîme est mon cœur!

Brûlant comme un volcan, profond comme le vide!
Rien ne rassasiera ce monstre gémissant
Et ne rafraîchira la soif de l'Euménide
Qui, la torche à la main, le brûle jusqu'au sang.

Have we committed then a strange, forbidden act?
Please, if you can, explain my trouble and my fright:
I shake and tremble when you say to me "my love!"
And still I feel my mouth is yearning at your call.

My heart's-ease and my dear, don't look at me that way!
O sister of my choice, you'll always be my love,
And even though you were an ambush ready-set,
The first disturbing step along the road to Hell!'

Delphine, then, rising up to shake her tragic mane,
As if before the tripod,* stamping furiously,
Flashing her fatal eye, answered in despot's voice:
—'Who in the face of love dares speak to me of Hell!

Accursed may he be, the one with useless dreams
Who in stupidity, promoting to the world
A sterile conundrum, impossible to solve,
First sought to mix the ways of virtue and of love!

Anyone who could join within a mystic bond
Shadow with glowing heat, the night-time with the day,
Never will come to warm his paralytic flesh
At this refulgent sun, which people know as love!

Go, if you will, and find some brutish fiancé;
Go give a virgin heart to torturous embrace;
And, livid, with your fill of horror and remorse,
Come running back to me with scars across your breasts . .

In this world only one true master can be served!'
But the unhappy child poured out a giant grief
As suddenly she cried:—'I feel within my soul
An opening abyss: this chasm is my heart!

Deep as the void, with a volcano's boiling heat!
This fierce and moaning monster nothing can assuage,
And nothing can refresh the Furies'* fiery thirst,
Who, torch in hand, will burn the flesh down to the blood!

Que nos rideaux fermés nous séparent du monde,
Et que la lassitude amène le repos!
Je veux m'anéantir dans ta gorge profonde,
Et trouver sur ton sein la fraîcheur des tombeaux!'

— Descendez, descendez, lamentables victimes,
Descendez le chemin de l'enfer éternel!
Plongez au plus profond du gouffre, où tous les crimes,
Flagellés par un vent qui ne vient pas du ciel,

Bouillonnent pêle-mêle avec un bruit d'orage.
Ombres folles, courez au but de vos désirs;
Jamais vous ne pourrez assouvir votre rage,
Et votre châtiment naîtra de vos plaisirs.

Jamais un rayon frais n'éclaira vos cavernes;
Par les fentes des murs des miasmes fiévreux
Filtrent en s'enflamment ainsi que des lanternes
Et pénètrent vos corps de leurs parfums affreux.

L'âpre stérilité de votre jouissance
Altère votre soif et roidit votre peau,
Et le vent furibond de la concupiscence
Fait claquer votre chair ainsi qu'un vieux drapeau.

Loin des peuples vivants, errantes, condamnées,
A travers les déserts courez comme les loups;
Faites votre destin, âmes désordonnées,
Et fuyez l'infini que vous portez en vous!

111. Femmes damnées

Comme un bétail pensif sur le sable couchées,
Elles tournent leurs yeux vers l'horizon des mers,
Et leurs pieds se cherchant et leurs mains rapprochées
Ont de douces langueurs des frissons amers.

Let our closed curtains, then, remove us from the world,
And let our lassitude allow us to find rest!
I would obliterate myself upon your throat
And find the coolness of the tombs within your breast!'

—Descend, you victims,* oh lamentably descend,
Descend along the path to the eternal Hell!
Plunge on into the gulf where all the shameful crimes,
Those foolish shadows, run at limits of desire,

Seething this way and that with a great thunderous noise,
Flogged by a heavy wind that never saw the sky;
There never will you find your passion satisfied,
And your torment will be your pleasure's awful child.

Never a freshening ray will shine within your caves;
Through cracks along the wall will filter deadly mists
That cast a lantern's glow of pale and dismal flame
And penetrate your bodies with perfumes of death.

The harsh sterility of all your acts of lust
Will bring a dreadful thirst and stiffen out your skin,
And your concupiscence become a furious wind
To snap your feeble flesh like an old, weathered flag.

Far from the living world, wandering and condemned,
Across the desert wastes, go running like the wolves;
Make out your destiny, you poor disordered souls,
And flee the infinite you carry in yourselves!

111. Condemned Women

Like pensive cattle lying on the sands
They gaze upon the endless seas, until
Feet grope for feet, and hands close over hands,
In languid sweetness or with quivering chill.

Les unes, cœurs épris de longues confidences,
Dans le fond des bosquets où jasent les ruisseaux,
Vont épelant l'amour des craintives enfances
Et creusent le bois vert des jeunes arbrisseaux;

D'autres, comme des sœurs, marchent lentes et graves
A travers les rochers pleins d'apparitions,
Où saint Antoine a vu surgir comme des laves
Les seins nus et pourprés de ses tentations;

Il en est, aux lueurs des résines croulantes,
Qui dans le creux muet des vieux antres païens
T'appellent au secours de leurs fièvres hurlantes,
Ô Bacchus, endormeur des remords anciens!

Et d'autres, dont la gorge aime les scapulaires,
Qui, recélant un fouet sous leurs longs vêtements,
Mêlent, dans le bois sombre et les nuits solitaires,
L'écume du plaisir aux larmes des tourments.

Ô vierges, ô démons, ô monstres, ô martyres,
De la réalité grands esprits contempteurs,
Chercheuses d'infini, dévotes et satyres,
Tantôt pleines de cris, tantôt pleines de pleurs,

Vous que dans votre enfer mon âme a poursuivies,
Pauvres sœurs, je vous aime autant que je vous plains,
Pour vos mornes douleurs, vos soifs inassouvies,
Et les urnes d'amour dont vos grands cœurs sont pleins!

112. Les Deux Bonnes Sœurs

La Débauche et la Mort sont deux aimables filles,
Prodigues de baisers et riches de santé,
Dont le flanc toujours vierge et drapé de guenilles
Sous l'éternel labeur n'a jamais enfanté.

Some, with full hearts from long and private talk
In deep groves, where the brooks will chide and tease,
Spell out the love of fretful girlishness,
Carving the fresh green wood of tender trees.

Others, like sisters, walk with stately pace
Where apparitions live in craggy piles,
Where rose like lava for St Anthony*
The naked, purple breasts of his great trial.

Some there may be, by sinking resin glow,
Deep in a cave where ancient pagans met,
Who call to help for fevers in a rage,
O Bacchus,* silencer of all regret!

And others, with a taste for monkish cloaks,
Who, secreting a lash beneath the cloth,
Within the woods, through solitary nights,
Mingle with tears of pain their passion's froth.

O maidens, demons, monsters—martyrs all,
Spirits disdainful of reality,
Satyrs and seekers of the infinite
With rain of tears or cries of ecstasy,

You whom my soul has followed to your hell,
Poor sisters, let me pity and approve—
For all your leaden griefs, for slakeless thi.sts,
And for your hearts, great urns that ache with love!

112. The Two Good Sisters

Debauch and Death are a fine, healthy pair
Of girls, whose love is prodigal and free.
Their virgin wombs, beneath the rags they wear,
Are barren, though they labour constantly.

Au poëte sinistre, ennemi des familles,
Favori de l'enfer, courtisan mal renté,
Tombeaux et lupanars montrent sous leurs charmilles
Un lit que le remords n'a jamais fréquenté.

Et la bière et l'alcôve en blasphèmes fécondes
Nous offrent tour à tour, comme deux bonnes sœurs,
De terribles plaisirs et d'affreuses douceurs.

Quand veux-tu m'enterrer, Débauche aux bras immondes?
Ô Mort, quand viendras-tu, sa rivale en attraits,
Sur ses myrtes infects enter tes noirs cyprès?

113. La Fontaine de sang

Il me semble parfois que mon sang coule à flots,
Ainsi qu'une fontaine aux rythmiques sanglots.
Je l'entends bien qui coule avec un long murmure,
Mais je me tâte en vain pour trouver la blessure.

A travers la cité, comme dans un champ clos,
Il s'en va, transformant les pavés en îlots,
Désaltérant la soif de chaque créature,
Et partout colorant en rouge la nature.

J'ai demandé souvent à des vins captieux
D'endormir pour un jour la terreur qui me mine;
Le vin rend l'œil plus clair et l'oreille plus fine!

J'ai cherché dans l'amour un sommeil oublieux;
Mais l'amour n'est pour moi qu'un matelas d'aiguilles
Fait pour donner à boire à ces cruelles filles!

To the arch poet, foe of families,
Hell's favourite, a cut-rate whore at court,
Brothels and tombs show in dark galleries
A bed never frequented by remorse.

And coffin, alcove, rich in blasphemy,
As two good sisters would, offer as treats
Terrible pleasures, horrifying sweets.

Debauch, when will your clutches bury me?
O rival Death, will you be coming now
To graft black cypress to her myrtle bough?*

113. The Fountain of Blood

Sometimes it seems my blood spurts out in gobs
As if it were a fountain's pulsing sobs;
I clearly hear it mutter as it goes,
Yet cannot find the wound from which it flows.

Then through the city, coursing in the lists,
It travels, forming islands in its midst,
Seeing that every creature will be fed
And staining nature its flamboyant red.

Oh, I have asked of wine the magic way
To drug my terrors, even for a day;
Wine clears the eye, makes hearing more distinct!

I've sought forgetfulness in love, but failed,
Since love for me is just a bed of nails
Made to provide these women* bloody drink!

114. Allégorie

C'est une femme belle et de riche encolure,
Qui laisse dans son vin traîner sa chevelure.
Les griffes de l'amour, les poisons du tripot,
Tout glisse et tout s'émousse au granit de sa peau
Elle rit à la Mort et nargue la Débauche,
Ces monstres dont la main, qui toujours gratte et fauche,
Dans ses jeux destructeurs a pourtant respecté
De ce corps ferme et droit la rude majesté.
Elle marche en déesse et repose en sultane;
Elle a dans le plaisir la foi mahométane,
Et dans ses bras ouverts, que remplissent ses seins,
Elle appelle des yeux la race des humains.
Elle croit, elle sait, cette vierge inféconde
Et pourtant nécessaire à la marche du monde,
Que la beauté du corps est un sublime don
Qui de toute infamie arrache le pardon.
Elle ignore l'Enfer comme le Purgatoire,
Et quand l'heure viendra d'entrer dans la Nuit noire,
Elle regardera la face de la Mort,
Ainsi qu'un nouveau-né, — sans haine et sans remord.

115. La Béatrice

Dans des terrains cendreux, calcinés, sans verdure,
Comme je me plaignais un jour à la nature,
Et que de ma pensée, en vaguant au hasard,
J'aiguisais lentement sur mon cœur le poignard,
Je vis en plein midi descendre sur ma tête
Un nuage funèbre et gros d'une tempête,
Qui portait un troupeau de démons vicieux,
Semblables à des nains cruels et curieux.
A me considérer froidement ils se mirent,

114. Allegory

Picture a beauty, shoulders rich and fine,
Letting her long hair trail into her wine.
Talons of love, the poison tooth of sin
Slip and are dulled against her granite skin.
She laughs at Death and flouts Debauchery;
Those fiends who in their heavy pleasantries
Gouge and destroy, still keep a strange regard
For majesty—her body strong and hard.
A goddess, or a sultan's regal wife—
A faithful Paynim of voluptuous life—
Her eyes call mortal beings to the charms
Of ready breasts, between her open arms.
She feels, she knows—this maid, this barren girl
By our desire fit to move the world—
The gift of body's beauty is sublime
And draws forgiveness out of every crime.
She knows no Hell, or any afterlife,
And when her time shall come to face the Night
She'll meet Death like a newborn, face to face
In innocence—with neither guilt nor hate.

115. A Beatrice*

One day in ashy, cindery terrains,
As I meandered, making my complaint
To nature, slowly sharpening the knife
Of thought against the whetstone of my heart,
In plainest day I saw around my head
A lowering cloud as weighty as a storm,
Which bore within a vicious demon throng
Who showed themselves as cruel and curious dwarfs.
Disdainfully they circled and observed

Et, comme des passants sur un fou qu'ils admirent,
Je les entendis rire et chuchoter entre eux,
En échangeant maint signe et maint clignement d'yeux:

— 'Contemplons à loisir cette caricature
Et cette ombre d'Hamlet imitant sa posture,
Le regard indécis et les cheveux au vent.
N'est-ce pas grand'pitié de voir ce bon vivant,
Ce gueux, cet histrion en vacances, ce drôle,
Parce qu'il sait jouer artistement son rôle,
Vouloir intéresser au chant de ses douleurs
Les aigles, les grillons, les ruisseaux et les fleurs,
Et même à nous, auteurs de ces vieilles rubriques,
Réciter en hurlant ses tirades publiques?'

J'aurais pu (mon orgueil aussi haut que les monts
Domine la nuée et le cri des démons)
Détourner simplement ma tête souveraine,
Si je n'eusse pas vu parmi leur troupe obscène,
Crime qui n'a pas fait chanceler le soleil!
La reine de mon cœur au regard nonpareil,
Qui riait avec eux de ma sombre détresse
Et leur versait parfois quelque sale caresse.

115a. Les Métamorphoses du vampire

La femme cependant, de sa bouche de fraise,
En se tordant ainsi qu'un serpent sur la braise,
Et pétrissant ses seins sur le fer de son busc,
Laissait couler ces mots tout imprégnés de musc:
— 'Moi, j'ai la lèvre humide, et je sais la science
De perdre au fond d'un lit l'antique conscience.
Je sèche tous les pleurs sur mes seins triomphants,
Et fais rire les vieux du rire des enfants.
Je remplace, pour qui me voit nue et sans voiles,
La lune, le soleil, le ciel et les étoiles!

And, as a madman draws a crowd to jokes,
I heard them laugh and whisper each to each,
Giving their telling nudges and their winks:

'Now is the time to roast this comic sketch,
This shadow-Hamlet, who takes the pose—
The indecisive stare and straying hair.
A pity, isn't it, to see this fraud,
This posturer, this actor on relief?
Because he plays his role with some slight art
He thinks his shabby whining entertains
The eagles, and the insects, brooks and flowers.
Even to us, who wrote these trite charades,
He mouths the speeches of his paltry show.'

I had authority (my giant pride
Can easily disperse that chattering rout)
And simply could have turned my sovereign head,
Had I not seen, among that filthy troupe,
O crime that did not make the sun to swerve!
My heart's bright queen, she of the matchless gaze,
Who laughed with those who fed on my distress,
And stroked them more than once with low caress.

115a. The Metamorphoses of the Vampire

Twisting and writhing like a snake on fiery sands,
Kneading her breast against her corset's metal bands,
The woman, meanwhile, from her mouth of strawberry
Let flow these fragrant words of musky mystery:
—'I have the moistest lip, and well I know the skill
Within a bed's soft heart, to lose the moral will.
I dry up all your tears on my triumphant bust
And make the old ones laugh like children, in their lust.
I take the place for those who see my naked arts
Of moon and of the sun and all the other stars.

Je suis, mon cher savant, si docte aux voluptés,
Lorsque j'étouffe un homme en mes bras redoutés,
Ou lorsque j'abandonne aux morsures mon buste,
Timide et libertine, et fragile et robuste,
Que sur ces matelas qui se pâment d'émoi,
Les anges impuissants se damneraient pour moi!'

Quand elle eut de mes os sucé toute la moelle,
Et que languissamment je me tournai vers elle
Pour lui rendre un baiser d'amour, je ne vis plus
Qu'une outre aux flancs gluants, toute pleine de pus!
Je fermai les deux yeux, dans ma froide épouvante,
Et quand je les rouvris à la clarté vivante,
A mes côtés, au lieu de mannequin puissant
Qui semblait avoir fait provision de sang,
Tremblaient confusément des débris de squelette,
Qui d'eux-mêmes rendaient le cri d'une girouette
Ou d'une enseigne, au bout d'une tringle de fer,
Que balance le vent pendant les nuits d'hiver.

116. Un voyage à Cythère

Mon cœur, comme un oiseau, voltigeait tout joyeux
Et planait librement à l'entour des cordages;
Le navire roulait sous un ciel sans nuages,
Comme un ange enivré d'un soleil radieux.

Quelle est cette île triste et noire? — C'est Cythère,
Nous dit-on, un pays fameux dans les chansons,
Eldorado banal de tous les vieux garçons.
Regardez, après tout, c'est une pauvre terre.

— Île des doux secrets et des fêtes du cœur!
De l'antique Vénus le superbe fantôme
Au-dessus de tes mers plane comme un arome,
Et charge les esprits d'amour et de langueur.

I am, my dear savant, so studied in my charms
That when I stifle men within my ardent arms
Or when I give my breast to their excited bites,
Shy or unrestrained, of passionate delight,
On all those mattresses that swoon in ecstasy
Even helpless angels damn themselves for me!'

When she had drained the marrow out of all my bones,
When I turned listlessly amid my languid moans,
To give a kiss of love, no thing was with me but
A greasy leather flask that overflowed with pus!
Frozen with terror, then, I clenched both of my eyes;
When I reopened them into the living light
I saw I was beside no vampire mannequin
That lived by having sucked the blood out of my skin,
But bits of skeleton, some rattling remains
That spoke out with the clacking of a weathervane,
Or of a hanging shop sign, on an iron spike,
Swung roughly by the wind on gusty winter nights.

116. A Voyage to Cythera*

My heart was like a bird that fluttered joyously
And glided free among the tackle and the lines!
The vessel rolled along under a cloudless sky—
An angel, tipsy, gay, full of the radiant sun.

What is that sad black isle? I asked as we approached—
They call it Cythera, land to write songs about,
Banal Utopia of veterans of love;
But look, it seems to be a poor land after all.

—Island of sweet intrigues, and feastings of the heart!
The ghost of ancient Venus the magnificent
Glides like a haunting scent above your swelling seas,
Enrapturing the soul in languishing and love.

Belle île aux myrtes verts, pleine de fleurs écloses,
Vénérée à jamais par toute nation,
Où les soupirs des cœurs en adoration
Roulent comme l'encens sur un jardin de roses

Ou le roucoulement éternel d'un ramier!
— Cythère n'était plus qu'un terrain des plus maigres,
Un désert rocailleux troublé par des cris aigres.
J'entrevoyais pourtant un objet singulier!

Ce n'était pas un temple aux ombres bocagères,
Où la jeune prêtresse, amoureuse des fleurs,
Allait, le corps brûlé de secrètes chaleurs,
Entre-bâillant sa robe aux brises passagères;

Mais voilà qu'en rasant la côte d'assez près
Pour troubler les oiseaux avec nos voiles blanches,
Nous vîmes que c'était un gibet à trois branches,
Du ciel se détachant en noir, comme un cyprès.

De féroces oiseaux perchés sur leur pâture
Détruisaient avec rage un pendu déjà mûr,
Chacun plantant, comme un outil, son bec impur
Dans tous les coins saignants de cette pourriture;

Les yeux étaient deux trous, et du ventre effondré
Les intestins pesants lui coulaient sur les cuisses,
Et ses bourreaux, gorgés de hideuses délices,
L'avaient à coups de bec absolument châtré.

Sous les pieds, un troupeau de jaloux quadrupèdes,
Le museau relevé, tournoyait et rôdait;
Une plus grande bête au milieu s'agitait
Comme un exécuteur entouré de ses aides.

Habitant de Cythère, enfant d'un ciel si beau,
Silencieusement tu souffrais ces insultes
En expiation de tes infâmes cultes
Et des péchés qui t'ont interdit le tombeau.

Sweet isle of greenery, myrtle and blooming flowers,
Perpetual delight of those in every land,
Where sighs of adoration from the hearts of lovers
Roll as incense does over a rosy bower,

Or like the constant crooning of a turtle-dove!
—Cythera was an island barren in terrain,
A mere deserted rock, disturbed by piercing cries.
But on it I could glimpse a curious device!

No temple was this thing, among the woodland shades,
Where the young worshipper, the flowers' devotee,
Would tarry, body burning, hot with secret lusts,
Her robe half-open to the fleeting wisps of breeze;

But as we skimmed the shore, fairly near enough
To agitate the birds with swelling of our sails,
What we saw was a gibbet, made of three great stakes.
It reared against the sky, black, as a cypress stands.

Ferocious birds were gathered, snatching at their food,
Raging around a hanging shape already ripe;
Each creature worked his tool, his dripping filthy beak,
Into the bleeding corners of this rottenness.

The eyes were two blank gaps, and from the hollow paunch
Its tangled guts let loose, spilling over the thighs,
And those tormentors, gorged with hideous delights,
Had castrated the corpse with snapping of their beaks.

Under the feet, a troupe of jealous quadrupeds,
The muzzle lifted high, eddied and prowled about;
One larger, bolder beast was restless all the more,
The leader of the pack, surrounded by his aides.

Dweller in Cythera,* child of a sky so clear,
In silence you endure these desecrations—
In expiation for your infamous beliefs
And crimes which have denied you proper burial.

Ridicule pendu, tes douleurs sont les miennes!
Je sentis, à l'aspect de tes membres flottants,
Comme un vomissement, remonter vers mes dents
Le long fleuve de fiel des douleurs anciennes;

Devant toi, pauvre diable au souvenir si cher,
J'ai senti tous les becs et toutes les mâchoires
Des corbeaux lancinants et des panthères noires
Qui jadis aimaient tant à triturer ma chair.

— Le ciel était charmant, la mer était unie;
Pour moi tout était noir et sanglant désormais,
Hélas! et j'avais, comme en un suaire épais,
Le cœur enseveli dans cette allégorie.

Dans ton île, ô Vénus! je n'ai trouvé debout
Qu'un gibet symbolique où pendait mon image...
— Ah! Seigneur! donnez-moi la force et le courage
De contempler mon cœur et mon corps sans dégoût!

117. L'Amour et le crâne

Vieux cul-de-lampe

L'amour est assis sur le crâne
    De l'Humanité,
Et sur ce trône le profane,
    Au rire effronté,

Souffle gaiement des bulles rondes
    Qui montent dans l'air,
Comme pour rejoindre les mondes
    Au fond de l'éther.

Le globe lumineux et frêle
    Prend un grand essor,
Crève et crache son âme grêle
    Comme un songe d'or.

Hanged man, ridiculous, your sorrows are my own!
I feel, in blinding view of your loose-hanging limbs,
A rising to the teeth, a building in my throat
Of a choking spew of gall, and all my ancient griefs;

Along with you, poor devil, dear to memory,
I suffered all the stabs of all the killer crows
And felt the grinding jaws of panthers, cruel and black,
Who once took such delight in feasting on my flesh.

—The sky was ravishing, the sea a very glass;
For me the world was black, and bloody would it be.
Alas! And as within a heavy shroud, I have
Entombed my heart in this perverse allegory!*

Venus, in your black isle not one thing was erect
But the symbolic tree whereon my image hung.
Ah, Lord! I beg of you the courage and the strength
To take without disgust my body and my heart!

117. Passion and the Skull

An Old Colophon*

Passion sits on the skull
    Of Humanity,
And this infidel enthroned
    Laughs shamelessly,

And gaily blows round bubbles
    That will fly,
As if to join with worlds
    Deep in the sky.

Rising on high, the frail
    Luminous globe,
Shatters and bursts its slim soul
    Like a dream of gold.

J'entends la crâne à chaque bulle
  Prier et gémir:
'Ce jeu féroce et ridicule
  Quand doit-il finir?

Car ce que ta bouche cruelle
  Éparpille en l'air.
Monstre assassin, c'est ma cervelle,
  Mon sang et ma chair!'

I hear at each bubble, the skull
   Moan and contend:
'This vicious, ridiculous game,
   When will it end?

What you are blowing away
   Again and again,
You murderous fiend, is my body
   My blood and my brain!'

Révolte

Revolt

118. Le Reniement de saint Pierre

Qu'est-ce que Dieu fait donc de ce flot d'anathèmes
Qui monte tous les jours vers ses chers Séraphins?
Comme un tyran gorgé de viande et de vins,
Il s'endort au doux bruit de nos affreux blasphèmes.

Le sanglots des martyrs et des suppliciés
Sont une symphonie enivrante sans doute,
Puisque, malgré le sang que leur volupté coûte,
Les cieux ne s'en sont point encore rassasiés!

— Ah! Jésus, souviens-toi du Jardin des Olives!
Dans ta simplicité tu priais à genoux
Celui qui dans son ciel riait au bruit des clous
Que d'ignobles bourreaux plantaient dans tes chairs vives,

Lorsque tu vis cracher sur ta divinité
La crapule du corps de garde et des cuisines,
Et lorsque tu sentis s'enfoncer les épines
Dans ton crâne où vivait l'immense Humanité;

Quand de ton corps brisé la pesanteur horrible
Allongeait tes deux bras distendus, que ton sang
Et ta sueur coulaient de ton front pâlissant,
Quand tu fus devant tous posé comme une cible,

Rêvais-tu de ces jours si brillants et si beaux
Où tu vins pour remplir l'éternelle promesse,
Où tu foulais, monté sur une douce ânesse,
Des chemins tout jonchés de fleurs et de rameaux,

Où, le cœur tout gonflé d'espoir et de vaillance,
Tu fouettais tous ces vils marchands à tour de bras,
Où tu fus maître enfin? Le remords n'a-t-il pas
Pénétré dans ton flanc plus avant que la lance?

118. St Peter's Denial

What, then, has God to say of cursing heresies,
Which rise up like a flood at precious angels' feet?
A self-indulgent tyrant, stuffed with wine and meat,
He sleeps to soothing sounds of monstrous blasphemies.

The sobs of martyred saints and groans of tortured men
No doubt provide the Lord with rapturous symphonies.
And yet the heavenly hosts are scarcely even pleased
In spite of all the blood men dedicate to them.

—Jesus, do you recall the grove of olive trees
Where on your knees, in your simplicity, you prayed
To Him who sat and heard the noise the nailing made
In your live flesh, as villains did their awful deed,

When you saw, spitting on your pure divinity,
Scum from the kitchens, outcasts, guardsmen in disgrace,
And felt the crown of thorns around your gentle face
Piercing your temples, home of our Humanity,

When, like a target, you were raised above the crowd,
When the appalling wrench of broken body's weight
Stretched out your spreading arms, and as your blood and sweat
Streamed down your body, and across your pallid brow,

Did you remember all the days of brilliant calm
You went forth to fulfil the promise made by God,
And on a gentle ass triumphantly you trod
The streets all strewn with blooms and branches of the palms,

When with your heart so full of hope and far from fear,
You lashed with all your might that money-changing lot,*
And were at last the master? O, and then did not
Chagrin strike through your side more keenly than the spear?

— Certes, je sortirai, quant à moi, satisfait
D'un monde où l'action n'est pas la sœur du rêve;
Puissé-je user du glaive et périr par le glaive!
Saint Pierre a renié Jésus ... il a bien fait!

119. Abel et Caïn

I

Race d'Abel, dors, bois et mange;
Dieu te sourit complaisamment.

Race de Caïn, dans la fange
Rampe et meurs misérablement.

Race d'Abel, ton sacrifice
Flatte le nez du Séraphin!

Race de Caïn, ton supplice
Aura-t-il jamais une fin?

Race d'Abel, vois tes semailles
Et ton bétail venir à bien;

Race de Caïn, tes entrailles
Hurlent la faim comme un vieux chien.

Race d'Abel, chauffe ton ventre
A ton foyer patriarcal;

Race de Caïn, dans ton antre
Tremble de froid, pauvre chacal!

Race d'Abel, aime et pullule!
Ton or fait aussi des petits.

—Believe it, as for me, I'll go out satisfied
From this world where the deed and dream do not accord;
Would I might wield the sword, and perish by the sword!
Peter rejected Jesus*... he was justified!

119. Abel and Cain*

I

Race of Abel, sleep and eat;
God smiles on you complacently.

Race of Cain, in mud and filth
You crawl and die in misery.

Abel's race, your sacrifice
Smells sweet to all the Seraphim!

Race of Cain, your punishment,
Will it be ever at an end?

Race of Abel, see your seed,
Your flocks, your cattle come to good;

Race of Cain, like some old dog
Your empty entrails howl for food.

Race of Abel, warm your belly
By the hearth of countrymen;

Race of Cain, you tremble, freezing,
Lonely jackal, in your den!

Race of Abel, multiply—
Even your gold proliferates;

Race de Caïn, cœur qui brûle,
Prends garde à ces grands appétits.

Race d'Abel, tu croîs et broutes
Comme les punaises des bois!

Race de Caïn, sur les routes
Traîne ta famille aux abois.

II

Ah! race d'Abel, ta charogne
Engraissera le sol fumant!

Race de Caïn, ta besogne
N'est pas faite suffisamment;

Race d'Abel, voici ta honte:
Le fer est vaincu par l'épieu!

Race de Caïn, au ciel monte
Et sur la terre jette Dieu!

120. Les Litanies de Satan

Ô toi, le plus savant et le plus beau des Anges,
Dieu trahi par le sort et privé de louanges,

Ô Satan, prends pitié de ma longue misère!

Ô Prince de l'exil, à qui l'on a fait tort,
Et qui, vaincu, toujours te redresse plus fort,

Ô Satan, prends pitié de ma longue misère!

Toi qui sais tout, grand roi des choses souterraines,
Guérisseur familier des angoisses humaines,

Race of Cain, O burning heart,
Take guard against your appetites.

Race of Abel, chew and swell
Like insects swarming through the woods!

Race of Cain, in deep distress
Your people lag on stony roads.

II

Race of Abel, see your shame:
The plough is conquered by the pike!*

Cain, your modern progeny
Have just begun to do your work;

Race of Abel, carrion,
Manure to feed the steaming sod!

Race of Cain, assault the skies
And drag him earthward—bring down God!

120. Litanies* of Satan

O Angel, the most brilliant and most wise,*
A God betrayed by fate, deprived of praise,

Satan, take pity on my misery!

O Prince of exile, you who have been wronged,
Who, even conquered, rises yet more strong,

Satan, take pity on my misery!

Great king who knows the lore the earth imparts,
Intimate healer of our anguished hearts,

Ô Satan, prends pitié de ma longue misère!

Toi qui, même aux lépreux, aux parias maudits,
Enseignes par l'amour le goût du Paradis,

Ô Satan, prends pitié de ma longue misère!

Ô toi qui de la Mort, ta vieille et forte amante,
Engendras l'Espérance,—une folle charmante!

Ô Satan, prends pitié de ma longue misère!

Toi qui fait au proscrit ce regard calme et haut
Qui damne tout un peuple autour d'un échafaud,

Ô Satan, prends pitié de ma longue misère!

Toi qui sais en quels coins des terres envieuses
Le Dieu jaloux cacha les pierres précieuses,

Ô Satan, prends pitié de ma longue misère!

Toi dont l'œil clair connaît les profonds arsenaux
Où dort enseveli le peuple des métaux,

Ô Satan, prends pitié de ma longue misère!

Toi dont la large main cache les précipices
Au somnambule errant au bord des édifices,

Ô Satan, prends pitié de ma longue misère!

Toi qui, magiquement, assouplis les vieux os
De l'ivrogne attardé foulé par les chevaux,

Ô Satan, prends pitié de ma longue misère!

Toi qui, pour consoler l'homme frêle qui souffre,
Nous appris à mêler le salpêtre et le soufre,

Ô Satan, prends pitié de ma longue misère!

Toi qui poses ta marque, ô complice subtil,
Sur le front du Crésus impitoyable et vil,

Ô Satan, prends pitié de ma longue misère!

Satan, take pity on my misery!

Who, even to the leprous, the despised,
Can teach by love the taste for Paradise,

Satan, take pity on my misery!

Who with your old and hardy mistress, Death,
Breeds Hope, a charming lunatic at best,

Satan, take pity on my misery!

Who gives the prisoner his calm disdain,
Who damns the crowds around the guillotine,

Satan, take pity on my misery!

Who knows which corners of the envious lands
The jealous God has picked to hide his gems,

Satan, take pity on my misery!

Whose clear eye sees the deepest-lying stores
Where, buried, sleep the metals and the ores,

Satan, take pity on my misery!

Whose large hand overrides the sudden edge
For the somnambulist who walks the ledge,

Satan, take pity on my misery!

Whose magic gives a strength to ancient bones
Of drunkards trampled on the cobblestones,

Satan, take pity on my misery!

Who, to console us in our fearful lot,
Taught us the mysteries of shell and shot,

Satan, take pity on my misery!

Whose mark, astute accomplice, will be found
On Croesus'* mean and unforgiving brow,

Satan, take pity on my misery!

Toi qui mets dans les yeux et dans le cœur des filles
Le culte de la plaie et l'amour des guenilles,

Ô Satan, prends pitié de ma longue misère!

Bâton des exilés, lampe des inventeurs,
Confesseur des pendus et des conspirateurs,

Ô Satan, prends pitié de ma longue misère!

Père adoptif de ceux qu'en sa noire colère
Du paradis terrestre a chassé Dieu le Père,

Ô Satan, prends pitié de ma longue misère!

Prière
Gloire et louange à toi, Satan, dans les hauteurs
Du Ciel, où tu régnas, et dans les profondeurs
De l'Enfer, où, vaincu, tu rêves en silence!
Fais que mon âme un jour, sous l'Arbre de Science,
Près de toi se repose, à l'heure où sur ton front
Comme un Temple nouveau ses rameaux s'épandront!

Who sees that women's hearts and eyes sustain
The love of rags, the cult of wounds and pain,

Satan, take pity on my misery!

Staff of the exiles, the inventor's lamp,
Confessor of the hanged, plotters and tramps,

Satan, take pity on my misery!

Adoptive father of those ostracized
By God, and banished from his paradise,

Satan, take pity on my misery!

Prayer
Glory and praise to Satan, where you reigned
In Heaven, and in depths of Hell the same,
Where now you dream in silent reverie!
And may my soul take rest beneath the Tree
Of Knowledge* with you, when above your head
Like a new Temple, those great branches spread!

La Mort

Death

121.　La Mort des amants

Nous aurons des lits pleins d'odeurs légères,
Des divans profonds comme des tombeaux,
Et d'étranges fleurs sur des étagères,
Écloses pour nous sous des cieux plus beaux.

Usant à l'envi leurs chaleurs dernières,
Nos deux cœurs seront deux vastes flambeaux,
Qui réfléchiront leurs doubles lumières
Dans nos deux esprits, ces miroirs jumeaux.

Un soir fait de rose et de bleu mystique,
Nous échangerons un éclair unique,
Comme un long sanglot, tout chargé d'adieux;

Et plus tard un Ange, entr'ouvrant les portes,
Viendra ranimer, fidèle et joyeux,
Les miroirs ternis et les flammes mortes.

122.　La Mort des pauvres

C'est la Mort qui console, hélas! et qui fait vivre;
C'est le but de la vie, et c'est le seul espoir
Qui, comme un élixir, nous monte et nous enivre,
Et nous donne le cœur de marcher jusqu'au soir;

A travers la tempête, et la neige, et le givre,
C'est la clarté vibrante à notre horizon noir;
C'est l'auberge fameuse inscrite sur le livre,
Où l'on pourra manger, et dormir, et s'asseoir;

C'est un Ange qui tient dans ses doigts magnétiques
Le sommeil et le don des rêves extatiques,
Et qui refait le lit des gens pauvres et nus;

121. The Death of Lovers

We will have beds imbued with mildest scent,
And couches, deep as tombs, in which to lie,
Flowers around us, strange and opulent,
Blooming on shelves under the finest skies.

Approaching equally their final light,
Our twin hearts will be two great flaming brands
That will be double in each other's sight—
Our souls the mirrors where the image stands.

One evening made of rose and mystic blue
We will flare out, in an epiphany
Like a long sob, charged with our last adieus.

And later, opening the doors, will be
An Angel, who will joyfully reglaze
The tarnished mirrors, and relight the blaze.

122. The Death of the Poor

It is death that consoles and allows us to live.
Alas! that life's end should be all of our hope;
It goes to our heads like a powerful drink,
And gives us the heart to walk into the dark;

Through storm and through snow, through the frost at our feet,
It's the pulsating beacon at limit of sight,
The illustrious inn* that's described in the book,
Where we'll sit ourselves down, and will eat and will sleep;

It's an Angel who holds in his magical grip
Our peace, and the gift of magnificent dreams,
And who makes up the bed of the poor and the bare;

C'est la gloire des Dieux, c'est le grenier mystique,
C'est la bourse du pauvre et sa patrie antique,
C'est le portique ouvert sur les Cieux inconnus!

123. La Mort des artistes

Combien faut-il de fois secouer mes grelots,
Et baiser ton front bas, morne caricature?
Pour piquer dans le but, de mystique nature,
Combien, ô mon carquois, perdre de javelots?

Nous userons notre âme en de subtils complots,
Et nous démolirons mainte lourde armature,
Avant de contempler la grande Créature
Dont l'infernal désir nous remplit de sanglots!

Il en est qui jamais n'ont connu leur Idole,
Et ces sculpteurs damnés et marqués d'un affront,
Qui vont se martelant la poitrine et le front,

N'ont qu'un espoir, étrange et sombre Capitole!
C'est que la Mort, planant comme un soleil nouveau,
Fera s'épanouir les fleurs de leur cerveau!

124. La Fin de la journée

Sous une lumière blafarde
Court, danse et se tord sans raison
La Vie, impudente et criarde.
Aussi, sitôt qu'à l'horizon

La nuit voluptueuse monte,
Apaisant tout, même la faim,
Effaçant tout, même la honte,
Le Poëte se dit: 'Enfin!

It's the glory of gods, it's the mystical loft,
It's the purse of the poor and their true native land,
It's the porch looking out on mysterious skies!

123. The Death of Artists

How many times must I jingle my little bells*
And kiss your ugly forehead, shabby substitute?
How many, o my quiver, spears and bolts to lose
Trying to hit the target, nature's mystic self?

We will wear out our souls concocting subtle schemes,
And we'll be wrecking heavy armatures we've done
Before we gaze upon the great and wondrous One,*
For whom we've often sobbed, wracked by the devil's dreams!

But some have never known their Idol face to face—
These poor, accursed sculptors, marked by their disgrace,
Who go to beat themselves about the breast and brow,

Have only but a hope, strange sombre Capitol!*
It is that Death, a new and hovering sun, will find
A way to bring to bloom the flowers of their minds!

124. Day's End

In evening as the sun goes down
She twists and dances mindlessly—
Life, in her brash effrontery.
But also, when above the town

The night has risen, charming, vast,
Blessing the hungry with its peace,
Obliterating all disgrace,
The Poet tells himself: 'At last!

Mon esprit, comme mes vertèbres,
Invoque ardemment le repos;
Le cœur plein de songes funèbres,

Je vais me coucher sur le dos
Et me rouler dans vos rideaux,
Ô rafraîchissantes ténèbres!'

125. Le Rêve d'un curieux

A F.N.

Connais-tu, comme moi, la douleur savoureuse,
Et de toi fais-tu dire: 'Oh! l'homme singulier!'
— J'allais mourir. C'était dans mon âme amoureuse,
Désir mêlé d'horreur, un mal particulier;

Angoisse et vif espoir, sans humeur factieuse.
Plus allait se vidant le fatal sablier,
Plus ma torture était âpre et délicieuse;
Tout mon cœur s'arrachait au monde familier.

J'étais comme l'enfant avide du spectacle,
Haïssant le rideau comme on hait un obstacle...
Enfin la vérité froide se révéla:

J'étais mort sans surprise, et la terrible aurore
M'enveloppait. — Eh quoi! n'est-ce donc que cela?
La toile était levée et j'attendais encore.

My spirit, like my backbone, seems
Intent on finding its repose;
The heart so full of mournful dreams,

I'll stretch out on my weary back
And roll up in your curtains, those
Consoling comforters of black!'

125. Dream of a Curious Man

for F.N.

Do you, as I do, know a zesty grief,
And is it said of you, 'curious man!'
—I dreamed of dying; in my spirit's heat
Desire and horror mixed, a strange mischance;

Anguish and ardent hope were tightly knit;
The more the fatal glass was drained of sand
The more I suffered, and I savoured it;
My heart pulled out of the familiar, and

I was a child, eager to see a play,
Hating the curtain standing in the way . . .
At last the chilling verity came on:

Yes, I was dead, and in the dreadful dawn
Was wrapped.—And what! That's all there is to tell?
The screen was raised, and I was waiting still.

126. Le Voyage

A Maxime du Camp

I

Pour l'enfant, amoureux de cartes et d'estampes,
L'univers est égal à son vaste appétit.
Ah! que le monde est grande à la clarté des lampes!
Aux yeux du souvenir que le monde est petit!

Un matin nous partons, le cerveau plein de flamme,
Le cœur gros de rancune et de désirs amers,
Et nous allons, suivant le rhythme de la lame,
Berçant notre infini sur le fini des mers:

Les uns, joyeux de fuir une patrie infâme;
D'autres, l'horreur de leurs berceaux, et quelques-uns,
Astrologues noyés dans les yeux d'une femme,
La Circé tyrannique aux dangereux parfums.

Pour n'être pas changés en bêtes, ils s'enivrent
D'espace et de lumière et de cieux embrasés;
La glace qui les mord, les soleils qui les cuivrent,
Effacent lentement la marque des baisers.

Mais le vrai voyageurs sont ceux-là seuls qui partent
Pour partir; cœurs légers, semblables aux ballons,
De leur fatalité jamais ils ne s'écartent,
Et, sans savoir pourquoi, disent toujours: Allons!

Ceux-là dont les désirs ont la forme des nues,
Et qui rêvent, ainsi qu'un conscrit le canon,
De vastes voluptés, changeantes, inconnues,
Et dont l'esprit humain n'a jamais su le nom!

126. Voyaging

for Maxime du Camp*

I

The wide-eyed child in love with maps and plans
Finds the world equal to his appetite.
How grand the universe by light of lamps,
How petty in the memory's clear sight.

One day we leave, with fire in the brain,
Heart great with rancour, bitter in its mood;
Outward we travel on the rolling main,
Lulling infinity in finitude:

Some gladly flee their homelands gripped in vice,
Some, horrors of their childhood, others still—
Astrologers lost in a woman's eyes—
Some perfumed Circe* with a tyrant's will.

Not to become a beast, each desperate one
Makes himself drunk on space and blazing skies;
The gnawing ice, the copper-burning sun
Efface the scars of kisses and of lies.

But the true voyagers set out to sea
Just for the leaving's sake; hearts lift aloft,
Nothing dissuades them from their destiny,
Something beyond their knowing cries, 'We're off!'

These, then, whose ecstasies are wide as air
As conscripts dream of cannons, have their dreams
Of luxuries beyond what man can bear,
Such as the soul has neither named nor seen.

II

Nous imitons, horreur! la toupie et la boule
Dans leur valse et leurs bonds; même dans nos sommeils
La Curiosité nous tourmente et nous roule,
Comme un Ange cruel qui fouette des soleils.

Singulière fortune où le but se déplace,
Et n'étant nulle part, peut être n'importe où!
Où l'Homme, dont jamais l'espérance n'est lasse,
Pour trouver le repos court toujours comme un fou!

Notre âme est un trois-mâts cherchant son Icarie;
Une voix retentit sur le pont: 'Ouvre l'œil!'
Une voix de la hune, ardente et folle, crie:
'Amour... gloire... bonheur!' Enfer! c'est un écueil!

Chaque îlot signalé par l'homme de vigie
Est un Eldorado promis par le Destin;
L'Imagination qui dresse son orgie
Ne trouve qu'un récif aux clartés du matin.

Ô le pauvre amoureux des pays chimériques!
Faut-il le mettre aux fers, le jeter à la mer,
Ce matelot ivrogne, inventeur d'Ameriques
Dont le mirage rend le gouffre plus amer?

Tel le vieux vagabond, piétinant dans la boue,
Rêve, le nez en l'air, de brillants paradis;
Son œil ensorcelé découvre une Capoue
Partout où la chandelle illumine un taudis.

III

Étonnants voyageurs! quelles nobles histoires
Nous lisons dans vos yeux profonds comme les mers!
Montrez-nous les écrins de vos riches mémoires,
Ces bijoux merveilleux, faits d'astres et d'éthers.

II

Our actions are grotesque—in leaps and bounds
We waltz like balls or tops; when day is done
Our curiosity rolls us around
As if a cruel Angel lashed the sun.

Strange thing it is, to chase a shifting fake—
A goal that's nowhere, anywhere at all!
Man, whose anticipation stays awake,
To find his rest goes racing like a fool!

Our soul's three-master seeks the blessed isle:*
A voice on deck shouts 'Ho there, have a look!'
Some crow's-nest spy cries in romantic style
'Love . . . glory . . . happiness!' Damn, just a rock!

Each isle is named the long-awaited sight,
The Eldorado* of our Destiny;
Fancy, that grows us orgies in the night,
Breaks on a reef in morning's clarity.

Oh, the inebriate of distant lands,
This sot who sees Americas at will,
Must he be chained, abandoned on the sands,
Whose visions make the gulf more bitter still?

So the old tramp who shuffles in the filth
Dreams of a paradise and lifts his head—
In his wild eyes, Capua* and her wealth
Wherever candle glow lights up a shed.

III

Fabulous voyagers! What histories
Are there behind your deep and distant stare!
Show us the treasures of your memories,
Those jewels and riches made of stars and air.

Nous voulons voyager sans vapeur et sans voile!
Faites, pour égayer l'ennui de nos prisons,
Passer sur nos esprits, tendus comme une toile,
Vos souvenirs avec leurs cadres d'horizons.

Dites, qu'avez-vous vu?

IV

'Nous avons vu des astres
Et des flots; nous avons vu des sables aussi;
Et, malgré bien des chocs et d'imprévus désastres,
Nous nous sommes souvent ennuyés, comme ici.

La gloire du soleil sur la mer violette,
La gloire des cités dans le soleil couchant,
Allumaient dans nos cœurs une ardeur inquiète
De plonger dans un ciel au reflet alléchant.

Les plus riches cités, les plus grands paysages,
Jamais ne contenaient l'attrait mystérieux
De ceux que le hasard fait avec les nuages,
Et toujours le désir nous rendait soucieux!

— La jouissance ajoute au désir de la force.
Désir, vieil arbre à qui le plaisir sert d'engrais,
Cependant que grossit et durcit ton écorce,
Tes branches veulent voir le soleil de plus près!

Grandiras-tu toujours, grand arbre plus vivace
Que le cyprès? — Pourtant nous avons, avec soin,
Cueilli quelques croquis pour votre album vorace,
Frères qui trouvez beau tout ce qui vient de loin!

Nous avons salué des idoles à la trompe;
Des trônes constellés de joyaux lumineux;
Des palais ouvragés dont la féerique pompe
Serait pour vos banquiers un rêve ruineux;

We're travellers afraid of steam and sail!
Here in our prison every day's the same.
Oh, paint across the canvas of our souls
Your memoirs, with horizon as their frame.

Tell us, what have you seen?

IV

'We've seen the stars
And waves, and we have seen the sandy shores;
Despite disasters, all our jolts and jars,
On sea, on land we find that we are bored.

The glorious sun across the violet sea,
Great sunlit cities dreaming as they lie,
Made our heart yearn with fierce intensity
To plunge towards those reflections in the sky.

Rich cities, and the grandest mountain spires
Somehow could never hold the same allure
As shifting clouds, the shape of our desires,
Which left us unfulfilled and insecure.

—Surely enjoyment quickens passion's spark.
Desire, old tree, that fattens on delight,
As you grow older, toughening your bark,
You want to see the sun from nearer height!

Do you grow always taller, grandest tree,
Older than cypress?—Still, we have with care
Brought sketch-book pieces from across the sea
For brothers who love all that's strange and rare!

Idols with trunks we've greeted in our time;
Great palaces enwrought with filigree
And jewelled thrones in luminous design,
To send your brokers dreams of bankruptcy;

Des costumes qui sont pour les yeux une ivresse;
Des femmes dont les dents et les ongles sont teints,
Et des jongleurs savants que le serpent caresse.'

V

Et puis, et puis encore?

VI

'Ô cerveaux enfantins!

Pour ne pas oublier la chose capitale,
Nous avons vu partout, et sans l'avoir cherché,
Du haut jusques en bas de l'échelle fatale,
Le spectacle ennuyeux de l'immortel péché:

La femme, esclave vile, orgueilleuse et stupide,
Sans rire s'adorant et s'aimant sans dégoût;
L'homme, tyran goulu, paillard, dur et cupide,
Esclave de l'esclave et ruisseau dans l'égout;

Le bourreau qui jouit, le martyr qui sanglote;
La fête qu'assaisonne et parfume le sang;
Le poison du pouvoir énervant le despote,
Et le peuple amoureux du fouet abrutissant;

Plusieurs religions semblables à la nôtre,
Toutes escaladant le ciel; la Sainteté,
Comme en un lit de plume un délicat se vautre,
Dans les clous et le crin cherchant la volupté;

L'Humanité bavarde, ivre de son génie,
Et, folle maintenant comme elle était jadis,
Criant à Dieu, dans sa furibonde agonie:
"Ô mon semblable, ô mon maître, je te maudis!"

Scant costumes that can stupefy the gaze
On painted women, every nail and tooth,
And subtle jugglers, wise in serpents' ways.'

V

And then, and then what more?

VI

'O childish dupes!

You want the truth? We'll tell you without fail—
We never thought to search it out, but saw
From heights to depths, through all the mortal scale
The numbing spectacle of human flaw.

Woman, vile slave, proud in stupidity,
Tasteless and humourless in self-conceit;
Man, greedy tyrant, lustful, slovenly,
Slave of the slave, a sewer in the street;

The hangman jokes, the martyr sobs and faints,
The feast of blood is seasoned perfectly;
Poison of power drains a tyrant's strength,
Whose subjects love the whip's brutality.

Religions like our own in most details
Climb skyward on their saints, who it is said
Indulge their lusts with hairshirts, or with nails,
As dainty fops sprawl on a feather bed.

Drunk on her genius, Humanity,
Mad now as she has always been, or worse,
Cries to her God in raging agony:
"Master, my image, damn you with this curse!"*

Et les moins sots, hardis amants de la Démence,
Fuyant le grand troupeau parqué par le Destin,
Et se réfugiant dans l'opium immense!
— Tel est du globe entier l'éternel bulletin.'

VII

Amer savoir, celui qu'on tire du voyage!
Le monde, monotone et petit, aujourd'hui,
Hier, demain, toujours, nous fait voir notre image:
Une oasis d'horreur dans un désert d'ennui!

Faut-il partir? rester? Si tu peux rester, reste;
Pars, s'il le faut. L'un court, et l'autre se tapit
Pour tromper l'ennemi vigilant et funeste,
Le Temps! Il est, hélas! des coureurs sans répit,

Comme le Juif errant et comme les apôtres,
A qui rien ne suffit, ni wagon ni vaisseau,
Pour fuir ce rétiaire infâme; il en est d'autres
Qui savent le tuer sans quitter leur berceau.

Lorsque enfin il mettra le pied sur notre échine,
Nous pourrons espérer et crier: En avant!
De même qu'autrefois nous partions pour la Chine,
Les yeux fixés au large et les cheveux au vent,

Nous nous embarquerons sur la mer des Ténèbres
Avec le cœur joyeux d'un jeune passager.
Entendez-vous ces voix, charmantes et funèbres,
Qui chantent: 'Par ici! vous qui voulez manger

Le Lotus parfumé! c'est ici qu'on vendange
Les fruits miraculeux dont votre cœur a faim;
Venez vous enivrer de la douceur étrange
De cette après-midi qui n'a jamais de fin?'

Not quite so foolish, bold demented ones
Flee from the feeding lot that holds the herd;
Their boundless shelter is in opium.
—From all the world, such always is the word.'

VII

How bitter, what we learn from voyaging!
The small and tedious world gives us to see
Now, always, the real horror of the thing,
Ourselves—that sad oasis in ennui!

Must one depart? or stay? Stand it and stay,
Leave if you must. One runs, one finds a space
To hide and cheat the deadly enemy
Called Time. Alas, some run a constant race—

The twelve apostles, or the Wandering Jew—*
For them no ship avails, no ways or means
To flee that gladiator; others know
From infancy how to defeat the fiend.

Finally, though, his boot is on our chest;
Then may we hope, and call out 'Onward ho!'
Even as once we set out for the East,
Our eyes fixed widely, hair blown to and fro,

Now sailing on the sea of shades we go,
With all the plans of passengers well-pleased
To hear the voice, funereal and low,
That sings: 'This way! Come here and take your ease

And eat the Lotus!* Here we gather in
These fruits for hearts that yearn for strange delights;
Intoxicate yourselves on alien
Enjoyment through these days without a night.'

A l'accent familier nous devinons le spectre;
Nos Pylades là-bas tendent leurs bras vers nous.
'Pour rafraîchir ton cœur nage vers ton Électre!'
Dit celle dont jadis nous baisions les genoux.

VIII

Ô Mort, vieux capitaine, il est temps! levons l'ancre!
Ce pays nous ennuie, ô Mort! Appareillons!
Si le ciel et la mer sont noirs comme de l'encre,
Nos cœurs que tu connais sont remplis de rayons!

Verse-nous ton poison pour qu'il nous réconforte!
Nous voulons, tant ce feu nous brûle le cerveau,
Plonger au fond du gouffre, Enfer ou Ciel, qu'importe?
Au fond de l'Inconnu pour trouver du *nouveau*!

We understand the phantom's friendly part,
That Pylades* who reaches out to tease:
'Swim towards Electra* now, to ease your heart!'
She cries, and long ago we kissed her knees.

VIII

O Death, old captain, time to make our trip!
This country bores us, Death! Let's get away!
Even if sky and sea are black as pitch
You know our hearts are full of sunny rays!*

Serve us your poison, sir, to treat us well!
Minds burning, we know what we have to do,
And plunge to depths of Heaven or of Hell,
To fathom the Unknown, and find the *new*!*

Les Épaves

The Waifs

I. Le Coucher du soleil romantique

Que le soleil est beau quand tout frais il se lève,
Comme une explosion nous lançant son bonjour!
— Bienheureux celui-là qui peut avec amour
Saluer son coucher plus glorieux qu'un rêve!

Je me souviens!... J'ai vu tout, fleur, source, sillon,
Se pâmer sous son œil comme un cœur qui palpite...
— Courons vers l'horizon, il est tard, courons vite,
Pour attraper au moins un oblique rayon.

Mais je poursuis en vain le Dieu qui se retire;
L'irrésistible Nuit établit son empire,
Noire, humide, funeste et pleine de frissons;

Un odeur de tombeau dans les ténèbres nage,
Et mon pied peureux froisse, au bord du marécage,
Des crapauds imprévus et de froids limaçons.

Galanteries

VIII. Le Jet d'eau

Tes beaux yeux sont las, pauvre amante!
Reste longtemps, sans les rouvrir,
Dans cette pose nonchalante
Où t'a surprise le plaisir.
Dans la cour le jet d'eau qui jase
Et ne se tait ni nuit ni jour,
Entretient doucement l'extase
Où ce soir m'a plongé l'amour.

I. The Setting of the Romantic Sun

How lovely is the sun fresh in the skies,
Blasting his good day to the world below!
—Happy the one who can with passion know
The sunset's glory, dreamlike to the eyes!

I have seen all: the flower, furrow, spring
Swoon in his beaming like a throbbing heart . . .
—Now it is late, run westward, let us start,
To trap one ray, at least one fading thing.

But I pursue the dying God in vain;
Remorseless Night establishes her reign,*
Black, damp and baneful, full of shivering;

At the swamp's edge swim odours of the tomb,
And where my bruising foot, there in the gloom,
Steps fearful, snails and toads* are quivering.

*Gallantries**

VIII. The Fountain

Poor tired love, your eyes are closed!
Stay through the night, and rest them well—
How nonchalant your sleeping pose
When lassitude has mastered you.
The fountain gossips in the square
Gently through the dark and day,
Speaks to the depths of ecstasy
Where I am plunged, tonight, by love.

La gerbe épanouie
  En mille fleurs,
Où Phoebé réjouie
  Met ses couleurs,
Tombe comme un pluie
  De larges pleurs.

Ainsi ton âme qu'incendie
L'éclair brûlant des voluptés
S'élance, rapide et hardie,
Vers les vastes cieux enchantés.
Puis, elle s'épanche, mourante,
En un flot de triste langueur,
Qui par une invisible pente
Descend jusqu'au fond de mon cœur.

La gerbe épanouie
  En mille fleurs,
Où Phoebé réjouie
  Met ses couleurs,
Tombe comme un pluie
  De larges pleurs.

Ô toi, que la nuit rend si belle,
Qu'il m'est doux, penché vers tes seins,
D'écouter la plainte éternelle
Qui sanglote dans les bassins!
Lune, eau sonore, nuit bénie,
Arbres qui frissonnez autour,
Votre pure mélancolie
Est le miroir de mon amour.

La gerbe épanouie
  En mille fleurs,
Où Phoebé réjouie
  Met ses couleurs,
Tombe comme un pluie
  De larges pleurs.

The sheaf opens out
  In a thousand flowers
That Phoebe,* delighted
  Touches with colours—
Arches and falls
  In a rain of tears.

And thus your passion's soul, which fires
The scorching lightning of delights,
Strikes forward swiftly, fearlessly
Toward the vast enchanted skies,
Then dying, overflows herself,
Becomes a mournful, languorous flood
Invisibly, mysteriously
Flowing into my deepest heart.

The sheaf opens out
  In a thousand flowers
That Phoebe, delighted,
  Touches with colours—
Arches and falls
  In a rain of tears.

My dear, made lovelier by the night,
How sweet to me when on your breast
To listen to the old lament
That softly sobs about the pools!
Moon, sounding water, quivering trees,
The blessed midnight all above—
Your melancholy purity
Becomes the mirror of my love.

The sheaf opens out
  In a thousand flowers
That Phoebe, delighted,
  Touches with colours—
Arches and falls
  In a rain of tears.

IX. Les Yeux de Berthe

Vous pouvez mépriser les yeux plus célèbres,
Beaux yeux de mon enfant, par où filtre et s'enfuit
Je ne sais quoi de bon, de doux comme la Nuit!
Beaux yeux, versez sur moi vos charmantes ténèbres!

Grands yeux de mon enfant, arcanes adorés,
Vous ressemblez beaucoup à ces grottes magiques
Où, derrière l'amas des ombres léthargiques,
Scintillent vaguement des trésors ignorés!

Mon enfant a des yeux obscurs, profonds et vastes,
Comme toi, Nuit immense, éclairés comme toi!
Leurs feux sont ces pensers d'Amour, mêlés de Foi,
Qui pétillent au fond, voluptueux ou chastes.

X. Hymne

A la très chère, à la très belle
Qui remplit mon cœur de clarté,
A l'ange, à l'idole immortelle,
Salut en l'immortalité!

Elle se répand dans ma vie
Comme un air imprégné de sel,
Et dans mon âme inassouvie
Verse le goût de l'éternel.

Sachet toujours frais qui parfume
L'atmosphère d'un cher réduit,
Encensoir oublié qui fume
En secret à travers la nuit,

IX. Bertha's Eyes

The most renowned of eyes you can despise,
Eyes of my child, where filter and take flight
Who knows what good, what sweetness like the Night!
Turn your dark charms to me, beautiful eyes!

My child's great eyes, mysteries so adored,
You much resemble those enchanted caves
Where, back behind the massed, lethargic shades
Will vaguely gleam an unknown treasure-hoard!

My child has sombre, deep and spacious eyes
Like thee, enormous Night, with lights like thine!
Their fires are thoughts of love and faith combined,
That sparkle, lewd or chaste, deep in their skies.

X. Hymn

To the dearest, to the most lovely
Who lights the heart in me,
To the angel immortal, the idol,
Praise to eternity!

She sifts through my intimate being
Like the tang of salt from the sea,
And into my famishing spirit
Pours a taste for the heavenly.

Sachet always fresh in perfuming
The air of a cherished retreat,
A censer diffusing its fragrance
By night, with a secret heat,

Comment, amour incorruptible,
T'exprimer avec vérité?
Grain de musc qui gis, invisible,
Au fond de mon éternité!

A la très bonne, à la très belle
Qui fait ma joie et ma santé,
A l'ange, à l'idole immortelle,
Salut en l'immortalité!

XI. Les Promesses d'un visage

J'aime, ô pâle beauté, tes sourcils surbaissés,
    D'où semblent couler des ténèbres,
Tes yeux, quoique très noirs, m'inspirent des pensers
    Qui ne sont pas du tout funèbres.

Tes yeux, qui sont d'accord avec tes noirs cheveux,
    Avec ta crinière élastique,
Tes yeux, languissamment, me disent; 'Si tu veux,
    Amant de la muse plastique,

Suivre l'espoir qu'en toi nous avons excité,
    Et tous les goûts que tu professes,
Tu pourras constater notre véracité,
    Depuis le nombril jusqu'aux fesses;

Tu trouveras au bout de deux beaux seins bien lourds,
    Deux larges médailles de bronze,
Et sous un ventre uni, doux comme du velours,
    Bistré comme la peau d'un bonze,

Une riche toison qui, vraiment, est la sœur
    De cette énorme chevelure,
Souple et frisée, et qui t'égale en épaisseur,
    Nuit sans étoiles, Nuit obscure!'

How can I, my perfect beloved,
Give word of you truthfully?
Grain of musk ineluctably hidden
In the holiest centre of me!

To the purest, to the most lovely,
My joy and my sanity,
To the angel immortal, the idol,
Praise to eternity!

XI. A Face Makes Promises

Pale beauty, I adore your curving brows
    That pour a darkness through the room;
Your eyes, though black, inspire thoughts and vows
    Not altogether full of gloom.

Your eyes, that speak in consort with your hair,
    Elastic mane of raven hues,
Your eyes in languor tell me: 'If you'd care,
    O lover of the plastic muse,

To exercise the fancies you profess
    And all the hopes we've raised, you'll find
You may go down, to prove our faithfulness,
    From navel to the cheeks behind;

There'll be a pair of lovely, heavy breasts,
    Bronze medals tipping each of these;
Below a belly, velvet to caress,
    As tawny as a Japanese,

Twines a rich fleece, true sister in delight
    Of those great, supple locks that are
The head of hair—your match in thickness, Night!
    O shrouded Night without a star!'

XII. Le Monstre
ou Le Paranymphe d'une nymphe macabre

I

Tu n'es certes pas, ma très chère,
Ce que Veuillot nomme un tendron.
Le jeu, l'amour, la bonne chère,
Bouillonnent en toi, vieux chaudron!
Tu n'es plus fraîche, ma très chère,

Ma vieille infante! Et cependant
Tes caravanes insensées
T'ont donné ce lustre abondant
Des choses qui sont très-usées,
Mais qui séduisent cependant.

Je ne trouve pas monotone
La verdeur de tes quarante ans;
Je préfère tes fruits, Automne,
Aux fleurs banales du Printemps!
Non! tu n'es jamais monotone!

Ta carcasse a des agréments
Et des grâces particulières;
Je trouve d'étranges piments
Dans le creux de tes deux salières
Ta carcasse a des agréments!

Nargue des amants ridicules
Du melon et du giraumont!
Je préfère tes clavicules
A celles du roi Salomon,
Et je plains ces gens ridicules!

XII. The Monster

or The Praise of a Macabre Nymph

I

Dearest, you certainly are not
What Veuillot* calls a tender shoot.
Gambling, lust and gluttony,
Old cauldron, boil away in you.
You are no longer fresh, my dear,

My old infanta! None the less
Your antics, your mad caravans
Have cast the lustre over you
Of things that have been often used
But which seduce us none the less.

I do not find monotonous
The acids of your forty years;
I favour the autumnal fruits
Over the banal blooms of Spring!
No! you are *not* monotonous!

Your carcass has its ornaments
And some particulars of grace;
I find strange spices flourishing
In hollows of your collar-bones;
Your carcass has its ornaments!

A fig for foolish lovers, who
Dote on the melon's juicy flesh!
I much prefer your clavicles
To those of old King Solomon,*
And pity all those doting fools!

Tes cheveux, comme un casque bleu,
Ombragent ton front de guerrière,
Qui ne pense et rougit que peu,
Et puis se sauvent par derrière,
Comme les crins d'un casque bleu.

Tes yeux qui semblent de la boue,
Où scintille quelque fanal,
Ravivés au fard de ta joue,
Lancent un éclair infernal!
Tes yeux sont noirs comme la boue!

Par sa luxure et son dédain
Ta lèvre amère nous provoque;
Cette lèvre, c'est un Éden
Qui nous attire et qui nous choque.
Quelle luxure! et quel dédain!

Ta jambe musculeuse et sèche
Sait gravir au haut des volcans,
Et malgré la neige et la dèche
Danser les plus fougueux cancans.
Ta jambe est musculeuse et sèche;

Ta peau brûlante et sans douceur,
Comme celle des vieux gendarmes,
Ne connaît pas plus la sueur
Que ton œil ne connaît les larmes.
(Et pourtant elle a sa douceur!)

II

Sotte, tu t'en vas droit au Diable!
Volontiers j'irais avec toi,
Si cette vitesse effroyable
Ne me causait pas quelque émoi.
Va-t'en donc, toute seule, au Diable!

Your head of hair, a blue-black casque,
Shadows your Amazonish brow
That hardly blushes, hardly thinks,
And then, behind, it flows away—
A mane, from under a blue casque.

Your eyes, the colour of the mud,
Where signal-lights are glimmering,
Revived in rouging of your cheek,
Cast an infernal lightning-flash!
Your eyes are black as any mud!

By luxury and by disdain
Your bitter lip arouses us;
An Eden is this very lip,
Offending as it captivates.
What luxury! and what disdain!

Your leg, both muscular and lean,
Knows how to climb volcanoes' heights,
And will, in snow or poverty,
Perform the cancan wickedly.
Your leg is muscular and lean;

Your torrid skin, no longer sweet
And like an old policeman's hide,
Seems not to be aware of sweat
As your eye never knows a tear.
(It has its sweetness, though, for me!)

II

Fool, you are headed straight for Hell!
I willingly would tag along
Were I not put in such a state
By this intimidating speed.
Go to the Devil, then, alone!

Mon rein, mon poumon, mon jarret
Ne me laissent plus rendre hommage
A ce Seigneur, comme il faudrait.
'Helas! c'est vraiment bien dommage!'
Disent mon rein et mon jarret.

Oh! très sincèrement je souffre
De ne pas aller aux sabbats,
Pour voir, quand il pète du soufre,
Comment tu lui baises son cas!
Oh! très sincèrement je souffre!

Je suis diablement affligé
De ne pas être ta torchère,
Et de te demander congé,
Flambeau d'enfer! Juge, ma chère,
Combien je dois être affligé,

Puisque depuis longtemps je t'aime,
Étant très logique! En effet,
Voulant du Mal chercher la crème
Et n'aimer qu'un monstre parfait,
Vraiment oui! vieux monstre, je t'aime!

Épigraphes

xiv. Vers pour le portrait de M. Honoré Daumier

Celui dont nous t'offrons l'image,
Et dont l'art, subtil entre tous,
Nous enseigne à rire de nous,
Celui'là, lecteur, est un sage.

C'est un satirique, un moqueur;
Mais l'énergie avec laquelle
Il peint le Mal et sa séquelle,
Prouve la beauté de son cœur.

My kidneys, lungs, my aching shanks
No longer let me celebrate
That great Lord as one ought to do.
'Alas, it truly is a shame!'
So say my kidneys and my shanks.

Oh! I'm sincerely suffering
To miss the sabbaths, not to see
When he lets his sulphurous blasts
You bend to kiss his filthy ass!*
Oh! I'm sincerely suffering!

I am afflicted hellishly,
Not being fit to hold your lamp,
Having to beg my leave of you,
Infernal torch! Please judge, my dear,
How sore afflicted I must be,

Since I, so logically, have loved
You years and years! Wishing, that is,
To skim the cream of Sin, to love
Only a pure monstrosity,
Oh yes! old monster, I love you!

Epigraphs

XIV. Poem on the Portrait of Honoré Daumier*

The man depicted on this page
Whose craft in all its subtleties
Teaches us our inanities,
That person, reader, is a sage.

Yes, mocking satire is his art,
But all the force at his command
To show us Evil and his band
But proves the beauty of his heart.

Son rire n'est pas la grimace
De Melmoth ou de Méphisto
Sous la torche de l'Alecto
Qui les brûle, mais qui nous glace.

Leur rire, hélas! de la gaîté
N'est que la douloureuse charge;
Le sien rayonne, franc et large,
Comme un signe de sa bonté!

xv. Lola de Valence

Entre tant de beautés que partout on peut voir,
Je comprends bien, amis, que le désir balance;
Mais on voit scintiller en Lola de Valence
Le charme inattendu d'un bijou rose et noir.

XVI. Sur *Le Tasse en prison* d'Eugène Delacroix

Le poëte au cachot, débraillé, maladif,
Roulant un manuscrit sous son pied convulsif,
Mesure d'un regard que la terreur enflamme
L'escalier de vertige où s'abîme son âme.

Les rires enivrants dont s'emplit le prison
Vers l'étrange et l'absurde invitent sa raison;
Le Doute l'environne, et la Peur ridicule,
Hideuse et multiforme, autour de lui circule.

Ce génie enfermé dans un taudis malsain,
Ces grimaces, ces cris, ces spectres dont l'essaim
Tourbillonne, ameuté derrière son oreille,

His smile is not like Melmoth's* bold
Grimace, or Mephistopheles'*
Pursued by the Erinyes*
Whose fiery torches leave us cold.

Their smile, alas, for gaiety
Is nothing but caricature;
His smile is frank and large, a sure
Sign of his magnanimity.

xv. Lola de Valence*

One sees such beauties everywhere one goes
I know, my friends, desire hesitates;
But in Lola de Valence radiates
The rare charm of a jewel of black and rose.

xvi. On *Tasso in Prison*, by Eugène Delacroix*

The poet in his cell, unbuttoned, sick,
Beneath his frantic foot a manuscript,
Takes measure with a terror-haunted gaze
Of giddy stairs that have his soul amazed.

A drunken laughter almost can be heard
To lead his reasoning towards the absurd;
While Doubt surrounds him, Fear, the imbecile,
The multiform, encircles him at will.

This genius locked in a filthy space,
These cries, these spectres swarming through the place
And whirling to their spot behind his ear,

Ce rêveur que l'horreur de son logis réveille,
Voilà bien ton emblème, Âme aux songes obscurs,
Que le Réel étouffe entre ses quatre murs!

Pièces diverses

XVII. La Voix

Mon berceau s'adossait à la bibliothèque,
Babel sombre, où roman, science, fabliau,
Tout, la cendre latine et la poussière grecque,
Se mêlaient. J'étais haut comme un in-folio.
Deux voix me parlaient. L'une, insidieuse et ferme,
Disait: 'La Terre est un gâteau plein de douceur;
Je puis (et ton plaisir serait alors sans terme!)
Te faire un appétit d'une égale grosseur.'
Et l'autre: 'Viens! oh! viens voyager dans les rêves,
Au delà du possible, au delà du connu!'
Et celle-là chantait comme le vent des grèves,
Fantôme vagissant, on ne sait d'où venu,
Qui caresse l'oreille et cependant l'effraie.
Je te répondis: 'Oui! douce voix!' C'est d'alors
Que date ce qu'on peut, hélas! nommer ma plaie
Et ma fatalité. Derrière les décors
De l'existence immense, au plus noir de l'abîme,
Je vois distinctement des mondes singuliers,
Et, de ma clairvoyance extatique victime,
Je traîne des serpents qui mordent mes souliers.
Et c'est depuis ce temps que, pareil aux prophètes,
J'aime si tendrement le désert et la mer;
Que je ris dans les deuils et pleure dans les fêtes,
Et trouve un goût suave au vin le plus amer;
Que je prends très souvent les faits pour des mensonges,
Et que, les yeux au ciel, je tombe dans des trous.
Mais la voix me console et dit: 'Garde tes songes:
Les sages n'en ont pas d'aussi beaux que les fous!'

This dreamer, sleepless from the horrors here,
Surely depicts the soaring Soul who falls
Into the Real, smothered within four walls!

Diverse Pieces

XVII. The Voice

My cradle rocked below the stacks of books—
That Babel* of instructions, novels, verse
Where Roman rubbish mixed with Grecian dust.
I was no taller than a folio,*
But heard two voices. One, beguiling, bold
Proclaimed, 'The world is just a sweetened cake!
And I, to give you endless joy, offer
You appetite to take it in a bite!'
But then the other: 'Come, dream-voyager,
Beyond the possible, beyond the known!'
And that one chanted like the seaside wind,
A wailing phantom out of God knows where,
Caressing, yet still frightening the ear.
I answered, 'Yes, sweet voice!' And from that time,
That date, my wound was named, my fate was sealed.
Behind the scenery of this immense
Existence, through abysmal blackness, I
Distinctly see the wonder of new worlds,
And, fervid victim of my clairvoyance,
I walk with serpents striking at my shoes.
And it is since that time that, prophet-like,
I love so tenderly the desert wastes;
I laugh in pain and cry on holidays
And tempt my palate with the sourest wine;
I take for truth what others call a lie
And, eyes to heaven, trip into a ditch.
But then my voice says, 'Madman, keep your dreams;
The wise have nothing beautiful as they!'

XVIII. L'Imprévu

Harpagon qui veillait son père agonisant,
Se dit, rêveur, devant ces lèvres déjà blanches:
'Nous avons au grenier un nombre suffisant,
    Ce me semble, de vieilles planches?'

Célimène roucoule et dit: 'Mon cœur est bon,
Et naturellement, Dieu m'a fait très belle.'
— Son cœur! cœur racorni, fumé comme un jambon,
    Recuit à la flamme éternelle!

Un gazetier fumeux, qui se croit un flambeau,
Dit au pauvre, qu'il a noyé dans les ténèbres:
'Où donc l'aperçois-tu, ce créateur du Beau,
    Ce Redresseur que tu célèbres?'

Mieux que tous, je connais certain voluptueux
Qui bâille nuit et jour, et se lamente et pleure,
Répétant, l'impuissant et le fat: 'Oui, je veux
    Être vertueux, dans une heure!'

L'horloge à son tour, dit à voix basse: 'Il est mûr,
Le damné! J'avertis en vain la chair infecte.
L'homme est aveugle, sourd, fragile comme un mur
    Qu'habite et que ronge un insecte!'

Et puis, Quelqu'un paraît, que tous avaient nié,
Et qui leur dit, railleur et fier: 'Dans mon ciboire,
Vous avez, que je crois, assez communié
    A la joyeuse Messe noir?

Chacun de vous m'a fait un temple dans son cœur;
Vous avez, en secret, baisé ma fesse immonde!
Reconnaissez Satan à son rire vainqueur,
    Énorme et laid comme le monde!

XVIII. The Unforeseen

Harpagon,* while his father wastes away,
Meditates, as those lips grow white and thin:
'Up in the loft we have somewhere, I'd say,
   Enough old boards to do for him.'

Célimène* coos: 'My heart is good; I am
Of course made beautiful by God as well.'
—Her heart! a shrivelled heart, smoked like a ham,
   Re-heated in the flames of Hell!

A gazetteer* who claims he's spreading light
Says to the poor, through smoke that suffocates:
'Where, then, do you perceive this lovely sight,
   This Saviour whom you celebrate?'

Of libertines, none knows as well as I
These men who yawn in ennui, grieve and vow
And in their fecklessness set up the cry:
   'I will be good, an hour from now!'

The Clock, in turn, says in a low voice: 'All
Are ripe, damned beings! Fragile Man, it's time.
You're deaf and blind, infected as a wall
   An insect gnaws and undermines!'

And then Someone denied by all appears,
And mocking, proud, he tells them: 'From my vast
Ciborium* you have communed for years
   In celebrating my Black Mass!

You all have built me temples deep inside,
And kissed my filthy buttocks! Now you must
Recognize Satan by his laugh of pride,
   Huge, ugly as this world of dust!

Avez-vous donc pu croire, hypocrites surpris,
Qu'on se moque du maître, et qu'avec lui l'on triche,
Et qu'il soit naturel de recevoir deux prix,
    D'aller au Ciel et d'être riche?

Il faut que le gibier paye le vieux chasseur
Qui se morfond longtemps à l'affût de la proie.
Je vais vous emporter à travers l'épaisseur,
    Compagnons de ma triste joie,

A travers l'épaisseur de la terre et du roc,
A travers les amas confus de votre cendre,
Dans un palais aussi grand que moi, d'un seul bloc,
    Et qui n'est pas de pierre tendre;

Car il est fait avec l'universel Péché,
Et contient mon orgueil, ma douleur et ma gloire!'
— Cependant, tout en haut de l'univers juché,
    Un ange sonne le victoire

De ceux dont le cœur dit: 'Que béni soit ton fouet,
Seigneur! que la douleur, ô Père, soit bénie!
Mon âme dans tes mains n'est pas un vain jouet,
    Et ta prudence est infinie.'

Le son de la trompette est si délicieux,
Dans ces soirs solennels de célestes vendanges,
Qu'il s'infiltre comme une extase dans tous ceux
    Dont elle chante les louanges.

XIX. La Rançon

L'Homme a, pour payer sa rançon,
Deux champs au tuf profond et riche,
Qu'il faut qu'il remue et défriche
Avec le fer de la raison;

You hypocrites, can you believe these lies—
That one may mock the Master, play him tricks,
That one may really win a double prize,
   To go to Heaven, and be rich?

I've thrilled and quivered, tracking down my prey,
Who now must pay the ancient hunter's fee,
As I transport you from the light of day,
   Guests of my mournful levity,

Through the dense darkness of the land and rock,
Across the midden where your bones are thrown,
Into a palace large as I, one block,
   And not of any tender stone,

Since it is made of universal Sin,
And of my glory, pain, and vanity!'
—But then on high an angel will begin
   To sound the note of victory

For those whose hearts say: 'Blest be your commands
O Lord! Your lash is for our benefit!
My soul is not a plaything in your hands,
   Whose providence is infinite.'

And so delicious is the trumpet's call
These evenings of the holy harvest days,
It filters like an ecstasy in all
   Who listen as it sings their praise.

xix. The Ransom

To pay his ransom, Man must take
Two fields of tufa, deep and rich,
And use the tools of reason, which
Are all he has, to dig and rake;

Pour obtenir la moindre rose,
Pour extorquer quelques épis,
Des pleurs salés de son front gris
Sans cesse il faut qu'il les arrose.

L'un est l'Art, et l'autre l'Amour.
— Pour rendre le juge propice,
Lorsque de la stricte justice
Paraîtra le terrible jour,

Il faudra lui montrer des granges
Pleines de moissons, et des fleurs
Dont les formes et les couleurs
Gagnent le suffrage des Anges.

xx. A une Malabaraise

Tes pieds sont aussi fins que tes mains, et ta hanche
Est large à faire envie à la plus belle blanche;
A l'artiste pensif ton corps est doux et cher;
Tes grands yeux de velours sont plus noirs que ta chair.
Aux pays chauds et bleus où ton Dieu t'a fait naître,
Ta tâche est d'allumer la pipe de ton maître,
De pourvoir les flacons d'eaux fraîches et d'odeurs,
De chasser loin du lit les moustiques rôdeurs,
Et, dès que le matin fait chanter les platanes,
D'acheter au bazar ananas et bananes.
Tout le jour, où tu veux, tu mènes tes pieds nus,
Et fredonnes tout bas de vieux airs inconnus;
Et quand descend le soir au manteau d'écarlate,
Tu poses doucement ton corps sur une natte,
Où tes rêves flottants sont pleins de colibris,
Et toujours, comme toi, gracieux et fleuris.
Pourquoi, l'heureuse enfant, veux-tu voir notre France,
Ce pays trop peuplé que fauche la souffrance,
Et, confiant ta vie aux bras forts des marins,

To grow a rose of shortest stem,
To wrest a few pathetic ears,
His grey head sheds its salty tears,
Which he must use to water them:

One field is Art, the other, Love.
—But then, in order that he may
Persuade the court, that awful day
Judgement is rendered from above,

He must display his barns, that teem
With harvest crops, with corn and grapes
And flowers of the shades and shapes
To earn the Angels' high esteem.

xx. To a Girl of Malabar

Your feet, fine as your hands, your large hips too
Make European beauties envy you;
The artist finds your body sweet and fresh;
Your velvet eyes are darker than your flesh.
Here in your blue and sultry native land
To light your master's pipe with gentle hand,
To serve fresh water in its scented flasks
And chase away mosquitoes are your tasks;
When morning makes the plane-trees sing, you are
To buy fresh pineapples at the bazaar;
You may direct your bare feet all day long
At will, and trill some half-forgotten song;
And when the sun in scarlet mantle sets,
You sweetly pose your body for its rest,
Where all your dreams are full of hummingbirds,
And gracious, like yourself, beyond all words.
O happy child, why do you want to see
Our France, a country reaped by misery,
And, subject to the seas' capricious winds,

Faire de grands adieux à tes chers tamarins?
Toi, vêtue à moitié de mousselines frêles,
Frissonnante là-bas sous la neige et les grêles,
Comme tu pleurerais tes loisirs doux et francs,
Si, le corset brutal emprisonnant tes flancs,
Il te fallait glaner ton souper dans nos fanges
Et vendre le parfum de tes charmes étranges,
L'œil pensif, et suivant, dans nos sales brouillards,
Des cocotiers absents les fantômes épars!

Bouffonneries

XXI. Sur les débuts d'Amina Boschetti
Au Théâtre de la Monnaie à Bruxelles

Amina bondit, — fuit, — puis voltige et sourit;
Le Welche dit: 'Tout ça, pour moi, c'est du prâcrit;
Je ne connais, en fait de nymphes bocagères,
Que celles de *Montagne-aux-Herbes-Potagères*.'

Du bout de son pied fin et de son œil qui rit,
Amina verse à flots le délire et l'esprit;
Le Welche dit: 'Fuyez, délices mensongères!
Mon épouse n'a pas ces allures légères.'

Vous ignorez, sylphide au jarret triomphant,
Qui voulez enseigner la valse à l'éléphant,
Au hibou la gaîté, le rire à la cigogne,

Que sur la grâce en feu le Welche dit: 'Haro!'
Et que, le doux Bacchus lui versant du bourgogne,
Le monstre répondrait: 'J'aime mieux le faro!'

To make goodbyes to dear old tamarinds?
There in your filmy muslin as you go
To freeze in France beneath the hail and snow,
How you will cry, regretful of the trip,
If, in the brutal corset's crushing grip,
You have to sell your beauty in the street,
Out of this muck to glean some food to eat,
While through our filthy mists your vision sees
The phantom spars of absent coco-trees.*

Buffooneries

XXI. On the Début of Amina Boschetti

At the Théâtre de la Monnaie, Brussels

Amina leaps and flies—then flutters smilingly;
The boorish Belgian says: 'All that is Greek to me;
Of wood-nymphs I know nothing other than affairs
Of those on the *Montagne-aux-Herbes-Potagères.*'*

From toe of her slim foot, and from her laughing eye,
Amina pours in waves spirit and ecstasy;
Says the barbarian: 'Be gone, you false delights!
My wife does not observe these trifling ways at night.'

You do not know, o sylph of the triumphant stance,
Who wants to teach the clumsy elephant to dance,
The sober stork to laugh, the owl to be gay,

How to a fiery grace the Belgian says: 'Away!'
And how, if Bacchus were to pour a vintage wine,
The monster would respond: 'Some Belgian beer for mine!'*

XXII. A M. Eugène Fromentin

A propos d'un importun
qui se disait son ami

Il me dit qu'il était très riche,
Mais qu'il craignait le choléra;
— Que de son or il était chiche,
Mais qu'il goûtait fort l'Opéra;

— Qu'il raffolait de la nature,
Ayant connu monsieur Corot;
— Qu'il n'avait pas encor voiture,
Mais que cela viendrait bientôt;

— Qu'il aimait le marbre et la brique,
Les bois noirs et les bois dorés;
— Qu'il possédait dans sa fabrique
Trois contremaîtres décorés;

— Qu'il avait, sans compter le reste,
Vingt mille actions sur le *Nord*;
— Qu'il avait trouvé, pour un zeste,
Des encadrements d'Oppenord;

— Qu'il donnerait (fût-ce à Luzarches!)
Dans le bric-à-brac jusqu'au cou,
Et qu'au Marché des Patriarches
Il avait fait plus d'un bon coup;

— Qu'il n'aimait pas beaucoup sa femme,
Ni sa mère;—mais qu'il croyait
A l'immortalité de l'âme,
Et qu'il avait lu Niboyet!

XXII. To M. Eugène Fromentin

Concerning a Bore
Who Called Himself His Friend

He told me he was very rich,
But had a fear of cholera;
—That mostly he was tight of fist,
But dearly loved the Opera;

—That nature carried him away,
Corot* had been a special friend;
—He had no carriage, sad to say,
But he was working towards that end;

—Marble he loved, and brickwork, then
He loved gold trim and ebony;
—That three much-decorated men
Helped him to run his factory;

—That in his large portfolio
Was an investment in the *Nord*;*
—That he'd discovered, priced too low,
Some handsome frames by Oppenord,*

—For the best curios he'd feel
Inclined to splurge (and at Luzarches!)
—That more than once he'd cut a deal
At the Marché des Patriarches;

—He didn't really like his wife,
Or mother—But would have to say
Their souls should find an afterlife,
And he had read his Niboyet!*

— Qu'il penchait pour l'amour physique,
Et qu'à Rome, séjour d'ennui,
Une femme, d'ailleurs phthisique,
Était morte d'amour pour lui.

Pendant trois heures et demie,
Ce bavard, venu de Tournai,
M'a dégoisé toute sa vie;
J'en ai le cerveau consterné.

S'il fallait décrire ma peine,
Ce serait à n'en plus finir;
Je me disais, domptant ma haine:
'Au moins, si je pouvais dormir!'

Comme un qui n'est pas à son aise,
Et qui n'ose pas s'en aller,
Je frottais de mon cul ma chaise,
Rêvant de le faire empaler.

Ce monstre se nomme Bastogne;
Il fuyait devant le fléau.
Moi, je fuirai jusqu'en Gascogne,
Ou j'irai me jeter à l'eau,

Si dans ce Paris, qu'il redoute,
Quand chacun sera retourné,
Je trouve encore sur ma route
Ce fléau, natif de Tournai.

—He did believe in love-affairs;
One boring time in Rome, a slim
Young woman of consumptive airs
Had pined away for love of him.

Three hours and a half I spent,
While this fool, native of Tournai,
Unloaded all his life's events;
My brain felt nothing but dismay.

Don't ask me to describe my pain,
I'd never finish with the task;
I told myself, to ease the strain:
'A little sleep is all I ask!'

Like any man who does not dare,
Though ill-at-ease, to stand and go,
I screwed my rump into my chair,
And dreamed of skewering my foe.

Bastogne is this monster's name;
He was escaping the disease.
Myself, I'd run as far as Spain,
Or throw myself into the seas,

If in this Paris he can't stand,
When everyone is back to stay,
I'd find again, on any hand,
This pestilence out of Tournai.

XXIII. Un cabaret folâtre

Sur la route de Bruxelles à Uccle

Vous qui raffolez des squelettes
Et des emblèmes détestés,
Pour épicer les voluptés,
(Fût-ce de simples omelettes!)

Vieux Pharaon, ô Monselet!
Devant cette enseigne imprévue,
J'ai rêvé de vous: *A la vue*
Du Cimetière, Estaminet!

XXIII. A Jolly Tavern

On the Road from Brussels to Uccle

You who are fond of skeletons
And emblems most of us detest,
To spice your pleasures, every one,
(Even a humble omelette!)

Old Pharoah, M. Monselet!*
I saw this sign and thought of you
While on the road the other day:
Tavern, Cemetery View!

Additions de la troisième édition
des *Fleurs du Mal* (1868)

Additional Poems from the Third Edition of *The Flowers of Evil* (1868)

1. Épigraphe pour un livre condamné

Lecteur paisable et bucolique,
Sobre et naïf homme de bien,
Jette ce livre saturnien,
Orgiaque et mélancolique.

Si tu n'as fait ta rhétorique
Chez Satan, le rusé doyen,
Jette! tu n'y comprendrais rien,
Ou tu me croirais hystérique.

Mais si, sans se laisser charmer,
Ton œil sait plonger dans les gouffres,
Lis-moi, pour apprendre à m'aimer;

Âme curieuse qui souffres
Et vas cherchant ton paradis,
Plains-moi!... Sinon, je te maudis!

2. A Théodore de Banville
1842

Vous avez empoigné les crins de la Déesse
Avec un tel poignet, qu'on vous eût pris, à voir
Et cet air de maîtrise et ce beau nonchaloir,
Pour un jeune ruffian terrassant sa maîtresse.

L'œil clair et plein du feu de la précocité,
Vous avez prélassé votre orgueil d'architecte
Dans des constructions dont l'audace correcte
Fait voir quelle sera votre maturité.

1. Epigraph for a Condemned Book

Reader, you of calm, bucolic,
Artless, sober bonhomie,
Get rid of this Saturnian* book
Of orgies and despondency.

Just throw it out! unless you've learned
Your rhetoric in Satan's school
You will not understand a word,
You'll think I am hysterical.

But if your eye can brave the depths
And not be lost in gulfs or skies,
Read me, and learn to love this text;

O questing soul who suffers and
Keeps searching for your paradise
Have pity on me ... or be damned!

2. To Théodore de Banville*

1842

You've gripped the hair the goddess had let down
In such a fist, one might take you to be,
Seeing your nonchalance, your mastery,
A roughneck boy who throws his whore around.

Your clear eye fired with precocity,
Builder, you show us structures in your pride
Whose bold correctness helps us to decide
What we may hope from your maturity.

Poëte, notre sang nous fuit par chaque pore;
Est-ce que par hasard la robe de Centaure,
Qui changeait toute veine en funèbre ruisseau

Était teinte trois fois dans les baves subtiles
De ces vindicatifs et monstrueux reptiles
Que le petit Hercule étranglait au berceau?

4. La Prière d'un païen

Ah! ne ralentis pas tes flammes;
Réchauffe mon cœur engourdi,
Volupté, torture des âmes!
Diva! supplicem exaudi!

Déesse dans l'air répandue,
Flamme dans notre souterrain!
Exauce une âme morfondue,
Qui te consacre un chant d'airain.

Volupté, sois toujours ma reine!
Prends le masque d'une sirène
Faite de chair et de velours,

Ou verse-moi tes sommeils lourds
Dans le vin informe et mystique,
Volupté, fantôme élastique!

5. Le Couvercle

En quelque lieu qu'il aille, ou sur mer ou sur terre,
Sous un climat de flamme ou sous un soleil blanc,
Serviteur de Jésus, courtisan de Cythère,
Mendiant ténébreux ou Crésus rutilant,

Poet, our blood flows out by every pore;
Could it be that the robe of the Centaur
That turned each vein into a stream of red,

Was dyed three times within the subtle slime
Of those same snakes, so spiteful and malign,
Hercules strangled in his cradle-bed?*

4. Prayer of a Pagan

Ah! never let your flame grow cold;
Fire my heart's torpidity,
*Voluptas,** torture of the soul!
*Diva! supplicem exaudi!**

Goddess who haunts the atmosphere,
Blaze in the nether regions too!
A soul benumbed begs you to hear
The brazen song he sings to you.

Be thou my queen! that is my prayer;
Take up a siren's mask to wear
Of flesh and velvet, soft and fine;

In vapours of your mystic wine
Pour out a heavy sleep for me,
O phantom, Sensuality!

5. The Pot Lid

Whatever place he goes, on land or sea,
Under a flaming or a chilling sun,
Servant of Jesus, courtier of Love,
Refulgent Croesus* or a dingy tramp,

Citadin, campagnard, vagabond, sédentaire,
Que son petit cerveau soit actif ou soit lent,
Partout l'homme subit la terreur du mystère,
Et ne regarde en haut qu'avec un œil tremblant.

En haut, le Ciel! ce mur de caveau qui l'étouffe,
Plafond illuminé par un opéra bouffe
Où chaque histrion foule un sol ensanglanté;

Terreur du libertin, espoir du fol ermite;
Le Ciel! couvercle noir de la grande marmite
Où bout l'imperceptible et vaste Humanité.

6. L'Examen de minuit

La pendule, sonnant minuit,
Ironiquement nous engage
A nous rappeler quel usage
Nous fîmes du jour qui s'enfuit:
— Aujourd'hui, date fatidique,
Vendredi, treize, nous avons,
Malgré tout ce que nous savons,
Mené le train d'un hérétique.

Nous avons blasphémé Jesus,
Des Dieux le plus incontestable!
Comme un parasite à la table
De quelque monstrueux Crésus,
Nous avons, pour plaire à la brute,
Digne vassale des Démons,
Insulté ce que nous aimons,
Et flatté ce qui nous rebute;

Contristé, servile bourreau,
Le faible qu'à tort on méprise;
Salué l'énorme Bêtise,
La Bêtise au front de taureau;

Set in his city or a vagabond,
Whether his little brain be quick or slow,
Man everywhere quakes at the mystery,
And looks up only with a trembling eye.

The sky above! this wall that stifles him,
A ceiling lit by the dramatic farce
In which each actor treads a bloody earth;

Libertines' terror, the mad hermit's hope:
The Sky! black lid of the enormous pot*
Where vast, amorphous Mankind boils and seethes.

6. Midnight Examination*

The clock chimes the midnight in,
And ironically gives us the charge
To remember the fleeting day,
What usage we made of our time:
—Today, that fateful day,
Friday the thirteenth, we have,
In spite of all that we know
Behaved like a heretic.

We have blasphemed Jesus, the most
Incontestable of all Gods!
Like a parasite at the feast
Of some monstrous profligate,
We have, to please the brute,
That worthy vassal of Hell,
Insulted what we love,
And flattered the one we scorn;

Vile torturer, we have afflicted
The weak, who are wrongly despised;
Have bowed to enormous Folly,
Folly with brow of a bull;

Baisé la stupide Matière
Avec grande dévotion,
Et de la putréfaction
Béni la blafarde lumière.

Enfin, nous avons, pour noyer
La vertige dans le délire,
Nous, prêtre orgueilleux de la Lyre,
Dont la gloire est de déployer
L'ivresse des choses funèbres,
Bu sans soif et mangé sans faim!...
— Vite soufflons la lampe, afin
De nous cacher dans les ténèbres!

7. Madrigal triste

I

Que m'importe que tu sois sage?
Sois belle! et sois triste! Les pleurs
Ajoutent un charme au visage,
Comme le fleuve au paysage;
L'orage rajeunit les fleurs.

Je t'aime surtout quand la joie
S'enfuit de ton front terrassé;
Quand ton cœur dans l'horreur se noie;
Quand sur ton présent se déploie
Le nuage affreux du passé.

Je t'aime quand ton grand œil verse
Une eau chaude comme le sang;
Quand, malgré ma main qui te berce,
Ton angoisse, trop lourde, perce
Comme un râle d'agonisant.

Made love to mindless Matter,
With pious devotion indeed,
And blessed the lurid glow
Of putrefaction's light;

Finally, trying to drown
In delirium, vertigo,
We have, proud priest of the Lyre,
Whose glory is to unfold
The transport of morbid things,*
Eaten and drunk like a swine! . . .
— O quickly, blow out the lamp
And hide us deep in the dark!

7. Sad Madrigal

I

What do I care if you be wise?
Be lovely! and be sad! For tears
Are as appealing on the face
As rivers in the countryside;
Flowers are freshened by the storm.

I love you most of all when joy
Escapes from your defeated brow;
Or when a horror drowns your heart;
When on your present day, a cloud
Out of the past deploys itself.

I love you when your great eye pours
A water warm as any blood;
When, under my consoling hand,
Your piercing anguish finds a voice—
The rattle of a dying throat.

J'aspire, volupté divine!
Hymne profond, délicieux!
Tous les sanglots de ta poitrine,
Et crois que ton cœur s'illumine
Des perles que versent tes yeux!

II

Je sais que ton cœur, qui regorge
De vieux amours déracinés,
Flamboie encor comme une forge,
Et que tu couves sous ta gorge
Un peu de l'orgueil des damnés;

Mais tant, ma chère, que tes rêves
N'auront pas reflété l'Enfer,
Et qu'en un cauchemar sans trêves,
Songeant de poisons et de glaives,
Éprise de poudre et de fer,

N'ouvrant à chacun qu'avec crainte,
Déchiffrant le malheur partout,
Te convulsant quand l'heure tinte,
Tu n'auras pas senti l'étreinte
De l'irrésistible Dégoût,

Tu ne pourras, esclave reine
Qui ne m'aimes qu'avec effroi,
Dans l'horreur de la nuit malsaine
Me dire, l'âme de cris pleine:
'Je suis ton égale, ô mon Roi!'

I breathe, a luxury divine!
Profound, delicious hymn to me!
All of the sobbing of your breast,
And I believe your heart will glow
With pearls your eyes have cast away!

II

I know your heart, that overflows
With all of your uprooted loves,
Flames always like a forge, and that
Beneath your breast you incubate
Some of the smugness of the damned;

But dear, as long as dreams of yours
Will not reflect the flames of Hell—
As long as in a nightmare's grip,
Dreaming of poisons, slashing blades,
In love with powder, cannon shot,

Dreading to answer any door,
Anatomizing misery,
Tormented by the tolling clock,
You will not suffer the embrace
Of irresistible Disgust—

You may not, oh my slave and queen
Who loves me only out of fear,
Horrified, in the fevered night,
With screaming soul proclaim to me:
'I am your equal, o my King!'

8. L'Avertisseur

Tout homme digne de ce nom
A dans le cœur un Serpent jaune,
Installé comme sur un trône,
Qui, s'il dit: 'Je veux!' répond: 'Non!'

Plonge tes yeux dans les yeux fixes
Des Satyresses ou des Nixes,
La Dent dit: 'Pense à ton devoir!'

Fais des enfants, plante des arbres,
Polis des vers, sculpte des marbres,
La Dent dit: 'Vivras-tu ce soir?'

Quoi qu'il ébauche ou qu'il espère,
L'homme ne vit pas un moment
Sans subir l'avertissement
De l'insupportable Vipère.

9. Le Rebelle

Un Ange furieux fond du ciel comme un aigle,
Du mécréant saisit à plein poing les cheveux,
Et dit, le secouant: 'Tu connaîtras la règle!
(Car je suis ton bon Ange, entends-tu?) Je le veux!

Sache qu'il faut aimer, sans faire la grimace,
Le pauvre, le méchant, le tortu, l'hébété,
Pour que tu puisses faire à Jésus, quand il passe,
Un tapis triomphal avec ta charité.

8. The Cautioner

Each man who's worth the name must know
A yellow Serpent is at home
Within his heart, as on a throne,
Which, if he says: 'I want!' says: 'No!'

Go plunge your eyes into the depths
Of Nixie's* eyes, or Satyress',*
'Your duty first!' the Tooth will say.

Engender children, nurture trees,
Sculpt marble, polish poetry,
The Tooth says, 'You may die today!'

Despite his hopes, the plans he makes,
Man does not live a moment free
From cautions offered knowingly
By that insufferable Snake.

9. The Rebel

A raging Angel in an eagle's flight
Swoops, grabs the sinner's hair in fisted hand
And shakes him, saying 'You know what is right!
(You hear your Angel?) This is my command!

I order you to love without a sneer
The mad, the wretched, those in poverty,
To make for Jesus, when he passes here,
A regal carpet, of your charity.

Tel est l'Amour! Avant que ton cœur ne se blase,
A la gloire de Dieu rallume ton extase;
C'est la Volupté vraie aux durables appas!'

Et l'Ange, châtiant autant, ma foi! qu'il aime,
De ses poings de géant torture l'anathème;
Mais le damné répond toujours: 'Je ne veux pas!'

10. Bien loin d'ici

C'est ici la case sacrée
Où cette fille très parée,
Tranquille et toujours préparée,

D'une main éventant ses seins,
Et son coude dans les coussins,
Écoute pleurer les bassins:

C'est la chambre de Dorothée.
— La brise et l'eau chantent au loin
Leur chanson de sanglots heurtée
Pour bercer cette enfant gâtée.

Du haut en bas, avec grand soin,
Sa peau délicate est frottée
D'huile odorante et de benjoin.
— Des fleurs se pâment dans un coin.

11. Le Gouffre

Pascal avait son gouffre, avec lui se mouvant.
— Hélas! tout est abîme, — action, désir, rêve,
Parole! et sur mon poil qui tout droit se relève
Mainte fois de la Peur je sens passer le vent.

That is real Love! So that you do not turn
Numb to God's glory, let your rapture burn,
And know true pleasure in the sensual way!'

Good God! the Angel, who corrects and loves,*
Twists in his fist the sinner from above;
Answers the damned soul, 'I will not obey!'

10. Very Far From France

Here is the place—the hut, the shrine,
Where this well-favoured girl reclines,
Tranquil, prepared for any guests.

Using a hand to fan her breasts,
Propped on a cushioned elbow, she
Can listen to the fountains cry:

This is the room of Dorothy.*
—The breeze and water far away
Carol their sobbing song all day
To bring this child a lullaby.

And carefully, from top to toe
Her skin is polished to a glow
With scented oils and perfume.
—The flowers in the corner swoon.

11. The Gulf

Pascal* had his gulf, moving where he moved.
Alas! all is abyss—all action, dream
Desire, speech! and many a time I feel
My hair stand up, brushed by the wind of Fear.

En haut, en bas, partout, la profondeur, la grève,
Le silence, l'espace affreux et captivant...
Sur le fond de mes nuits Dieu de son doigt savant
Dessine un cauchemar multiforme et sans trêve.

J'ai peur du sommeil comme on a peur d'un grand trou,
Tout plein de vague horreur, menant on ne sait où;
Je ne vois qu'infini par toutes les fenêtres,

Et mon esprit, toujours du vertige hanté,
Jalouse de néant l'insensibilité.
— Ah! ne jamais sortir des Nombres et des Êtres!

12. Les Plaintes d'un Icare

Les amants des prostituées
Sont heureux, dispos et repus;
Quant à moi, mes bras sont rompus
Pour avoir étreint des nuées.

C'est grâce aux astres nonpareils,
Qui tout au fond du ciel flamboient,
Que mes yeux consumés ne voient
Que des souvenirs de soleils.

En vain j'ai voulu de l'espace
Trouver la fin et le milieu;
Sous je ne sais quel œil de feu
Je sens mon aile qui se casse;

Et brûlé par l'amour du beau,
Je n'aurai pas l'honneur sublime
De donner mon nom à l'abîme
Qui me servira de tombeau.

On high, low, everywhere, the depth, the shore
The silence, frightening and bewitching space...
Deep in my nights, God with a master's hand
Draws me a nightmare, ceaseless, manifold.

Sleep frightens me, as one feels loathing at
A great hole leading who knows where; I see
Only the infinite through all windows,

And my spirit, haunted by vertigo,
Envies non-being its insentience.
—Ah! never from beings, numbers to be free!

12. Lament of an Icarus*

Those men who cuddle whores for love
Are sated by their darlings' charms,
But I have only tired arms
From having hugged the clouds above.

Thanks to the stars, the matchless ones
That flame within the depths of skies,
All I can see with burnt-out eyes
Are dark remembrances of suns.

In vain I've tried to find the heart
Of space, to venture deeper, higher;
Under who knows what eye of fire
My weary wings will break apart;

And burned by love of beauty, I
Will not achieve my poignant wish,
To give my name to the abyss,
The tomb below, to which I fly.

13. Recueillement

Sois sage, ô ma Douleur, et tiens-toi plus tranquille.
Tu réclamais le Soir; il descend; le voici:
Une atmosphère obscure enveloppe la ville,
Aux uns portant la paix, aux autres le souci.

Pendant que des mortels la multitude vile,
Sous le fouet de Plaisir, ce bourreau sans merci,
Va cueillir des remords dans la fête servile,
Ma Douleur, donne-moi la main; viens par ici,

Loin d'eux. Vois se pencher les défuntes Années,
Sur les balcons du ciel, en robes surannées;
Surgir du fond des eaux le Regret souriant;

Le Soleil moribond s'endormir sous une arche,
Et, comme un long linceul traînant à l'Orient,
Entends, ma chère, entends la douce Nuit qui marche

14. La Lune offensée

Ô Lune qu'adoraient discrètement nos pères,
Du haut des pays bleus où, radieux sérail,
Les astres vont te suivre en pimpant attirail,
Ma vieille Cynthia, lampe de nos repaires,

Vois-tu les amoureux, sur leurs grabats prospères,
De leur bouche en dormant montrer le frais émail?
Le poëte buter du front sur son travail?
Ou sous les gazons secs s'accoupler les vipères?

13. Meditation

Be good, my Sorrow, quiet your despair.
You call for Evening; it descends, is here;
Around the town, a darkness in the air
Promising peace to some, to others care.

While most, the rabid multitude of men,
Lashed by their Lust, in merciless torment,
Gather remorse on slavish holiday,
My Sorrow, take my hand and come away,

Away from them. Look, as the Years lean down
From heaven's porches, clothed in ancient gowns;
Regret, in smiles, looms from the water's depths;

Under an archway sleeps the dying Sun.
And, like a shroud swept to the Orient,
Listen, my dear, the sweet Night walks along.

14. The Insulted Moon

O moon our ancestors discreetly praised,
Out of the high blue country, where the stars,
Your harem, trail their elegant arrays,
Old Cynthia,* lamp of these lairs of ours,

Do you see lovers on their thriving beds,
Their bright teeth flashing as they snore away?
Frustrated poets buffeting their heads?
Or ardent vipers writhing in the hay?

Sous ton domino jaune, et d'un pied clandestin,
Vas-tu, comme jadis, du soir jusqu'au matin,
Baiser d'Endymion les grâces surannées?

— 'Je vois ta mère, enfant de ce siècle appauvri,
Qui vers son miroir penche un lourd amas d'années,
Et plâtre artistement le sein qui t'a nourri!'

With padded foot, behind your yellow mask,
From sunset to the dawn, do you pursue
Endymion's* pale charms, as formerly?

—'Child of this wretched century,* I see
Your mother towards her mirror lean a mass
Of years, rouging the teat that nourished you!'

EXPLANATORY NOTES

The arrangement of the poems is that of the 1861 second edition of the *Flowers*, supplemented by 16 poems from *The Waifs* (1866), and also by the poems added to the 1868 third edition of the *Flowers*. I follow the arrangement in the Gallimard edition of *Les Fleurs du Mal* (1972), except that I have returned the six pieces condemned by the court in 1857 from their place in *The Waifs* to their original placement in the first edition. Thus, 'The Jewels', coming after poem no. 21, 'Hymn to Beauty', has been numbered 21a, to show that it has been inserted, and I have numbered the other inserted pieces similarly. The numbering of the 1861 edition has therefore been preserved, but the reader can also readily see the original context in which Baudelaire had located the poems.

I have found the following sources particularly useful in compiling these notes:

ADAM, ANTOINE, ed., *Baudelaire: 'Les Fleurs du Mal'* (Paris: Garnier Frères, 1961).

CHÉRIX, ROBERT-BENOIT, ed., *Commentaire des 'Fleurs du Mal'*, Collection d'Études et de Documents Littéraires (Genève: Pierre Cailler, 1949).

DELABROY, JEAN, ed., *Charles Baudelaire: 'Les Fleurs du Mal'*, Collection Textes et Contextes (La Creuse, France: Louis Magnard, 1989).

DUPONT, JACQUES, ed., *Charles Baudelaire: 'Les Fleurs du Mal'* (Paris: Flammarion, 1991).

PICHOIS, CLAUDE, *Baudelaire*, trans. Graham Robb (London: Hamish Hamilton, 1989).

—— ed., *Charles Baudelaire: 'Les Fleurs du Mal'*, *Édition de 1861*, Collection Poésie (Paris: Gallimard, 1972).

I also thank Jonathan Culler for his suggestions and additions. References to Culler in the notes below pertain to our correspondence during the preparation of this book, unless otherwise noted.

The references to Baudelaire's prose poems apply specifically to Rosemary Lloyd, trans., *Charles Baudelaire: The Prose Poems and 'La Fanfarlo'*, The World's Classics (New York and Oxford: Oxford University Press, 1991).

3 *Théophile Gautier*: (1811–72) one of the foremost French poets of the generation previous to Baudelaire's. Baudelaire admired

Gautier's mastery of the French language and perfection of form, but the two poets also shared enthusiasms for the grotesque, as well as for such matters as the painting of Delacroix and seventeenth-century poetry. This dedication to Gautier was originally much longer, but was reduced according to Gautier's preference. Baudelaire expected, as his *Flowers* were about to be published, that readers would rank his poetry with that of Hugo, Gautier, and Byron.

It is of some interest that the 1857 edition of the *Flowers* had as epigraph a passage from *Les Tragiques*, book II of the baroque poet Théodore Agrippa d'Aubigné (1550–1630): 'It's said that one must sink all execrable things | Closed in a sepulchre, deep in oblivion, | And that by written works, evil brought back to life | Will taint the moral will of our posterity. | But Vice is mothered not by Knowledge, not at all, | And Virtue's surely not the child of Ignorance.'

To the Reader

5 *the alchemist* | *Satan Thrice-Great*: Satan is seen as an alchemist, in the tradition of Hermes Trismegistus (thrice-great), associated with the Egyptian god Thoth, by legend the author of works on alchemy and other medieval sciences.

7 *Ennui*: frequently translated into English as 'boredom', but 'boredom' seems not forceful enough for what Baudelaire intends. 'Ennui' in Baudelaire is a soul-deadening, pathological condition, the worst of the many vices of mankind, which leads us into the abyss of non-being. Baudelaire recognizes Ennui in himself, and insists in this poem that the reader shares this vice. Here he personifies Ennui as a being drugging himself, smoking his water-pipe (hookah).

SPLEEN AND THE IDEAL

Ennui and 'Spleen', a word in English, are closely related concepts in this volume: they drag man down towards the abyss, while a contrary tendency would elevate man away from evil; this is man's yearning towards the 'Ideal'. 'Spleen' in medieval psychology was one of the four 'humours' thought to control human behaviour. It became associated in the eighteenth century, especially in England, with deep, suicidal depression, which seems to have led to Baudelaire's associating it with the soul-deadening spiritual condition he calls 'ennui'.

1. Benediction

11 *my penance*: the baby; the young poet.

Gehenna: the Valley of Hinnon, south of Jerusalem, where sacrifices of children were made in ancient times. The word has become a synonym for 'Hell'.

13 *harpies' talons*: in Greek mythology, a Harpy was a vicious, winged monster with the head and body of a woman, but the talons of a bird of prey.

15 *Virtues, Powers, Dominations, Thrones*: the reference here is to the angelic orders, as they were understood in medieval angelology. There were nine orders: in descending importance, Seraphim, Cherubim, Thrones, Dominations, Virtues, Powers, Principalities, Archangels, and Angels.

old Palmyra's wealth: Palmyra was the opulent ancient capital of Syria, located north-east of Damascus.

2. The Albatross

17 *He cannot walk, his wings are in the way*: an albatross is a large sea bird with exceptionally long, narrow wings which enable it to soar at great heights, but which are virtually useless on the ground.

4. Correspondences

Baudelaire had at least a passing familiarity with the doctrines of the Swedish mystical theologian and scientist, Emanuel Swedenborg (1688–1772), pertaining to direct correspondences between the physical and spiritual realms, physical objects being symbols of spiritual realities. Baudelaire's *alter ego*, Samuel Cramer, in his story 'The Fanfarlo', has a volume of Swedenborg in his study. Baudelaire would also have been well aware of Balzac's interest in Swedenborg, an interest shared by Romantic poets and philosophers in Europe and America. In fact many previous writers, including Hugo and Lamartine, had compared nature to a temple, and treated the physical world as the reflection of a spiritual one. To Jonathan Culler, Baudelaire's poem is an ironic reflection on this tradition; see the Introduction to this volume.

19 *Odours there are... green as meadow grass*: an example of synaesthesia (the mixing of the senses), and a reminder that Baudelaire was a great poet of odours, of the sense of smell. The bringing together in this poem of odours, colours, sounds to produce a kind of rapture beyond everyday reality made this an important work for the later French symbolists.

5. 'I love the thought...'

Phoebus: Phoebus Apollo, son of Zeus, was the Greek god associated with (among other things) the sun.

Cybele: in Greek mythology, the goddess of Nature. The worship of Cybele originated in Phrygia, in Asia Minor.

she-wolf... fed the universe: there are legends from various cultures of wolves raising human children, including the founders of Rome, Romulus and Remus. See also no. 89, ll. 47–8.

21 *Utility*: this is the 'god' of the industrial, commercial bourgeois society, which to Baudelaire and many of his contemporaries in the arts was the enemy of all they valued. Jacques Dupont suggests that the 'brazen wraps' in which Utility 'swaddles his progeny' are, for women, corsets, and for men tight-fitting frock coats.

6. The Beacons

Rubens: Peter Paul Rubens (1577–1640) was an immensely prolific Flemish painter, known for his particularly fleshy nudes.

23 *Leonardo*: Leonardo da Vinci (1452–1519), Italian artist and scientist, was perhaps the quintessential 'Renaissance man' in his versatility and achievement. He painted the *Mona Lisa*, and other female figures with enigmatic smiles.

Rembrandt: Rembrandt van Rijn (1606–69) has become perhaps the most celebrated painter of a great age of art in The Netherlands. He was known for his religious paintings, and for his effects of light on a basically dark canvas.

Michelangelo... forms of Christ: Michelangelo Buonarotti (1475–1564), born in Florence, was a sculptor, architect, painter, and poet. The reference to Hercules mingling with forms of Christ refers to the very muscular bodies of Michelangelo's figures in his religious works.

Puget: French sculptor Pierre Puget (1622–94).

23 *Watteau*: Antoine Watteau (1684–1721), the Flemish painter, was perhaps the foremost artist of the rococo period.

Goya: Francisco Goya (1746–1828), a Spanish painter known for exploring the dark side of human experience.

Delacroix: Eugène Delacroix (1798–1863), the French painter. Baudelaire knew Delacroix, and in his art criticism was a champion of Delacroix's romantic style.

Weber: Carl Maria von Weber (1786–1826), German composer and conductor.

Te Deum: 'Thee, Lord', the beginning of the hymn of praise sung in the Catholic mass, and on occasions of celebration.

7. The Sick Muse

25 *succubus*: an evil spirit or demon, especially one that takes a woman's form to tempt a man; it has been suggested that Baudelaire intended 'incubus' (a spirit in male form) here.

Minturnes: Minturnae, a city in Latium, surrounded by swamps, where Marius, an official of the Roman Republic, sought refuge from persecution in the first century BC.

Apollo, and the harvest-lord, great Pan: among his other attributes, Apollo was associated with music and poetry, and was master of the lyre. Pan—part man and part goat—was associated with nature and fertility; he played on the pan-pipes, which he made out of reeds, and though he was a superior musician, he was no match for Apollo in a contest between them. According to some sources, Apollo was the father of Pan.

8. The Venal Muse

27 *Te Deums*: hymns of praise sung in the Catholic mass, and on occasions of celebration. See note to no. 6.

9. The Wretched Monk

29 *cenobite*: a member of a religious community.

10. The Enemy

The Enemy in this poem has been variously identified as the Devil, or as Time personified.

11. Ill Fortune

29 *Ill Fortune*: in French, 'Guignon'. Writing of the American poet Edgar Allan Poe, many of whose prose works he translated, Baudelaire commented that in the literature of every country there are men who carry the word 'guignon' written in mysterious characters on their foreheads.

Sisyphus: for the crime of (temporarily) outwitting Death, Sisyphus was condemned in Erebus (the Hell of Greek mythology) endlessly to push a huge rock up a hill: just when it should topple over the summit, it instead rolls backwards, and Sisyphus has to start all over again.

Time . . . so long: the axiom, 'art is long and time is fleeting', has been a commonplace since ancient times: Baudelaire said he first found it in Hippocrates (Greek physician ?460–?377 BC). Later it was expressed in an American poem, Longfellow's 'Psalm of Life': 'Art is long and time is fleeting, | And our hearts, though stout and brave, | Still, like muffled drums, are beating | Funeral marches to the grave.' This passage is the basis for ll. 4–8 of Baudelaire's poem. Lines 9–14 are based on a passage from another poem in English, Thomas Gray's 'Elegy Written in a Country Churchyard': 'Full many a gem of purest ray serene | The dark unfathomed caves of ocean bear; | Full many a flower is born to blush unseen | And waste its sweetness on the desert air.'

13. Gypsies Travelling

This poem was inspired by a print by Jacques Callot, having the same title as the poem (*Bohémiens en voyage*).

33 *chimeras*: a chimera is a female monster, lion-like, but with the attributes as well of goat and serpent. Here 'chimeras' are impossible fancies, creations of the imagination.

Cybele: goddess of Nature. See note to no. 5.

15. Don Juan in Hell

This poem was also entitled 'The Impenitent', which allies it in theme to the succeeding poem, about a man punished for his pride. Don Juan was a legendary seducer of women and a favourite subject for many dramatists, including Molière and Mozart (the libretto for Mozart's *Don Giovanni* was by Lorenzo da Ponte). In their versions, the story ends with Don Juan's being condemned to Hell; this poem, then, picks up where that story leaves off. J. Dupont points out that around 1853 Baudelaire was contemplating writing an opera entitled *The End of Don Juan*.

35 *coin for Charon's chores*: Charon was the boatman in Greek and Roman mythology who ferried the souls of the dead to the Underworld (called Erebus or Tartarus) across the river Acheron, or in some versions, the Styx. A coin to pay Charon was placed between the lips of the dead.

A beggar with Antisthenes' proud gaze: Antisthenes was a Greek philosopher, disciple of Socrates, who became the head of the school of the Cynics. It is not clear why the philosopher is referred to in this poem, but there appears in Molière's *Dom Juan*, Act III, pursuing the hero, a beggar who might have taken 'an avenger's grip around the oars' (l. 4).

Sad women: Don Juan has become the prototype of the heartless philanderer, having no regard, for example, for the vows he made to his wife Elvira, or to any of his many mistresses.

Sganarelle ... Don Luis ... Elvira ... A great stone man: all characters in Molière's comedy *Dom Juan*; Sganarelle was Don Juan's servant, Don Luis his father, Elvira his wife. The 'great stone man' recalls the statue of the Commander, the agent for condemning Don Juan to Hell in the traditional story.

16. Punishment for Pride

37 *A celebrated doctor*: the thirteenth-century theologian Simon of Tournai, who, according to medieval commentators, became so proud of himself for having demonstrated the truth of the dogma of the Holy Trinity that he defied Jesus, and was punished as Baudelaire describes in this poem.

17. Beauty

39 *a stone-fashioned dream*: beauty as a statue of metal or stone, cold and remote, is one of Baudelaire's recurring images, for instance in 'I give to you these verses ...' or in the prose poem 'The Jester and the Goddess'.

sphinx: a monster in Greek mythology with the face of a woman, the body of a lion, and the wings of a bird; in the story of King Oedipus, the Sphinx would ask a riddle of passers-by, and those who could not solve it would be devoured.

18. The Ideal

39 *vignettes*: decorative, illustrative book designs.

chlorosis: a kind of anaemia often afflicting adolescent girls.

Gavarni: a fashionable cartoonist and engraver of frivolous subjects.

Aeschylus' dream: Lady Macbeth as an Aeschylean heroine transplanted to northern climes. Aeschylus' Clytemnestra would certainly be another example of the type of woman Baudelaire is invoking here, one who does not shrink from bloodshed. Delacroix's *Lady Macbeth* was exhibited at the Salon of 1850.

41 *great Night of Michelangelo's*: refers to Michelangelo's statue of Night as a powerful nude female in the Chapel of the Medicis in Florence. Night was the mother of the Titans.

19. The Giantess

times: Baudelaire is referring to vaguely mythological ancient times.

20. The Mask

Ernest Christophe, sculptor: a friend of Baudelaire's, whose work *The Human Comedy* serves as the basis for this poem. Later Christophe renamed the statue *The Mask* in commemoration of Baudelaire's poem; the statue is now on display at the Musée D'Orsay in Paris.

43 *exquisite air*: this refers to the mask; the true head behind it shows an expression of deep distress.

21a. The Jewels

It is generally, though not universally, assumed that this poem refers to Jeanne Duval. Its placement here would make it the first of the Jeanne Duval cycle (see note to no. 22).

47 *those clusters on my vine*: a direct allusion to the Song of Solomon, 7:8.

49 *Antiope*: the sister of the Amazon queen, Hippolyta (see note to no. 35), and consort of the Athenian king, Theseus. Baudelaire would certainly have known paintings by Ingres and Watteau of which she was the subject. In this poem Antiope is mentioned as a figure with full, womanly hips.

22. Exotic Perfume

Here begins, in the 1861 edition, what critics have called the cycle of the 'Black Venus', Baudelaire's long-time companion, Jeanne Duval (also known as Jeanne Lemer, or Jeanne Prosper) Jeanne Duval was a mulatto actress and sometime prostitute Baudelaire first mentions in a letter of 1843. In 1852 he broke with her, but the break was not permanent. Manet painted her portrait, entitling the picture *Baudelaire's Mistress*, in 1862. She was by no means Baudelaire's intellectual equal and cared little for his poetry, but her body and her temperament fascinated the poet. Jeanne's cycle runs from no. 22 to no. 39, but probably excludes no. 25.

49 *Inviting shorelines*: the landscape described in 'Exotic Perfume' relates to a sea journey Baudelaire took in 1841 to Mauritius and Réunion, islands in the Indian Ocean.

23. Head of Hair

51 *Of sails, of oarsmen, waving pennants, masts*: this recalls the landscape of the previous poem, and is also echoed in the prose poem, 'A Hemisphere in a Head of Hair': 'Your hair contains an entire dream, full of sails and masts.' One of Jeanne's features most fascinating to Baudelaire was her great mane of dark hair, and he mentions it often.

24. 'I love you as I love . . .'

53 *lachrymal*: vase found in ancient Roman tombs, once thought to be for the tears of mourners.

This iciness so beautiful to me: we might be reminded of Baudelaire's characteristic image of Beauty as a statue of stone or metal, something beyond the purely physical and natural.

25. 'You'd entertain the universe . . .'

Foul woman: there is testimony from Baudelaire's contemporaries that this poem was inspired by Baudelaire's first mistress, Sara, a Jewish prostitute also known as Louchette. Sara seems likely to be the 'monstrous Jewish whore' of poem no. 32.

26. *Sed non satiata*

55 *Sed non satiata*: 'but not satisfied'—a reference to the Roman poet Juvenal's description of the sexual appetite of Valeria Messalina, wife of the Emperor Claudius

55 *Faust*: the legendary student of magic who made a bargain with
the Devil. Baudelaire would have known Gerard de Nerval's
translation, published in 1840, of Goethe's *Faust* (Part I, 1808;
Part II, 1833).

pavane: a stately dance.

Styx: legendary river that circles Hell nine times. J. Dupont
notes in addition a possible echo from Ovid's *Loves*, III. 26,
pertaining to remarkable virility: the sustaining of the assault nine
times.

Megaera: one of the Furies, female divinities who live in the
Underworld (Erebus) and pursue and punish human
transgressors.

Persephone: as the wife of Hades, god of Erebus, she ruled
over the Furies. She also presided over the yearly cycle of death
and rebirth, and so became goddess of resurrected vigour, or of
debauchery (J. Dupont). Critics have taken this last line, along
with the reference to 'nine times' in l. 11, to mean that the
speaker cannot make love to his mistress as insatiably as a
goddess might; there seems also to be an indication of lesbian
tendencies in the mistress.

27. 'The way her silky garments . . .'

57 *sphinx*: see note to no. 17.

29. A Carcass

Because of the notoriety attending this poem, Baudelaire said
that he could be considered the 'Prince of Carcasses'.

63 *the form, and the essence divine*: though the human body must die
and decay, the poet or artist may provide it with a permanent
form, that captures a spiritual essence.

30. *De profundis clamavi*

De profundis clamavi: 'from the depths, I cried out.' Psalm 130,
which begins with this phrase in the Latin Bible, was used in the
Catholic funeral liturgy, the 'office of the dead'. One of this
poem's earlier titles was 'The Spleen', and certainly the mood of
deep despair the poem represents demonstrates the way
Baudelaire employs the term 'spleen'.

31a. Lethe

This poem was most probably inspired by Jeanne Duval, and was originally located here within her cycle.

67 *Lethe*: the river of forgetfulness in the Underworld, described by Plato and Virgil; here souls drink and forget their spiritual existence, in preparation for their being born again into earthly bodies. See also nos. 60 and 77.

nepenthe: legendary drug to bring oblivion as a remedy for grief.

32. 'Beside a monstrous Jewish whore . . .'

69 *monstrous Jewish whore*: according to tradition, Sara, called Louchette, Baudelaire's first mistress.

beauty my desire had turned away: the poem presents the situation of the speaker having returned to an earlier mistress, but thinking of another—it is assumed Jeanne Duval—as he lies with her.

34. The Cat

Baudelaire was a cat-lover. In this poem the cat is likened to the speaker's mistress.

35. *Duellum*

71 *Duellum*: the archaic form of *bellum*, or war; here it simply means combat between two adversaries: duel.

73 *Amazon*: Amazons were female warriors of ancient Greek legend; Homer mentions them as allies of Troy in *The Iliad*.

36. The Balcony

This poem employs the *strophe encadrée*, or enveloped stanza, in which the first and last lines of each stanza are identical, or nearly so. Baudelaire also used the enveloped stanza in nos. 44, 54, 62, 110a, and XII.

37. The Possessed

75 *Beelzebub*: the root meaning in Hebrew is 'Lord of the Flies'. It has become another name for Satan. The speaker represents himself as possessed by the demonic spirit of his mistress, whom he also compares to a dagger in l. 8.

38. A Phantom

This is a relatively late poem (1860), written about the memory or ghost of Baudelaire's love, quite evidently Jeanne Duval.

39. 'I give to you these verses...'

This poem plays off the tradition of poets promising their mistresses immortality in their verses. This mistress will be immortalized uniquely as a 'damned being', the memory of whom will 'bore the reader'.

40. *Semper eadem*

This is the first of a cycle of nine poems, nos. 40–48, inspired by the 'White Venus', Apollonie Sabatier, born Aglaé-Joséphine Savatier, called 'La Présidente' in her circle of friends. Mme Sabatier at the time Baudelaire knew her in the 1850s was the mistress of the wealthy Belgian Alfred Mosselman; she presided over a kind of salon of artists and intellectuals, which undoubtedly included some of her former lovers. Baudelaire, knowning full well her physical generosity, none the less chose to regard her as his ideal of pure beauty. He wrote her poems in anonymous letters, extolling her virtue in a manner close to idolatry. When three years after seeing the poems Mme Sabatier offered herself physically, Baudelaire was much dismayed; physical love was not at all what he had wanted from the woman, whom he had chosen to regard as his 'Guardian, Madonna, Muse' (no. 42). Interestingly, though, some of the 'White Venus' poems show complexities in this relationship beyond pure idealization.

83 *Semper eadem*: she is always the same.

So let my heart be lost within a lie: the emphasis of 'lie' is Baudelaire's. Love is a lie that conceals life's evils, and the fact of death.

41. Completely One

the objects, black or rose: the Devil wants to focus on the beloved's physical, particularly sexual, attributes, but the poet responds by describing her transcendent grace and beauty, the harmony of the whole. This poem plays on the tradition of the Blazon, where the excellencies of the beloved, the beauty of her eyes, hair, shoulders, and so on, were detailed.

43. The Living Torch

87 *You sing Awakening, they praise the Dead*: 'you' refers to the eyes of the beloved; 'they' to the 'tapers lit at noon' (l. 10). Critics have noted similarities to Poe's 'To Helen' in tone and language.

43a. To One Who Is Too Cheerful

Baudelaire presented this poem to Mme Sabatier in an anonymous letter dated 9 December 1852.

89 *my venom*: Baudelaire explained in a note that he intended this 'venom' to refer to his melancholy or splenetic temperament, rejecting his prosecutors' interpretation that the 'venom' was syphilis.

44. Reversibility

91 *David in dying might have claimed the health*: refers to King David in the Bible (I Kings 1–4); David in his old age could not get warm, so his servants found a young maiden, Abishag the Shunammite, to wait on him and to lie next to him.

46. The Spiritual Dawn

Baudelaire sent this poem, unsigned, undated, to Mme Sabatier with a brief preface written in English: 'After a night of pleasure and desolation, all my soul belongs to you.'

47. The Harmony of Evening

This poem, in form, is a pantoum (though irregular, because the poem does not begin and end with the same line); the pantoum is a Malayan verse form involving patterned repetition of lines, which was used effectively by Victor Hugo, de Banville, and other poets of Baudelaire's acquaintance.

97 *monstrance*: in the Roman Catholic Church, a receptacle that displays the host (the wafer that is the body of Christ).

48. The Flask

99 *Lazarus*: raised from the dead by Jesus; see John 11: 38–44

49. Poison

This poem begins the cycle of works, poems nos. 49–57, addressed to a third woman in Baudelaire's life, the actress

Marie Daubrun, the so-called 'Green-eyed Venus'. This relationship took place in the mid-1850s, at the same time as Baudelaire was writing his letters to Mme Sabatier.

101 *Opium*: in 1860 Baudelaire published a serious study of the effects of opium, based in part on his translation of Thomas De Quincey's *Confessions of an English Opium-Eater*, entitled *Artificial Paradises* (*les Paradis artificiels*).

51. The Cat

105 *seraphic*: the Seraphim were the highest among the orders of angels; see note to no. 1.

52. The Splendid Ship

107 *moire*: a fabric presenting a watery or wavelike appearance (the adjective form is 'moiré', sometimes used as a noun in English).

infant Hercules: Hercules (or Heracles) was the son of Zeus and a mortal woman; Zeus' wife Hera in a fit of jealousy sent two serpents to kill the baby Hercules, but he strangled both of them.

53. Invitation to the Voyage

There is a closely related Baudelaire prose poem with the same title, translated 'The Invitation to a Journey' by Lloyd.

111 *canals*: Baudelaire seems to have had the landscape of Holland in mind, but in a larger sense it is an imaginary land to which the poet is inviting his beloved, a 'land of Cockaigne' in the prose poem.

54. The Irreparable

113 *The irremissible*: the unpardonable sin.

115 *Sometimes I've seen within a theatre*: in 1847 Marie Daubrun acted the leading role in a play entitled *The Girl With the Golden Hair*, in which a fairy (not played by Daubrun) defeats diabolical forces. Baudelaire seems deliberately to have blended the two roles of heroine and fairy for the purposes of this poem. In its first publication in 1855, the poem was entitled 'To the Girl with the Golden Hair'.

55. Conversation

you want it still: 'it' refers to the speaker's heart, only the 'meagre scraps' of which are left.

57. To a Madonna

119 *Votive in the Spanish Style*: 'votive' means 'offered with a vow'.
The Spanish Baroque style ran to extremes, as in the images of
this poem. Antoine Adam comments that this is a baroque poem,
'where passion borrows the vocabulary of the most fanatical piety,
makes appeal to the most sumptuous and refined images to speak
of its adorations and its transports'. J. Dupont refers to three
types of representations of the Virgin in the Spanish tradition: the
hieratic Virgin; the immaculate Virgin with a moon and serpent
under her feet; and the Virgin of the Sorrows, pierced by seven
swords.

a Moon where you may stand: frequently in the iconography
associated with Mary she is standing on a quarter-moon.

bruise him with your tread: in Genesis 15, God punishes Adam
and Eve for their disobedience, but He also proclaims that Eve's
progeny will 'bruise the head' of the serpent who tempted Eve.

121 *The seven deadly sins*: pride, covetousness, lust, anger, gluttony,
envy, and sloth. Catholics are often taught that when one sins,
one penetrates the heart of the Virgin Mary, and Jonathan Culler
has mentioned 'the devotional tradition, reflected in art, which
represented the seven deadly sins committed by men as seven
daggers thrust into the Virgin Mary's heart'. This, then, is the
Virgin of the Sorrows, mentioned by Dupont. For Baudelaire to
create his perfect Mary, he must subject her to this combination
of 'the sumptuous and the barbarian' (Antoine Adam's words);
describing her first in the imagery of the Immaculate Virgin, he
then plants the deadly sins like daggers in her heart.

58. Song of the Afternoon

This poem begins a series of works apparently inspired by
various women of Baudelaire's acquaintance, not all of whom
have been identified by biographers. Both Jeanne and Marie have
been suggested as possible recipients of this poem.

123 *my Siberian night*: Siberia is an arctic region subject in winter to
an almost permanent darkness.

59. Sisina

125 *Sisina*: this is the name Baudelaire gives to an Italian friend of
Mme Sabatier, Elisa Nieri (or Neri, or Guerri), whose expression
of sympathy for the Italian revolutionaries led by Orsini, who

made an attempt on the life of Napoleon III, was a radical position at the time.

125   *Diana*: goddess of the hunt.

Théroigne: Théroigne de Méricourt, a heroine of the French Revolution, who stormed the staircase at Versailles. She became known as 'the Amazon of Liberty'.

60. Praises for My Francisca

This is the one poem in *The Flowers* not written in French, but in Latin. As a schoolboy, Baudelaire had won prizes for Latin verse. This poem in the 1857 edition had as its subtitle, 'verses written for a learned and devout milliner'.

125   *Lethe*: the river of forgetfulness in the classical Underworld. See note to nos. 31a and 77.

127   *Lodestar*: Polaris; a star that serves as a guide or fixed point of reference.

61. For a Creole Lady

129   *a Creole Lady*: the lady was the wife of M. Autard de Bragard, Emmeline de Carcenac, whom Baudelaire had met in Mauritius. He discreetly conveyed the poem to the lady in a letter to her husband.

62. Mœsta et errabunda

Mœsta et errabunda: sorrowful and wandering (Latin).

Agatha: unknown to biographers. There is an Agatha mentioned in a notebook Baudelaire used in the 1860s, but this poem was first published in 1855.

64. Autumn Sonnet

133   *Eros in his den*: the god of Love, often depicted as the child Cupid, ambushing unsuspecting mortals with his bow and arrows, to make them fall in love.

Marguerite: a Marguerite Bellegard is mentioned in a notebook of Baudelaire's, but one suspects the Marguerite, or Gretchen, of Goethe's *Faust* should be in our minds here. Baudelaire makes allusions to Faust and to Marguerite in the prose poems (see Lloyd, p. 22 and note; p. 76 and note), and he used the name Faust in no. 26 (see notes to this poem). The Marguerite of *Faust* was 'pale' indeed as she met her end in Part I of Goethe's drama, and she knew well of 'crime, madness, horror', awaiting execution for having murdered her newborn child. The first 'marguerite' in this poem is not capitalized in the French, referring probably to the daisylike flower of that name.

66. Cats

135 *Erebus*: in Greek mythology, the son of Chaos, brother of Night, father of the Styx and of the Fates; also, the classical Underworld or Hell: Tartarus.

Great sphinxes . . . desert solitudes: Baudelaire seems to be thinking of the famous ancient statue of the Sphinx, in the Egyptian desert. See note to no. 17.

67. Owls

137 *the punishment . . . change of place*: here Baudelaire could be calling to mind axioms from La Bruyère (French moralist, 1645–96) and Pascal (French philosopher and mathematician, 1623–62) pertaining to the evils of restlessness, given in the prose poem 'Solitude', in which he condemns the 'bustle . . . of the age I live in'.

68. The Pipe

the Kaffir race: a Kaffir is a member of a South African Bantu-speaking Negroid race of people. The point in the poem is that the pipe is dark from having been smoked frequently.

69. Music

Baudelaire, a great admirer of the music of Richard Wagner (1813–83), wrote to the composer of his music's granting a 'truly sensual pleasure, resembling that of mounting on the air, or rolling on the sea'.

71. A Fantastical Engraving

This poem represents closely the images in an engraving designed by John Mortimer, engraved by Joseph Haynes in 1784, entitled *Death on a Pale Horse*.

72. The Happy Corpse

143 *philosophes*: the word could be translated 'philosophers', but I have not translated it in order to maintain the sense the French

word conveys in English. *Philosophes* were men and women of the Enlightenment who spread and popularized the new scientific knowledge. Noted *philosophes* in France included Voltaire, Diderot, and Condorcet. Baudelaire seems to be using the word in this poem to refer ironically to the worms as 'sophisticated creatures'.

73. The Cask of Hate

143   *the Danaïdes*: these were the 49 daughters of Danaus who, for killing their husbands on their wedding night, were sentenced in Tartarus to an eternity of trying to carry water in bottomless containers. Baudelaire uses this image to represent Hate as a being that can never be filled up or satisfied.

Hydra's heads: the reference is to Hercules' combat with the Lernean Hydra, a serpent-like monster with nine heads; if one were cut off, two others would grow in its place.

75. Spleen (I)

145   *Pluvius*: the French Republic, starting 22 September 1792, established a new calendar. Pluvius (*Pluviôse*) was the name given the period from 21 January to 19 February. The word also means 'rainy', and Baudelaire personifies Pluvius as one who pours 'great waves of chilling rain' out of his 'urn'; the reference to 'mortality in gloomy district streets' seems another reminiscence of revolutionary times. Napoleon abolished this calendar, beginning 1 January 1806.

76. Spleen (II)

147   *faded old Bouchers*: François Boucher (1703–70) was a French painter and decorator of the rococo period.

Ennui... Takes on the size of immortality: in this poem, as elsewhere in Baudelaire, the concepts of 'spleen' and 'ennui' are seen as virtual synonyms; see also no. 78.

An ancient sphinx... glow of setting sun: the Statue of Memnon, in Egypt, was supposed to sing when struck by the rays of the rising sun. Here Baudelaire modifies the legend by having the statue of a forgotten sphinx sing to the setting sun, in an image of the poet isolated and ignored by the world.

77. Spleen (III)

149   *Nothing can cheer him*: such a prince—full of ennui—is described in the prose poem 'A Hero's Death'.

149   *those baths of blood*: it was a Roman belief that bathing in blood
could restore vigour and force to the body.

   Lethe: the river of forgetfulness in the classical Underworld. See
note to no. 31a; see also no. 60.

79. Obsession

151   *De Profundis*: see note to no. 30.

81. Alchemy of Suffering

153   *Hermes*: Hermes Trismegistus; see note to 'To The Reader'.

   Midas' counterpart: King Midas of Phrygia foolishly asked Diony-
sus to grant him the wish that everything he touched might
turn to gold; the wish granted, he could neither eat nor drink.
Dionysus had him remove the curse of the 'golden touch' by
washing in the river Pactolus. Baudelaire's curse is the opposite
of Midas': touching gold, he gets iron. The Pactolus is referred
to again in no. 105.

82. Congenial Horror

155   *Ovid ... expelled from Rome*: the poet Ovid was banished from
Rome by Augustus and forced to live in wild Scythia. He never
ceased lamenting his explusion from 'paradise', the city of Rome.

83. *Heautontimoroumenos*

   Heautontimoroumenos: literally (in Greek), 'that which punishes
itself'. It is also the title of a play by the Roman dramatist
Terence.

   for J.G.F.: Baudelaire's study of the effects of opium, *The
Artificial Paradises*, is also dedicated to J.G.F., but biographers
have not yet identified this person. In fact, Baudelaire himself
remarked in the latter case, 'I want this dedication to be
unintelligible'.

   Moses smote the rock: in Exodus 17; Moses, directed by God,
provided water for his people in the wilderness by striking a rock
with his staff.

157   *To laugh, but who can smile no more*: very likely a reference to the
last line of Poe's 'The Haunted Palace', an allegory of a
disordered mind. J. Dupont also sees a reference to Maturin's
novel *Melmoth* (see note to no. XIV), where it is written that the

nature of the vampire betrays itself notably in that it cannot smile, and we recall that the speaker of this poem is '[his] own blood's epicure' (l. 25).

84. The Irremediable

Part I of this poem contains a series of images drawn from diverse sources in romantic literature which, as the poem says, give the impression that the Devil does his work well, and that mankind is trapped, imprisoned, oppressed. Jonathan Culler offers the following commentary on Part II: 'The images of part I suggest that we are trapped in a realm of evil. Part II's description of self-reflection as a heart mirroring itself is another image of entrapment; this self-consciousness offers no way out, but it is a light in darkness, a source of both diabolic, ironic torment and of Satanic glory that is the only sort of consolation we have.'

159 *the Stygian slough*: the Styx, a river of the Underworld. See note to no. 26.

85. The Clock

161 *The way a sylphid flits into the wings*: a sylph or sylphid is a spirit of the air; here we are to think of a graceful actress or ballerina exiting the stage. The romantic ballet *Les Sylphides* dates from 1832.

PARISIAN SCENES

This is a section of poems created for the 1861 edition, including both new poems and poems moved from the 'Spleen and the Ideal' section.

86. Landscape

167 *my eclogues*: eclogues are pastoral poems, but Baudelaire's setting is a strictly urban one. An idyll (l. 20) is similar to an eclogue.

Riot: Baudelaire had some experience with public riots: he had witnessed one as a schoolboy in Lyons (his school caught fire), and had himself participated in the 1848 uprisings in Paris.

87. The Sun

169 *my quaint swordsmanship alone*: a curious image of the poet as solitary fencer.

chlorosis: a kind of anaemia. The 'fighter of chlorosis' is the sun.

88. To a Red-Haired Beggar Girl

169 *Pale girl with russet hair*: this same young woman is the subject of
the masterpiece of Baudelaire's friend, the painter Émile Deroy.
She was an itinerant guitar-player and street singer who
circulated through the Latin Quarter and was noticed for her
beauty by several among Baudelaire's circle of friends.

171 *Belleau*: Rémi Belleau (1528–77), noted love poet.

173 *Ronsards*: Pierre Ronsard (1524–85), the great poet of sixteenth-
century France. This poem is in a form associated with Ronsard,
and some of its words in French are archaic, from Ronsard's
time. Baudelaire was particularly fascinated by, and know-
ledgeable in French poetry of the fifteenth to the seventeenth
centuries.

Valois: the French ruling family from 1328 to 1589. The beggar
girl is whimsically being treated as though she were a sixteenth
century beauty.

Backstreet Véfour: ironic; the Véfour, of the Palais-Royal, was a
celebrated and expensive restaurant of Baudelaire's time, as it is
in ours.

89. The Swan

Victor Hugo: (1802–85); the great French poet and novelist.
Baudelaire first attempted to make his acquaintance in a letter
written in 1840. Later Hugo supported Baudelaire when the first
edition of the *Flowers* was put on trial in 1857, and soon
thereafter he wrote an open letter as a preface to a long essay of
Baudelaire's on the poet Gautier. Baudelaire dedicated 'The
Swan' and the two poems succeeding it to Hugo, in self-imposed
political exile on the island of Guernsey, and he also sent Hugo a
copy of the 1861 edition of the *Flowers*, which Hugo praised
generously. Baudelaire responded by praising Hugo's novel *Les
Misérables*, though in private he expressed serious reservations.
There was, then, a tension between the older and younger poet.
Still, they were not enemies, and they took the appropriate public
occasions to show their mutual respect.

Andromache: wife of the Trojan warrior Hector in *The Iliad*.
Baudelaire is drawing largely on book III of Virgil's *Aeneid*, which
tells the story of Andromache after the death of Hector and the
fall of Troy; the Greek Pyrrhus (see l. 38), claimed Andromache,
since his father Achilles had killed her husband in battle.

173 *This fraudulent Simois*: Andromache, in exile after the defeat of Troy, looked at a 'meagre stream' which reminded her of the river Simois of her native land.

175 *the modern Carrousel*: this is the area between the two wings of the Louvre and the Carrousel Arch. Before 1852 it had been a warren of small streets, but in Baudelaire's time the area was cleared for a monumental square. The speaker, crossing the modern Carrousel, recalls the time when it was a building site (the 'busy camp of huts') and when a menagerie was situated there.

The old Paris is gone: Paris, especially on the right bank of the Seine, was being completely done over under the supervision of Baron Haussmann (1809–91); many of the wide boulevards of present-day Paris date from this reconstruction work of the mid-nineteenth century.

Ovid's book: probably the *Metamorphoses*, book I, verses 84–5.

177 *wife of Helenus*: Andromache. When the usurping Pyrrhus decided to marry Hermione, he gave Andromache to Helenus, Hector's brother, also Pyrrhus' slave.

90. The Seven Old Men

Of this and the next poem, Hugo wrote to Baudelaire: 'you have created a new thrill' (*frisson*).

179 *Judas*: the betrayer of Christ, thought to be a wanderer on the earth like the Wandering Jew, probably alluded to in l. 25 (see note to no. 126). Judas was commonly depicted as having a beard.

181 *Phoenix*: a bird in Egyptian mythology that rose, living, from its own ashes.

91. The Little Old Women

There is very similar material to some of the passages in this poem in the prose poem 'The Widows'; see also the prose poem 'The Old Woman's Despair'.

Eponine or Laïs: Eponine was a woman of Gaul, rebellious against Rome, who, though finally executed, became the symbol of great patriotism and virtue. Laïs was a beautiful Greek courtesan, mistress of the soldier-politican Alcibiades (?450–404 BC). These women, then, are opposite types, but both distinguished.

183   *Vestal of love*: ironic; the Vestal Virgins were Roman priestesses of the temple of Vesta, the goddess of the hearth.

old Frascati's rooms: Frascati was a gaming house, closed in 1836 when such establishments were abolished.

Priestess of Thalia: celebrant of the Muse of comedy; therefore, a comedienne.

Tivoli: a large pleasure-garden of Paris, most renowned during the Restoration period.

185   *Hippogriffe*: a mythical winged monster, half horse, half griffon, capable of conveying a human being into the sky.

93. To a Woman Passing By

189   *Tall, slim, in mourning*: such a woman is also described by Baudelaire in his prose poem 'The Widows'; there, however, no possibilities for romance are suggested.

94. Skeletons Digging

anatomical designs: Baudelaire was interested in sixteenth- and seventeenth-century drawings of skeletons, but it is not clear that he had one specific design in mind while writing this poem.

95. Dusk

The prose poem 'Evening Twilight' has a similar general subject, but quite different imagery.

97. Danse macabre

197   *Danse macabre*: dance of death. This poem was inspired by a statuette done by Ernest Christophe, which Baudelaire described in his *Salon of 1859* as 'a large feminine skeleton ready to get out for a ball'. Christophe's work also inspired no. 20.

199   *Alembic*: glass vessel used in the distilling process.

hetaera: in ancient Greece, a trained courtesan.

Antinous: a beautiful boy, favourite of the Emperor Hadrian.

many a lovelace: Lovelace was a central character in Samuel Richardson's novel, *Clarissa*. We have Baudelaire's own testimony in a letter that he wanted the concept of 'a lovelace' to function in this poem: it means an unprincipled seducer.

99. 'I have not forgotten . . .'

This and the next poem were addressed to Baudelaire's mother. They recall the years of her widowhood (1827–9), when young Charles lived with her in a small house in Neuilly, before she married her second husband, Major Aupick. These were the happiest days of Baudelaire's youth.

203 *Pomona*: the ancient Roman goddess of fruit-trees.

100. 'That kind heart you were jealous of . . .'

my nurse: Mariette, a servant employed by Baudelaire's mother when he was a child. In his 'Intimate Journals' the poet speaks of praying, as an adult, to Edgar Allan Poe and to Mariette, as intercessors.

102. Parisian Dream

205 *Constantin Guys*: French painter, contemporary, and friend of Baudelaire's, whom Baudelaire mentioned prominently in a famous essay, 'The Painter of Modern Life'. The imagery of this poem comes, however, not from Guys, but from Poe, De Quincey, and Gautier.

207 *Nature and the irregular*: see the reference to Lisbon in the prose poem 'Any Where Out of the World', where it is said 'its people have such a hatred of the vegetable kingdom that they uproot all the trees' (Lloyd, p. 102).

naïads: water-spirits inhabiting lakes, streams, rivers.

the narcissistic gaze: in Greek mythology Narcissus was a youth who fell in love with his own image, reflected in the water; when he tried to grasp his beloved, he was drowned.

103. Dawn

211 *Aurora*: the goddess of the dawn (Roman).

WINE

Baudelaire published in 1851 a serious study entitled 'Concerning Wine and Hashish'; wine, he decided in that work, functions best as consolation for the working class (as in no. 105), but ultimately drunkenness is blameable as an artificial attempt to escape from the problems of being human. The poems in this section, though, sometimes take a different view

105. The Ragman's Wine

217 *Pactolus*: the river in which Midas washed to remove his 'golden touch'; the river, then, became lined with gold flecks. See note to no. 81.

106. The Murderer's Wine

The situation presented in this poem was also to be the subject for a play Baudelaire made several attempts to write, but never finished.

107. The Solitary's Wine

223 *Adeline*: a name possibly chosen for the rhyme, since no pertinent literary allusion has been identified.

FLOWERS OF EVIL

This nearly oxymoronic title has been attributed to Hippolyte Babou, novelist, critic, and friend of Baudelaire. It first appears over work by Baudelaire in 1855, when the *Revue des deux mondes* gathered for publication 18 diverse Baudelaire poems. The section, 'Flowers of Evil', appears in the 1857 *Flowers*, and in subsequent editions.

109. Destruction

The original title of this poem was 'Volupté' (sensual pleasure), an allusion to Sainte-Beuve's novel of that name, in which temptation is ubiquitous.

229 *The Fiend*: as in 'To The Reader', a demonstration of the destructive power of the Devil in connection with the vice of Ennui.

110. A Martyr

Drawing by an Unknown Master: no particular drawing has been identified as the inspiration for this poem.

233 *His appetite gratify*: it is remarkable that this poem, with its imagining of necrophilia, was not condemned, as six of the original *Flowers* were, for outrage to public decency.

110a. Lesbos

Lesbos: the Greek island associated with the poet Sappho. On her love poetry was based the cult of female ('lesbian') love.

235 *Phrynes*: Phryne was a beautiful Greek courtesan of the fourth century BC.

Paphos: a village on the island of Cyprus associated with the worship of Aphrodite (Venus).

Venus envies Sappho: because Sappho is worshipped on Lesbos as avidly as is Venus on Cyprus.

some dry Plato: possibly Plato is invoked here because he argued against physical love, in favour of spiritual, an idea counter to the rites of Sappho or Venus.

237 *Leucas' peak*: Sappho committed suicide by leaping into the sea from a cliff on the island of Leucas. The poem goes on to indicate that she had blasphemed against the rites of the cult by accepting a male lover. Baudelaire is departing from the legend that she killed herself over unrequited love for the boatman, Phaon.

110b. Condemned Women: Delphine and Hippolyta

See the other poem with this title, no. 111. Sources for the names of the two women have not clearly been identified.

243 *the tripod*: the priestess of Apollo at Delphi proclaimed her oracles while seated on a three-legged stool.

Furies: female divinities who live in the Underworld of Greek mythology (Erebus) and pursue and punish human transgressors.

245 *Descend, you victims*: according to a letter from Baudelaire to his publisher Poulet-Malassis, this and the subsequent stanzas were written and revised a few days before the publication of the *Flowers*, in the hope of making its message more acceptable in anticipation of prosecution.

111. Condemned Women

247 *St Anthony*: St Anthony of Egypt (*fl. c.* AD 300), considered the father of Christian monasticism. An ascetic, he lived in the desert and was frequently beset by demons who sometimes took the forms of tempting women. The 'temptations of St Anthony' ('his great trial') have often been represented by artists.

Bacchus: the Roman god of wine.

112. The Two Good Sisters

249 *graft black cypress to her myrtle bough*: cypress is the tree most conventionally associated with cemeteries, therefore with death; myrtle is the tree sacred to Venus.

113. The Fountain of Blood

249   *these women*: possibly a reference to 'the two good sisters' of the previous poem: Debauch and Death.

114. Allegory

Some critics take this to be an allegory of prostitution.

115. A Beatrice

251   *Beatrice*: Beatrice Portinari was the ideal love of Dante's life, and the inspiration of his poetry. The 'Beatrice' presented in this poem is undeserving of the poet's idolatry.

116. A Voyage to Cythera

255   *Cythera*: a Greek island south of the Peloponnese; it is the legendary island of love, and as such, subject of a famous painting by Watteau (see note to no. 6). The poem 'can be read as a reply to a section of Gerard de Nerval's *Voyage en Orient*, which contrasted the splendid past of the island with its nineteenth-century oppression as an English colony. Victor Hugo wrote "Cérigó" as an optimistic reply to Baudelaire's pessimistic poem' (Culler).

257   *Dweller in Cythera*: the corpse hanging on the gibbet.

259   *this perverse allegory*: as in no. 89, the investing of scenes with allegorical meaning is a form of self-torture for the speaker.

117. Passion and the Skull

An Old Colophon: two engravings by Hendrik Goltzius (1558–1617) are very directly represented in the imagery of this poem.

REVOLT

Baudelaire explained in a note that, like an actor, he was simply taking on the role of spiritual rebel in order to depict this reprehensible and blasphemous attitude in the poems of the 'Revolt' section of the *Flowers*. This disclaimer did not deter the prosecution of Baudelaire and his publisher for outrage to public morals.

118. St Peter's Denial

Most of the biblical events related in this poem may be found in John 13–19 and Matthew 26.

265 *that moneychanging lot*: a reference to Jesus in Jerusalem casting the moneychangers out of the temple, saying they had turned it into 'a den of robbers'. See Mark 11.

267 *Peter rejected Jesus*: as Jesus had prophesied, Peter denied three times that he knew Jesus, in order to save himself from Jesus' persecutors.

119. Abel and Cain

Abel and Cain: see Genesis 4. Abel and Cain were the two sons of Adam and Eve; Abel was a shepherd and Cain a farmer. Both made offerings to God, but Cain's was not accepted. Jealous of his brother, Cain killed Abel. God sentenced Cain to be a perpetual fugitive and wanderer on the earth. Like other poets and artists in the Romantic tradition, including Byron, Baudelaire identifies with the outcast Cain and his progeny. Part I gives a traditional account; Part II draws new inferences.

269 *The plough is conquered by the pike*: that is, in A. Adam's reading, the smug and comfortable existence of Abel's race will be overthrown by the militant uprising of Cain's 'modern progeny'.

120. Litanies of Satan

litanies: a litany is a form of prayer consisting of supplication and response.

O Angel, the most brilliant and most wise: rebellious Romantics were likely to favour the energetic and assertive Satan over the God with all the answers, and Milton's vivid depiction of Satan in *Paradise Lost* provided a model for both poets and artists.

271 *Croesus*: fabulously wealthy King of Lydia in the sixth century BC; here a rich, miserly person.

273 *the Tree Of Knowledge*: Eve was tempted by Satan to eat the forbidden fruit from the Tree of Knowledge in the Garden of Eden; here Baudelaire's speaker takes the Tree to be within Satan's province, which he hopes to enter.

121. The Death of Lovers

This poem was set to music by the young Villiers de l'Isle-Adam, who was also to be a collaborator in the play Baudelaire planned to write based on 'The Murderer's Wine' (see note to no. 106). Villiers later became famous as a writer associated with the Symbolist movement.

122. The Death of the Poor

277   *The illustrious inn*: spiritual consolation and sustenance represented as an inn or tavern is seen also in nos. 54 and 60. J. Dupont finds allusions in this passage to Luke 10: 34–5, and 22.

123. The Death of Artists

279   *my little bells*: we are to imagine the artist-speaker costumed as a court jester, or fool.

great and wondrous One: 'nature's mystic self' of l. 4.

strange sombre Capitol: perhaps the reference is to the Capitoline Hill in Rome, and therefore to the triumphs of antiquity (J. Dupont).

125. Dream of a Curious Man

281   *F.N.*: Félix Nadar, cartoonist, pioneer photographer, and friend of Baudelaire.

126. Voyaging

283   *Maxime du Camp*: a secondary literary figure, never one of Baudelaire's close friends, who had published a poem entitled 'The Voyager' in his *Chants modernes*, the preface of which extols technological progress. Thus there is an irony involved in this dedication: Baudelaire knew well that his poem mocks du Camp's facile confidence in progress.

Circe: the enchantress in Homer's *Odyssey*, capable of turning men into swine.

285   *the blessed isle*: the 'Isles of the Blessed', where heroes went after death, was one of the concepts of the afterlife in Greek mythology. Here it simply stands for any imaginary Utopia.

Eldorado: city of gold; this is another expression of the soul's imaginary destiny.

285 *Capua*: an ancient Roman city on the Appian Way near Naples, noted for its wide streets.

289 '*Master, my image, damn you with this curse!*': people take their Master (God) to be comparable to themselves as they curse Him.

291 *the Wandering Jew*: a legendary figure who, for mocking Christ at His crucifixion, was condemned to wander the world until Judgement Day; see note to no. 90. He and the twelve apostles are compared to Christians in a Roman arena, forced to flee a gladiator to survive.

eat the Lotus: in the *Odyssey*, some of Odysseus' crew became drugged in the Land of the Lotus Eaters, and lost all interest in their voyage. Baudelaire is probably thinking specifically of Tennyson's poem 'The Lotos-Eaters'.

293 *Pylades*: friend of Orestes in Greek legend; symbol of the faithful friend.

Electra: the faithful sister of Orestes; in one version of the legend she married Pylades.

sunny rays: Maxime du Camp's blandly optimistic voyager 'carries in his heart God's sunny rays'.

To fathom the Unknown, the find the new: similar to the sentiment in the prose poem 'Any Where Out of the World'.

THE WAIFS

This was a volume brought out by Poulet-Malassis, publisher of *The Flowers*, in 1866, the year before Baudelaire's death. It was a miscellany of poems which, according to the announcement, Baudelaire did not wish to place in the definitive edition of the *Flowers*, but it had the great virtue of including the six poems condemned by the court from the 1857 *Flowers*, which I have in this edition returned to their original placement. *The Waifs* was arranged in sections. The volume began with the single poem 'The Setting of the Romantic Sun', which was followed by the six condemned pieces in a section of their own. Other sections were 'Gallantries', 'Epigraphs', 'Diverse Pieces', and 'Buffooneries'. Published in Brussels (though the cover said Amsterdam), copies of *The Waifs* had to be smuggled into France. 'Editor's Notes' attached to many of the poems were frequently by Baudelaire himself, indicating that he played a major part in assembling the collection.

I. The Setting of the Romantic Sun

297 *Remorseless Night establishes her reign*: Baudelaire's comment on his time as a literary dark age.

snails and toads: an expression of Baudelaire's contempt for other writers of his time.

II–VII. *Gallantries*

These were the condemned pieces I have removed to their original context in the *Flowers*. The last poem of the 'Gallantries' section was 'Praises for My Francisca', also no. 60 of the *Flowers* See Note on the Text, pp. xxxviii–xlviii.

VIII. The Fountain

299 *Phoebe*: the moon; the 'sheaf' of the fountain is likened to flowers, since the moonlight touches the water with colours.

IX. Bertha's Eyes

A 'Bertha'—only her first name is known—was Baudelaire's mistress in Brussels, but there is strong conjecture that this poem he gave to her could originally have been written for Jeanne Duval, who may have used 'Bertha' as a stage name.

X. Hymn

The poem comes from an anonymous letter to Mme Sabatier dated 8 May 1854; it was not included in either the 1857 or the 1861 *Flowers*.

XII. The Monster

It is not clear who inspired this poem, but Jeanne Duval certainly seems a possibility. Félix Fénéon, Baudelaire's acquaintance, quoted from this poem in commenting on Manet's portrait of Jeanne.

305 *Veuillot*: Louis Veuillot, Catholic writer and journalist, contemporary of Baudelaire.

I much prefer . . . of old King Solomon: the reference is to a book of magic, *The Clavicles of Solomon*, attributed to the biblical King Solomon.

309 *kiss his filthy ass*: part of the ritual of the Black Mass, the celebration of Satan, referred to also in no. XVIII.

XIV. Poem on the Portrait of Honoré Daumier

309 *Honoré Daumier*: painter and cartoonist, whose realistic works were dedicated to social criticism. Daumier once indicated that Baudelaire could have been a great painter had he made the attempt. The portrait of Daumier was in Champfleury's *History of Modern Caricature* (1865), for which Baudelaire wrote this poem.

311 *Melmoth*: in the novel by the Rev Charles Robert Maturin, Melmoth was a Satanic character, known by his prideful smile, who made a pact with the Devil; see the note to no. 83.

Mephistopheles: the Devil with whom Faust made a pact in Goethe's *Faust*, a work frequently referred to by Baudelaire.

Erinyes: another name for the Furies; see the note to no. 26.

XV. Lola de Valence

Lola de Valence: a celebrated Spanish dancer who made her début in Paris in 1862, the same year Manet painted a portrait of her. Baudelaire's short poem was attached to the painting when it was exhibited.

XVI. On *Tasso in Prison*, by Eugène Delacroix

Torquato Tasso was a sixteenth-century Italian poet. Delacroix, the great French romantic painter of Baudelaire's time, did several studies of the subject of Tasso in prison.

XVII. The Voice

313 *Babel*: a confusion of voices; the reference is to the Old Testament which records that God confounded the languages of men when he found them overreaching themselves, building a tower to heaven: the Tower of Babel.

no taller than a folio: probably two feet or less; the point the speaker is making is that he was quite young when he heard the two voices.

XVIII. The Unforeseen

This poem was dedicated to Barbey d'Aureville, who had predicted in an article that Baudelaire would have to either turn Christian or blow his brains out.

315 *Harpagon*: the type of a cheapskate, from Molière's play *The Miser*.

315   *Célimène*: the type of a self-satisfied flirt, from Molière's play *Th.*
Misanthrope.

A gazetteer: a sceptic; a 'Voltairean journalist' (J. Dupont).

Ciborium: a container for holding the host for the service of
communion; Satan is referring to that parody of the Christian
service, the Black Mass; see note to no. XII.

XX. To a Girl of Malabar

This is an early poem, inspired by a 'Dorothy', the foster-sister
of Mme Autard de Bragard, for whom Baudelaire wrote no. 61.
This Dorothy is not to be confused with the young prostitute
Dorothy of no. 10 of the Additional Poems, whom Baudelaire
knew from the island of Réunion, not Mauritius.

321   *absent coco-trees*: image and language here are similar to a passage
in no. 89.

XXI. On the Début of Amina Boschetti

Montagne-aux-Herbes-Potagères: a notorious street in the red-light
district of Brussels.

'*Some Belgian beer for mine!*': Baudelaire treated the Belgian beer,
'faro', with nothing but disgust, explaining that it was brewed
from the waters of a river which served as a public sewer;
therefore it was 'twice-drunk'. Baudelaire had arrived in Belgium
in April 1864, and he spent the last two productive years of his
life there. As this poem and others demonstrate, he had little love
for the Belgians, believing them cultureless boors.

XXII. To M. Eugène Fromentin

Eugène Fromentin was a painter and friend of Baudelaire.

323   *Corot*: Jean Baptiste Camille Corot (1796–1875), great French
landscape painter and realist.

Nord: a prominent railway company.

Oppenord: French architect, designer, and cabinet-maker in the
rococo style, born in the Netherlands (1639–1715).

Niboyet: a diplomat and author of moralistic novels.

XXIII. A Jolly Tavern

327   *M. Monselet*: this poem is ironically addressed to Baudelaire's
poet friend Charles Monselet, known to be fastidious and to
prefer the joyful to the macabre.

ADDITIONAL POEMS FROM
THE THIRD EDITION OF
THE FLOWERS OF EVIL (1868)

1.(3rd ed.) Epigraph for a Condemned Book

This poem was projected as an epigraph for the second edition of *Flowers*, after the court had condemned the 1857 edition, but it was not used. It was mistakenly inserted in the third edition at the beginning of the 'Flowers of Evil' section (Culler).

331 *Saturnian*: pertaining to the planet Saturn and its astrological influence, or to the Roman god Saturn. Baudelaire in this first stanza seems to be combining two Saturnian associations: 'orgies', in l. 4, probably pertains to the Roman Saturnalia, an unrestrained seven-day celebration beginning on 17 December; 'despondency' seems rather to refer to the 'saturnine' or melancholy disposition.

2.(3rd ed.) To Théodore de Banville, 1842

Théodore de Banville: Baudelaire's friend the poet Banville was one of the editors of the posthumous third edition of the *Flowers*, and he included this poem to himself, hitherto uncollected. The poem was actually written in 1845, rather than 1842.

333 *Poet . . . cradle-bed*: the last two stanzas of this poem contain a complicated allusion to two events in the legendary life of Hercules. The 'robe of the Centaur' (i.e. of Nessus) in l. 10, when Hercules put it on, caused his blood to flow from a thousand wounds. So Baudelaire felt Banville, himself, and all true poets were being assaulted by mediocrities, by the slime of 'snakes, so spiteful and malign', like those the infant Hercules had so hardily dispatched 'in his cradle-bed' (see note to no. 52).

3.(3rd ed.) The Peace Pipe

Poem no. 3 was Baudelaire's translation of a passage from Longfellow's 'The Song of Hiawatha', entitled 'Le Calumet de paix' ('The Peace Pipe'). The story is that in 1860 the American composer Robert Stoepel arrived in Paris needing a translator to render Longfellow's 'Song of Hiawatha' into French. Baudelaire agreed to do the work, but misunderstandings arose, and the work was not finished, nor was the poet paid; 'The Peace Pipe' in rhyming alexandrines is all that remains.

4.(3rd ed.) Prayer of a Pagan

Voluptas: sensual pleasure personified.

Diva! supplicem exaudi!: Goddess! hear (attend to) my plea! (Latin)

5.(3rd ed.) The Pot Lid

333 *Croesus*: see note to no. 120.

335 *The Sky! black lid of the enormous pot*: Baudelaire used a similar image memorably in no. 78.

6.(3rd ed.) Midnight Examination

Examination: an examination of conscience in going over the events of the day. See the prose poem 'One O'Clock in the Morning'.

337 *Proud priest . . . morbid things*: Baudelaire's capsule self-portrait as author of *The Flowers of Evil*.

7.(3rd ed.) Sad Madrigal

This poem dates from the early 1860s; it is not known to whom it is addressed.

8.(3rd ed.) The Cautioner

341 *Nixie*: in German mythology, a female water-spirit, sometimes half-human, half-fish: a mermaid.

Satyress: satyrs were part human, part goat, and notably lecherous; a satyress here is a temptress.

9.(3rd. ed.) The Rebel

343 *the Angel, who corrects and loves*: the specific reference is to the angel of the church in Laodicea, Revelation 3: 19.

10.(3rd ed.) Very Far From France

Dorothy: see note to no. XX. This Dorothy, from the island of Réunion, is also commemorated in the prose poem 'Beautiful Dorothea'.

11.(3rd ed.) The Gulf

Pascal: Blaise Pascal (1623–62), French mathematician and

philosopher; his 'gulf' had to do with his inability to believe that reason could provide certitude in life.

12.(3rd ed.) Lament of an Icarus

345 *Icarus*: in Greek mythology Icarus was the son of the great artificer, Daedalus, who made wings for them both so that they might fly in escape from Crete. Daedalus warned his son not to fly too high, but Icarus did not heed this warning, and the heat of the sun melted the wax in his wings, so that he fell to his death in what came to be called the Icarian Sea.

13.(3rd ed.) Meditation

The beginning of Longfellow's 'Hymn to the Night', 'I heard the trailing garments of the Night | Sweep through her marble halls', is reflected in the last line of this poem.

14.(3rd ed.) The Insulted Moon

347 *Cynthia*: the moon.

349 *Endymion*: in Greek mythology Endymion was a shepherd with whom the moon fell in love, and slept beside through the nights; Zeus granted him eternal youth and beauty.

Child of this wretched century: the moon, insulted by the cavalier attitude of the poet, responds by depicting his mother, the 'wretched century', as an ageing, overweight prostitute.

INDEX OF TITLES

INDEX OF FIRST LINES

	Till Eulenspiegel: His Adventures
	Eight German Novellas
GEORG BÜCHNER	Danton's Death, Leonce and Lena, and Woyzeck
J. W. VON GOETHE	Elective Affinities
	Erotic Poems
	Faust: Part One and Part Two
E. T. A. HOFFMANN	The Golden Pot and Other Tales
J. C. F. SCHILLER	Don Carlos and Mary Stuart

American Literature

British and Irish Literature

Children's Literature

Classics and Ancient Literature

Colonial Literature

Eastern Literature

European Literature

History

Medieval Literature

Oxford English Drama

Poetry

Philosophy

Politics

Religion

The Oxford Shakespeare

A complete list of Oxford Paperbacks, including Oxford World's Classics, OPUS, Past Masters, Oxford Authors, Oxford Shakespeare, Oxford Drama, and Oxford Paperback Reference, is available in the UK from the Academic Division Publicity Department, Oxford University Press, Great Clarendon Street, Oxford OX2 6DP.

In the USA, complete lists are available from the Paperbacks Marketing Manager, Oxford University Press, 198 Madison Avenue, New York, NY 10016.

Oxford Paperbacks are available from all good bookshops. In case of difficulty, customers in the UK can order direct from Oxford University Press Bookshop, Freepost, 116 High Street, Oxford OX1 4BR, enclosing full payment. Please add 10 per cent of published price for postage and packing.